DATE DUE

Pears Encyclopaedia

of

Myths and Legends

Pears Encyclopaedia
of
Myths and Legends

Oceania and Australia
The Americas

BY SHEILA SAVILL

ADVISORY EDITOR: PROFESSOR GEOFFREY PARRINDER

GENERAL EDITORS: MARY BARKER AND CHRISTOPHER COOK

PELHAM BOOKS

First published in Great Britain by
Pelham Books Ltd
52 Bedford Square
London WC1B 3EF
1978

Picture research by Philippa Lewis

ISBN 0 7207 1050 2

Filmset and printed in Great Britain by
BAS Printers Limited, Over Wallop, Hampshire
and bound by Hunter and Foulis Ltd, Edinburgh

Contents

Illustrations

6

A skull-bone *tiki*. British Museum. (*Photo: British Museum.*) p. 104

Tjuringa stones from the central Australian desert. (*Photo: Axel Poignant.*) p. 105

The upper part of a *Batak Tunggal Panaluan*. Museum für Völkerkunde, Munich. (*Photo: Michael Holford.*) p. 106

Javanese *Wayang Golek* puppets. British Museum. (*Photo: British Museum.*) p. 108

Carved head of a rattle used in shamanistic ritual dances by *Haida* Indians of the North West Coast. James Hooper Collection, Watersfield. (*Photo: Werner Forman Archive.*) p. 113

An Eskimo *shaman's* magical necklace. Ottawa Museum. (*Photo: Werner Forman Archive.*) p. 114

Mica figure of a snake, found in the Turner Mound, Hamilton County, Ohio. It dates from the ancient Indian Hopewell culture (200–300 A.D.). Peabody Museum of Archaeology and Ethnology, Harvard University. (*Photo: Peabody Museum, Harvard University.*) p. 115

Tlingit headdress of copper inlaid with abalone shell. Masks of this type were worn by chiefs and *shamans* at *potlach* ritual exchanges. Portland Art Museum. (*Photo: Werner Forman Archive.*) p. 118

Tsimshian totem pole at Skeena River, British Columbia. (*Photo: Werner Forman Archive.*) p. 119.

Pueblo cliff dwellings in the Mesa Verde National Park, SW Columbia. (*Photo: Werner Forman Archive.*) p. 120

Tlingit rattle with a raven's head and figure of a man lying along the bird's back. The beak of another raven lies parallel with his knees, while a third bird's head forms the lower side of the rattle. British Museum. (*Photo: British Museum.*) p. 121

Kwakiutl rattle carved to represent the Thunderbird carrying a pair of human beings *in copulo* on its back. Royal Scottish Museum, Edinburgh. (*Photo: Photoresources.*) p. 122

Olmec jadeite axe head carved in the figure of a god decorated with jaguar motifs. Dallas Museum of Fine Art. (*Photo: Werner Forman Archive.*) p. 123

Late seventh-century lintel from a *Maya* ceremonial centre at Yaxchilán, Guatemala, shows a worshipper kneeling to a double-headed snake-god. British Museum. (*Photo: British Museum.*) p. 124

Aztec greenstone figure of Quetzalcóatl between the jaws of the feathered serpent. British Museum. (*Photo: Werner Forman Archive.*) p. 126

Mosaic of mother-of-pearl on stone shows a warrior in a coyote helmet. Found at Tula it is sometimes called Quetzalcóatl of Tula. Instituto Nacional de Antropología e Historia, Mexico City. (*Photo: Werner Forman Archive.*) p. 127

Early carved stone figure from Chavin de Huántor. Private Collection. (*Photo: Michael Holford.*) p. 129

Painted stirrup vase from Chimor decorated with a sea-god. Private Collection. (*Photo: Werner Forman Archive.*) p. 130

Beaten silver pectoral from Chimor showing god or god-king wearing solar or lunar headdress and attended by stylised monsters, possibly sea-gods. Museum of the American Indian, New York. (*Photo: Werner Forman Archive.*) p. 131

Detail from an *Inca* painted and lacquered wooden beaker (*keru*) showing *conquistadores* and a Peruvian, with birds flying above. British Museum. (*Photo: Photoresources.*) p. 132

Detail from a nineteenth-century engraved walrus tusk, showing Eskimo hunting caribou. British Museum. (*Photo: Photoresources.*) p. 136

Detail of nineteenth-century engraved walrus tusk showing Eskimo hunters in kayaks and canoes. British Museum. (*Photo: British Museum.*) p. 137

Navajo ritual sandpainting shows the Earth-Mother and Sky-Father. On her body are symbols of the four sacred plants, growing from the 'place of emergence', on his symbols of the sun, moon and Milky Way. Museum of *Navajo* Ceremonial Art, Santa Fé. p. 139

Navajo ritual sandpainting shows the fourth world into which the people ascended (**45**). From the 'place of emergence' grow the four sacred plants, between the mountains of the cardinal points, which have tiered clouds beneath them, birds on their summits. Arching round the world is the body of the rainbow-goddess. Museum of *Navajo* Ceremonial Art, Santa Fé. p. 141

Navajo blanket, c. 1880, shows two spirits invoked in the Shooting Chant ritual flanking the sacred maize plant. The body of the rainbow-goddess frames them. Schindler Coll. New York. (*Photo: Werner Forman Archive.*) p. 142

Pawnee buckskin chart of the night sky. Field Museum of Natural History, Chicago. (*Photo: Werner Forman Archive.*) p. 144

Nineteenth-century whalebone knife handle carved with a raven's head, inlaid with abalone shell, made by *Haida* Indians of the NW Coast. Hooper Collection, Watersfield. (*Photo: Werner Forman Archive.*) p. 149

Tlingit house screen, c. 1840, with the brown-bear clan-symbol. Denver Art Museum. (*Photo: Denver Art Museum.*) p. 150

NW Coast copper mask of a killer-whale. British Museum. (*Photo: Photoresources.*) p. 151

Birchbark pictorial record of a *Midewiwin* society seating-plan. *Ojibwa* Indians, Leech Lake, Minnesota. Field Museum of Natural History, Chicago. (*Photo: Werner Forman Archive.*) p. 153

Payatami—*Zuñi* gods of music, flowers and butterflies, c. 1900. Brooklyn Museum. (*Photo: Brooklyn Museum.*) p. 158

Detail of a late ninth-century relief from the southern ballcourt at El Tajín, Mexico, showing the sacrifice of a ballplayer. (*Photo: Werner Forman Archive.*) p. 165

Zapotec clay mask of the bat-god known to the *Maya* as Camátoz. Note the feline features, relating the god to the deadly jaguar-god. Royal Scottish Museum, Edinburgh. (*Photo: Photoresources.*) p. 167

Aztec greenstone 'mask' of Tezcatlipoca, 1507, A.D. Over one ear is a smoke-wreathed mirror, the god's symbol. Dumbarton Oaks Research Library and Collections, Washington. (*Photo: Dumbarton Oaks Research Library and Collections.*) p. 169

Figure of Mictlantecuhtli, the Lord of Death. Museo de Antropologia de la Universidad Veracruzana, Jalapa. (*Photo: Werner Forman Archive.*) p. 170

Aztec stone head of the goddess Chalchiuhtlicue. British Museum. (*Photo: British Museum.*) p. 171

Aztec stone head of the moon-goddess Coyolxauhqui. Instituto Nacional de Antropología e Historia, Mexico City. (*Photo: Werner Forman Archive.*) p. 173

Aztec relief from Tenoctlitlán shows the feathered serpent, with whom Quetzalcóatl is identified, between two yearsymbols. (*Photo: Werner Forman Archive.*) p. 175

Twelfth-thirteenth-century gourd from Chimor inlaid with mother-of-pearl symbols of deities. Museum für Völkerkunde, Munich. (*Photo: Michael Holford.*) p. 183

Beaten gold funerary mask inlaid with emeralds, from Chimor. Mujica Gallo Collection, Lima. (*Photo: Michael Holford.*) p. 184

Drawing of *kuarup* logs by the *Xingu* artist Wacupiá. *Xingu, The Indians and Their Myths*, Villas Boas, pub. Souvenir Press. p. 186

Mochican pottery trumpet in the form of a jaguar. N. Cummings Collection, Chicago. (*Photo: Giraudon.*) p. 187

Kwakiutl mask of Bokwus. Denver Art Museum. (*Photo: Denver Art Museum.*) p. 191

Aztec basalt statue of the goddess Chalchiuhtlicue. British Museum. (*Photo: Michael Holford.*) p. 192

Aztec stone figure of the goddess Chicomecóatl wearing maize cobs in her headdress. British Museum. (*Photo: Michael Holford.*) p. 193

Fragment of *Aztec* pottery figurine showing the wind-god Ehécatl. (*Photo: Werner Forman Archive.*) p. 195

Iroquoian False-Face Society mask. Peabody Museum of Salem. (*Photo: M. W. Sexton.*) p. 196

Tenth-century bowl from Snaketown, Arizona, decorated with dancing flute-players, possibly precursors of the *Hopi* Flute Dancers. Arizona State Museum. (*Photo: Werner Forman Archive.*) p. 197

A set of *Apache gans* masks. Their designs are based on drawings attributed to the *gans* spirits. Maxwell Museum of Anthropology, Albuquerque. (*Photo: Maxwell Museum of Anthropology.*) p. 198

Kwakiutl mask representing the monstrous Hokhokw. Private Collection, Kansas City. p. 200

Eskimo *inua* mask representing the spirit of the salmon. Musée de Guimet, Paris. (*Photo: Hamlyn Picture Library.*) p. 201

Drawing of Jakuí by Wacupiá. *Xingu, The Indians and Their Myths*, Villas Boas, pub. Souvenir Press. p. 202

Hopi painted wooden *katchina* figure, c. 1850. Its eyes are said to symbolise rain clouds, its eyelashes rain. Private Collection. (*Photo: Werner Forman Archive.*) p. 203

Late eighteenth-century *Nootka* wolf headdress used in *Klukwala* rites. Denver Art Museum, Denver, Colorado. (*Photo: Denver Art Museum.*) p. 204

Kwakiutl mask of Komokwa. John H. Hauberg Collection, Seattle. p. 205

Drawing of *mamaé* spirits by Wacupiá. *Xingu, The Indians and Their Myths*, Villas Boas, pub. Souvenir Press. p. 206

Wooden Eskimo mask of Negakfok. Museum of the American Indian, New York. (*Photo: Museum of the American Indian, Heye Foundation.*) p. 208

Painted wooden mask of the *Kwakiutl* spirit Noohlmahl. Originally it was decorated with human hair. British Museum. (*Photo: British Museum.*) p. 209

Aztec stone carving of Ometecuhtli in his aspect as Tonacatecuhtli. Museum für Völkerkunde, Basle. (*Photo: Werner Forman Archive.*) p. 210

Hide painting of the Sun Dance, the Plains Indians' greatest ritual. Brown Museum, Providence, Rhode Island. (*Photo: Werner Forman Archive.*) p. 213

Cowichan (*Salish*) wooden comb decorated with a figure of Swaixwe. British Museum. (*Photo: British Museum.*) p. 215

Panel from the *Codex Fejervary-Mayer* shows Tezcatlipoca fishing for the Earth Monster with his foot as bait. The date symbols with dots denote eras which Tezcatlipoca dominated. Liverpool City Museum. (*Photo: Werner Forman Archive.*) p. 216

Stele of the Teotihuacán period, from the neighbouring city of Atzcapotzalco, shows the water-god Tláloc. (*Photo: Werner Forman Archive.*) p. 217

Aztec statue of the solar-god Tonatiuh. The symbol on his back denotes an earthquake. Museum für Völkerkunde, Basle. (*Photo: Werner Forman Archive.*) p. 218

Kwakiutl mask, c. 1870, of the ogress Tsonoqua. Mr and Mrs Morton I. Sosland Collection. p. 219

Basalt statue of the Aztec goddess Xilonen. Private Collection. (*Photo: Hamlyn Picture Library.*) p. 220

Colour Plates

Foreword

In modern times comparative studies of religion and mythology, strongly supported by psychology, have revealed again the importance of myths. And one 'fact' that confronts us immediately is that myths have universally been thought to express truth, not mere detail of present existence but primordial and eternal reality. The myth is real and sacred, and it serves as an example in providing a pattern for human behaviour and an explanation of its mysteries. These elements can be seen in great modern myths. In Communism, quite apart from economic theory, there is a revival of Jewish and Christian mythical themes in the redemptive role of the innocent, the proletariat, the inevitable struggle of good and evil, and faith in a coming Golden Age. At a lower level the Nazi myths, held recently by millions of intelligent and educated people, propounded the myth of the chosen people, the master-race, and tried to revive Nordic paganism, with its doom of the world and destruction in chaos. Other myths, about the Empire on which the Sun never Set, or the American Way of Life, had their potency but were also subject to the weakness of modern mythology in not being sufficiently anchored in age-old symbolism and therefore inadequate to represent lasting reality. But psychology has shown also that the dreams and fantasies of modern men, formerly dismissed by rationalists as nonsensical, often repeat great themes of mythology and produce their effect upon the unconscious and half-conscious behaviour of individuals.

An authoritative and comprehensive collection of myths such as this book provides, therefore, is of absorbing interest and topical significance.

This volume begins with the setting of the myths, relates them in detail, and provides comprehensive index and bibliography. It is a splendid work, for reading and reference, and enlightened by illustrations. Now the four volumes are completed they will be an unrivalled and up-to-date source for knowledge of these age-old mythologies.

GEOFFREY PARRINDER
Emeritus Professor of the Comparative Study of Religions,
University of London

General Introduction

The standard reference book of world myths, *The Mythology of All Races* (ed.: Louis Herbert Grey and John Arnott MacCulloch), appeared between 1916 and 1932. It comprises thirteen weighty volumes and its price, more than one hundred pounds, puts it beyond the means of most readers. Moreover, although this great work, which has recently been reissued, contains material of lasting importance and interest, much new knowledge has become available since it was compiled. The researches of the linguist and archaeologist have extended our knowledge and understanding of the myths and legends of the ancient civilisations, such as Sumer, Greece and China. Anthropologists and ethnographers have done the same for those of Africa, and parts of the Americas, Oceania and Australia. A number of books offer information on particular aspects of this new knowledge, but much of it remains tucked away in specialised libraries, the pages of learned journals and academic theses. Here therefore we have aimed to provide an up-to-date yet reasonably compact encyclopaedia for the growing number of readers who share our interest in this perennially fascinating subject.

This volume is the fourth and final one of a series. Each volume contains two chapters, each dealing with the myths and legends of a particular region:

Vol. 1
   Chapter 1 The Ancient Near and Middle East
   Chapter 2 Classical Greece and Rome
Vol. 2
   Chapter 3 Northern Europe
   Chapter 4 Southern and Central Africa
Vol. 3
   Chapter 5 Ancient Iran, India and S.E. Asia
   Chapter 6 Northern and Eastern Asia
          (Tibet, China, Korea, Japan)
Vol. 4
   Chapter 7 Oceania and Australia
   Chapter 8 The Americas

Each chapter is divided into four parts. The first gives a brief introduction to the historical, religious and cultural background of the region's myths and legends, the second outlines the chief stories of each area, in so far as these are known, or, as in the case of Africa and India, offers a representative selection from them. The third part of each chapter consists of an index and glossary, referring particularly to the numbered paragraphs of the second part and also including brief details of many other myths and legends of the region. Finally comes a bibliography and guide to further reading. This pattern is based on that devised for the original section on Greek myths and legends, first published in *Pears Cyclopaedia*. Many readers said how helpful they found the scheme, which enables any character or story easily to be pinpointed.

Examples of reference:

    23 refers to paragraph **23** of part 2 of the current chapter;

    4.1 refers to chapter 4, part 1;

    vol. 2: 4.2.**23** refers to volume 2, chapter 4, part 2, paragraph **23**;

    vol. 3: 7.3 refers to volume 3, chapter 7, part 3.

The terms *myth* and *legend* are often used rather ambiguously. Here *myth* is a particular kind of fictional narrative, legend is a story of a similar kind but with perhaps some historical foundations.

In speaking of fictional narratives we do not imply that myths and legends offer false images of the world. They have a serious function and express a people's feelings and intuitions about the significance of their lives, the nature of human relationships and human potentialities for good or ill.

It used to be thought that myths were stories devised to explain or to accompany rituals, but, although the evidence suggests that many did originate in this way, it is now accepted that the theory does not account for the origin of all myths, whose genesis remains a matter of speculation.

Certain mythological paradigms (mythologems) and symbols such as those of the flood, the theft of fire, the monster/dragon in its cave, the ladder from earth to heaven, appear to have a very widespread and potent significance for mankind. This fact was noted by Jung and forms the basis of his influential theory of the Collective Unconscious, which has done much to illuminate our understanding of the world's myths and legends.

More recently, studies of animal behaviour have led to the suggestion that perhaps some of the power of these archetypal images is analogous to that of the stimuli which provoke automatic responses in less highly developed species. A newly hatched chick will immediately cower if it sees a hawk or even an image of hawk shape, though it shows no fear of gulls or similar birds.

Each society gives its own particular form to such 'archetypal images' or stimuli, for myths and legends are expression of communal feelings and intuitions.

During the past century scholars have made us increasingly aware of the important part myths and legends have played in shaping our own culture. The influence of Greek and Roman mythology had long been acknowledged but critical consideration of Jewish and Christian myths and legends was taboo, while very little was known of those earlier stories of the Near and Middle East from which many of our most compelling myths seem to have originated. Nor did we know much of the myths and legends of primitive peoples, or of the geographically remote Chinese and Indians.

The disciplines of archaeology, linguistics, psychology, anthropology, ethnography, sociology, comparative mythology, comparative religion and religious history have all played a part in helping to extend our knowledge and understanding of the world's myths and legends. Some of their discoveries and theses are discussed in the introductions to the various chapters.

It is impossible in a work of this size to incorporate detailed discussion of various theories regarding the provenance and significance of individual myths and legends, but wherever possible we have included brief details, and referred the reader to the appropriate scholarly works.

The following general studies are particularly recommended:

CAMPBELL, Joseph *The Masks of God*, 3 vols. New York: The Viking Press. 1959–65.

DUMÉZIL, Georges *Mythe et epopée*. 3 vols. Paris: Gallimard. 1974.

ELIADE, Mircea *The Sacred and the Profane*. New York: Harcourt Brace & World Inc. 1959.

——*Myths, Dreams and Mysteries*. Harvill Press. 1960.

——*From Primitives to Zen*. Collins. 1967.

HUXLEY, Francis *The Way of the Sacred*. Aldus/Jupiter Books. 1974.

JUNG, Carl *Psychology of the Unconscious*. Kegan Paul, Trench Trubner & Co. 1919.

——*Symbols of Transformation*. Vol. 5 of *Collected Works*. Routledge & Kegan Paul. 1956.

——*Archetypes and the Collective Unconscious*. Vol. 9, Part 1 of *Collected Works*. Routledge & Kegan Paul. 1959.

JUNG, Carl and FRANZ, M. L. von (eds.) *Man and His Symbols*. George Allen & Unwin. 1964.

LÉVI-STRAUSS, Claude *Mythologies*. 3 vols. Translated as *An Introduction to the Science of Mythology*. Vol. 1 *The Raw and the Cooked*, Vol. 2 *From Honey to Ashes*. Jonathan Cape. 1970–73.

LOMMEL, Andreas *Masks Their Meaning and Function*. Paul Elek Books. 1972.

SCOTT-LITTLETON, C. *The New Comparative Mythology*. Revised ed. New York & London: University of California Press. 1974. (This book outlines the main ideas of Dumézil and critical reactions to them.)

CHAPTER 7

Oceania and Australia

PART 1

Introduction

This chapter covers the myths and legends of Australia and the island communities of the Pacific and South East Asia. These latter are grouped into four areas determined by ethnic and cultural rather than political boundaries. The reader may find it helpful to consult the map on page 20. In the eastern Pacific lies Polynesia, whose boundaries run from New Zealand to Easter Island, the Marquesas, the Hawaiian or Sandwich Islands, the Society and Tongan Islands. To the north west is Micronesia, enclosing the Marianas, the Gilbert and Ellice Islands and the Marshalls. To the south west lies Melanesia, incorporating the whole of New Guinea and stretching south to the Santa Cruz and the Solomon Islands, the Bismarck Archipelago and the Admiralty Isles. Indonesia, as a cultural rather than a political unit, stretches from the Andaman Islands in the Bay of Bengal, through the Malay Archipelago and north to the Philippines and Taiwan.

THE LIMITS AND SOURCES OF OUR KNOWLEDGE

Only in parts of New Guinea and remote areas of the Indonesian islands have Oceanic peoples been able to preserve many of their traditional beliefs and ways of life. To the east, where communities are either smaller or, as in New Zealand and Australia, made comparatively defenceless by the terrain, their culture has been disrupted, in many cases utterly destroyed. Since the time of Magellan, Western invaders have come seeking land, goods for their markets, labour for their mines and plantations, converts for their religion, (and, more recently, sights for their tourists), bringing with them European diseases which have often decimated those native populations that had otherwise managed to survive European fire-power. Our ignorance of the *Chamorro* traditions of the Mariana Islands stems from the brutality of the Spanish *conquistadores*; our ignorance of the Aborigine cultures of Tasmania and south-eastern Australia results from the genocide of those Aborigines at the hands of land-hungry Englishmen; the 'mystery' of Easter Island remains insoluble chiefly because of the treatment Easter Islanders received from their Peruvian conquerors, who in the 1860s enslaved the majority of the male population and transported them to the Chincha Islands. Those few who survived to return home took smallpox with them.

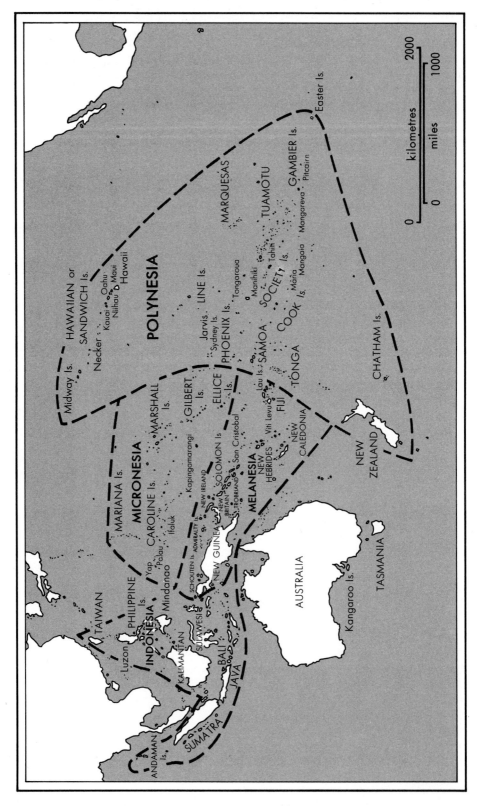

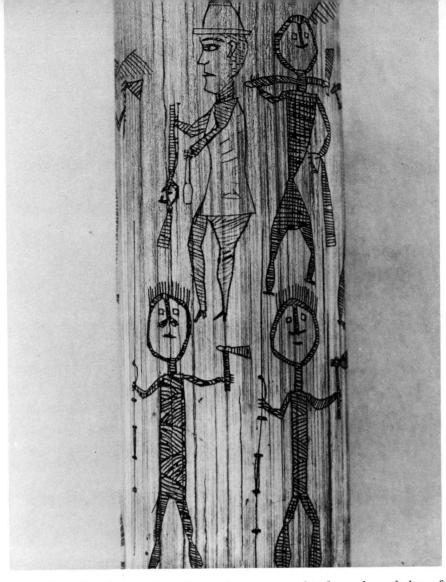

Nineteenth-century bamboo engraving from New Caledonia shows a European visitor among native islanders. British Museum. (*Photo: British Museum.*)

On the other hand, throughout the area, much of our knowledge of traditional beliefs and stories derives from the patient researches of benign administrators, following the pioneer footsteps of Sir Thomas Stamford Raffles, Governor-General of Java, 1811–15, and of Sir George Grey, Governor-General of New Zealand, 1845–54. They learned the native languages and studied their traditions the better to understand the people they governed. Raffles became the acknowledged authority on Javanese history and culture. Grey's *Polynesian Mythology* (1855) remains the basic study of *Maori* beliefs. Raffles and Grey were later to be emulated by Fornander in Hawaii, Grimble in the Gilbert Islands and Gilland and Spencer in Australia.

The impact of missionaries was as ambivalent as that of secular authorities. In general, Catholic missions were less inimical to native traditions than were the Protestants, who tended to be of rigid evangelical views, encouraging their converts to destroy religious images and all other traces of native beliefs. Yet all students of Oceanic mythology are indebted to the Protestant

London Missionary Society's William Ellis, J. M. Orsmond, W. Wyatt Gill and R. Codrington who, like the French Catholic Père Laval, recorded all they could discover of native beliefs. (See the bibliography for their works.)

In the southern Indonesian islands of Java, Sumatra and Bali, in which, from about the beginning of the Christian era, the courts at least came under the influence of Buddhist, and later of Hindu and Islamic teaching, literary remains date from the early eleventh century, when Mpu Kanwa, court poet to King Airlangga of East Java, composed his epic *Arjunavivaha*, which transforms the *Mahābhārata* into an allegory of Airlangga's career and even today provides the basis of many of the *Wayang Purwa* shadow-dramas (see below). Other early Indonesian epics in which Hindu beliefs are assimilated to native traditions include the quasi-historical *Parakaton* or *Book of Kings* (see **19–22**). Even in Indonesia however, literacy was the prerogative of a small minority and began to reach most other Oceanic peoples only at the end of the last century, with the advent of mission schools.

In Polynesia, though not for some reason in other areas, once the islanders could write they began themselves to record their traditions, a task in which some Europeans encouraged them. Thus King Kalakua of Hawaii was spurred by Adolf Bastian to write down the *Kulimpo Chant of Creation*, while in New Zealand a group of *Maoris* commissioned two scribes to record all that their priest Te Matarohanga could tell of *Maori* religion. This work was later translated as *The Lore of the Whare Whananga* (1913).

More recently, anthropologists and enthnographers have published studies of eastern Melanesian peoples and the Berenice Pauhi Bishop Museum in Honolulu has been established as the co-ordinating centre for research into Oceanic civilisations. The museum has a large collection of artefacts and publishes an invaluable series of books and papers.

The origins of the different racial groups of Oceania and their dispersal over thousands of islands remain controversial matters. The eastern islands were some of the last areas of the world to be populated. A minority view, popularised by Heyerdahl, holds that the Polynesians came from South America, but most scholars, while not entirely ruling out the possibility of late arrivals from South America, believe that the south-east Asian mainland was the chief source of Oceanic settlement, and the island peoples themselves believed their original homeland lay in this direction. It is clear that wherever the inhabitants originated, the native population is now a mixture of Caucasian, Mongoloid and Negrito peoples and that waves of settlers reached the islands over a long period, beginning at least as early as 18 000 B.C. and ending as late as A.D. 1000–1300, with the settlement of New Zealand. As there are considerable differences between the cultures of the various zones it is convenient to consider each in turn.

INDONESIA

The Indonesians comprise a mixture of races and creeds. Small groups of primitive Negrito hunters still inhabit the Andaman Islands and remote areas

Buddhist frieze from a temple in Bali. (*Photo: FCA International.*)

of Philippine Luzon and Mindanao. The bulk of the population is however of mixed *Malay* stock, descendants of Mongoloid peoples who began to enter the region some 3,000 years ago, intermarrying with the earlier immigrants who were already established in the area. (The term *Malay* is also sometimes used in a more restricted sense to mean those Indonesians who have adopted the Islamic faith.)

The Malay immigrants were talented sailors and seem to have spread as far afield as Polynesia to the east and Malagasy to the west. Some scholars, pointing to similarities between Indonesian and West African musical instruments and batik work, believe that the Malays even penetrated as far as Nigeria, a thesis which might also claim some support from the striking similarities existing between some West African and Indonesian myths (see **10–12** and vol. 2: 4.2. **82**).

Their nautical skill and the fact that their home lay at the centre of important trade routes, meant that the Indonesians early came under the influence of other cultures from mainland Asia, notably Hinduism and Mahāyāna Buddhism (see vol. 3), both of which, being polytheistic, were easily assimilated to native animistic beliefs.

This Balinese figure of the eagle-god Garuda killing a *nāga* (snake deity) illustrates the persistence of Hindu beliefs in this Indonesian island. (*Photo: FCA International.*)

At present the majority of Filipino islanders profess Catholicism, while in the rest of Indonesia, except for Bali which remains predominantly Hindu, most of the people are nominally Moslems. Throughout the region however, the more sophisticated creeds are to a greater or lesser extent combined with animistic practices, particularly in the villages of the interior.

The Soul and the Rice Mother

One of the most distinctive features of Indonesian animism is its concept of the soul, which is held to be a property not only of people and animals, but also of plants, most notably of the rice plant, whose soul is often given the same name as the human one; both are called *tondi* by the Sumatran *Bataks*, *toradja* in Sulawesi, *sumange*, *sumangat* or *semangat* in Java.

While present in every particle of rice, the soul is concentrated in a particular, ritually gathered plant that is treasured as the Rice Mother (Grandmother, Grandfather, Uncle), the remaining crop being spoken of as its children (grandchildren, nephews). The Rice Mother thus guards the rest of the crop and gathers to herself the soul of any plant eaten by predators. The Indonesians identify her with the Hindu spirit known as Dewī Shrī (Devī Shrī).

Hindu influences

Modern Balinese figure of the rice-goddess made from rice straw. (*Photo: Axel Poignant.*)

This is but one example of the widespread survival of Hindu names for the gods and spirits of the southern Indonesian islands, where most of the chief deities' names are of Hindu origin, as is the common belief in a trinity of great gods: Batara Guru, Soripata and Mangalubulan (qq.v.). Other Hindu concepts which have become assimilated to Indonesian beliefs and have passed on to the more easterly Oceanic islands include the idea of a number of heavens, seven or more, and such notions as the world's emergence from an egg. However, the most notable survival of early Indonesian Hindu traditions is to be found in the *Wayang Purwa* shadow-plays of Java and Bali,

Wayang Purwa puppet figure of the hero Bima. British Museum. (*Photo: British Museum.*)

which from early times were one of the chief means whereby Hindu spiritual concepts were transmitted to the uneducated masses. Over the centuries, the Javanese and Balinese have reinterpreted and developed the tradition until it has become distinctively their own, but the *wayang* dramas are still based on myths and legends of Hindu origin as well as upon native stories and traditions. Readers interested in this fascinating dramatic mode are referred to J. Scott-Kemball's easily available pamphlet *Javanese shadow puppets* and to the British Museum's Raffles' Collection.

POLYNESIA AND MICRONESIA

The Polynesians are an aristocratic race of tall, light-skinned people. The more hybrid Micronesians are rather shorter and darker, but a number of similarities exist between the two cultures, perhaps because at least some of the Micronesian islands, those of which we know the most, were conquered by Polynesians from Samoa.

Within Polynesia itself, there are some differences between the cultures of the western islands, Samoa and Tonga, and those to the south and east, which were probably all settled from the Marquesas and Society Islands. However, throughout Polynesia and in Micronesia also, though less rigidly, all the island societies were highly stratified, with aristocratic and priestly castes. The chiefs and kings traced their descent from gods and culture-heroes, so

providing a direct link with their peoples' mythological past. In Samoa and Tonga the so-called Talking Chiefs were the guardians of the community's traditions, which they handed down from one generation to another. In the rest of Polynesia the priesthood was divided into two groups: prophets and diviners, and ceremonial priests. Here, knowledge of tribal lore was shared among the priests and the aristocrats, who were formally instructed by the ceremonial clergy. Their education was often conducted in special buildings, like the Whare Wananga, or sacred colleges, of the New Zealand *Maoris*.

Religious festivals included dances, dramatic performances and, in Hawaii and Tahiti, marionette shows, organised by special groups of talented individuals. These were known as *Arioi* (q.v.) in Tahiti, *Ka'ioi* in the Marquesas, and *Hula* in Hawaii. The organisations had various ranks and

Interior of a *Maori* meeting house at Mandiapoto, New Zealand. The carved panels and figures represent tribal ancestors. (*Photo: Axel Poignant.*)

Hawaiian stool in the form of a *Hula* dancer. British Museum. (*Photo: British Museum.*)

Engraving made from a drawing by J. Webber on Captain Cook's third voyage shows a Hawaiian *Hula* dancer wearing dog-tooth leg ornaments and carrying a feather shield. (*Photo: Axel Poignant.*)

divisions and as membership seems to have depended on talent rather than birth, it probably offered a means for the clever but lowly-born to rise in society. At least one group, the Tahitian *Arioi*, was also a fertility-cult organisation. Some of its ceremonies were witnessed by Captain Cook. It seems likely that the society known as the *Uritoy* in the Micronesian Mariana Islands was a similar organisation, but it was early destroyed and little is known about it.

Gods and Spirits

The Polynesian and Micronesian pantheons are large and complicated since, for reasons of geography, each island society developed in comparative isolation. A deity of one island may be regarded as a hero or trickster in another. Conversely, gods or heroes may be credited with similar attributes and deeds, but given different names. As a result the mythology of the whole area can be confusing, but within each of the main zones certain themes and stories predominate. These are outlined in Part 2.

Sometimes, as in Tonga and Tahiti, one god was held to be chief of all the others, but there was no real concept of a supreme being. The great gods (Polynesian *atua* or *atea*) ruled various aspects of nature. Their importance to man was determined by their effect on his daily life. For example, the war-god Tu was of more immediate concern than the sky-god Rangi.

Apart from the great gods, ancestral spirits (*varua*) played an important part in religious beliefs and practices. It was thought they could embody themselves in creatures and artefacts, and fish-hooks and other utensils were carved in their likenesses, which also appeared on canoes and the doorposts of houses etc. Spirits of the recently dead were also believed to exert influence on man's daily life and it was most important that mortuary rituals should be properly observed, so that the ancestors were not dangerously offended. After death the spirit lingered near its human home and might become malevolent if due funeral rites were neglected. After they had been performed, the soul journeyed west (or, in northern New Zealand, north) to the junction of the spirit world and chaos. This 'Leaping place' (*Reinga*) was usually associated with a tree and it was commonly believed that spirits who grasped the green branches would descend into nothingness, while those who took hold of a seemingly dead bough went to the spirit world.

Various concepts of this afterworld existed, and it was usually held to be divided into several regions, mirroring the class divisions of earthly life. These regions were believed to exist either on islands below the horizon in the far west, or in the sky, or underground. The islanders also conceived of a paradisal home of the great gods and spirits. In eastern Polynesia this was

Ancient gable boards and entrance post from a *Maori* meeting house in the East Cape district, New Zealand, carved with ancestral figures. Auckland Museum. (*Photo: Werner Forman Archive.*)

called Hawaiki, but western peoples gave that name to their mythical homeland and usually called the spirit world Pulotu, while to the Micronesians it was known as the paradise of Matang (98–101).

Although the ancestors journeyed to the afterworld, they were also held to return to visit their human homes and take a continuing and intimate interest in their descendants' welfare and daily lives. In Micronesia, ancestral skulls were carefully preserved, sometimes in special gardens, where they were buried with the cranium exposed. On certain occasions this was tenderly anointed with oil. Grimble tells a story of a Gilbert Islander taking his grandfather's skull out with him into the canoe shed for a smoke. Cradling the skull in his elbow, he blew the tobacco fumes between its jaws, chatting to grandfather meanwhile. He explained to Grimble that he had chosen this particular gift for the old man as he knew that tobacco was unobtainable in the spirit world, and he wanted to give grandfather something he would particularly relish. Every now and then he enquired of the skull how it was enjoying the smoke.

Mummified, tatooed head of a *Maori* ancestor. Museum für Völkerkunde, Munich. (*Photo: Werner Forman Archive*.)

Mana

The Polynesian word *mana* signifies a spiritual power which all people were held in some measure to embody. Any special talent or achievement was attributed to the individual's possessing more *mana* than his fellows. Kings, chiefs and priests were naturally endowed with unusually high quantities, while the culture-heroes and gods possessed superhuman amounts, hence their distinction. For the Polynesians, the difference between men, culture-heroes and gods was therefore a matter of degree rather than of kind. Similar beliefs were held in the Micronesian and Melanesian islands, and indeed to some extent they still are. The cannibalism which prevailed among many of these peoples sprang from their desire to imbibe their victims' *mana*.

Bones from a Fijian cannibal feast fastened into a tree cleft. British Museum. (*Photo: British Museum.*)

MELANESIA

In Melanesia successive waves of immigrants produced more hybrid populations than those further east, and their cultural patterns are correspondingly diverse. Parts of the interior of New Guinea and much of its north and south-west coasts are inhabited by *Papuans*, a mixed race of comparatively tall, dark, frizzy-haired people. In the central highlands live pigmy tribes of *Negrito* hunters, about whom until recently little was known. The inhabitants of the east coast and its contiguous islands are a mixture of *Papuan* stock with the generally smaller and lighter-skinned 'true' Melanesians. In the islands farther to the south and east the Melanesian element predominates, but these people are still much darker than their copper-coloured Polynesian neighbours.

Most Melanesian societies are divided into kinship or *totem* groups (pp. 37–38), rather than into classes or castes. Hereditary chiefdoms existed in parts of the New Hebrides and New Caledonia, but in general Melanesian communities were, and are, comparatively democratic, decisions being reached by discussion among all adult men, and the rôle of the chief being here very much that of a *primus inter pares*.

All Melanesian cultures tend to be materialistic and organised so as to allow innumerable occasions for the reciprocal exchange of goods, a custom which reached its apogee in the *Kula* rites described by Malinowski in *Argonauts of the Western Pacific*. Anyone who possesses a large quantity of goods, or some article of high intrinsic value, achieves social status, but his ability to do so is attributed to his possessing unusually high *mana*, which has enabled him to discern the rituals most pleasing to the spirits, who respond by increasing his possessions. This is the basis of the respect given to the chiefs or so-called Big Men of New Guinea, who win their position by accumulating sufficient wealth to provide one or more huge feasts for the rest of the populace. In some areas, such as the Banks Islands, initiation into men's societies depends on being able to buy one's way in with pigs and by feasting other members. On the other hand, anyone who, in the ordinary

Carved 'stool' from a men's house in the Sepik River district of Papua-New Guinea. The figure probably represents a spirit. Museum für Völkerkunde, Basle. (*Photo: Axel Poignant.*)

Figure of a protective spirit, from Bougainville, Solomon Islands, probably used as a canoe-prow ornament. Museum für Völkerkunde, Basle. (*Photo: Axel Poignant.*)

course of commercial exchange, deliberately puts his fellow in a position where he must lose face by being unable to reciprocate, makes himself exceedingly unpopular, while he who refuses to engage in the exchanges, casts himself completely outside the pale. Indeed, the *Tangu* of New Guinea apply the word *ranguma* not only to such men but also to sorcerers and criminals.

Gods, Spirits and Demons

Although most Melanesians believe in gods and culture-heroes, each community has its own and men are interested in the origins of their particular environment and group rather than in those of the world and mankind as a whole. Their religion is dominated by animistic beliefs in which demons and ancestral spirits play roughly equal rôles. Ancestor cults

33

Preparing for a great pig feast in the Central Highlands of New Guinea. (*Photo: Axel Poignant.*)

and associated fertility rites in which large numbers of pigs are sacrificed to feed the spirits and, in some cases, to placate them, form a central part of religious festivals in many areas. The spirits are believed to take the forms of animals and reptiles at will, and sometimes to embody themselves in artefacts and natural phenomena, but the sacred statues and stones are hardly idols, since the worship is offered not to those things in themselves but to the spirits inhabiting them.

It is confidently believed that if men perform the correct rituals, the gods and spirits have no option but to respond. If no response is forthcoming, the fault lies with the man who performed the ritual, inadequately or incorrectly.

Cargo Cults

The extraordinary Cargo Cults that have sprung up in western Melanesia since the advent of white settlers, have their genesis in the Melanesians' practice of reciprocal exchange and in their confidence that the gods always respond to correctly-performed rituals.

The material prosperity of the white people and their refusal to partake in exchanges has placed the natives in a position where they feel both helpless and inferior. In some cases they have sought to explain their dilemma by myths telling how, in the remote past, two brothers, one white, the other dark, were separated by the darker one's folly or sin, so the white brother retained the gods' favour and is more prosperous. In many cases however, cults have sprung up based on a curious amalgam of native and Christian beliefs and rituals, designed to induce the Christian God and Jesus, who are conceived in terms of traditional deities, to send the natives goods like the white men's, which are believed to come ready-made from heaven. Heaven itself is held to be situated somewhere in Australia, in Sydney for example, or in the sky immediately above it, in which case it is joined to earth by a ladder, down which ancestral spirits carry the goods, packed in crates addressed to specific individuals. Participators in the cults confidently expect such crates to arrive by ship, plane or lorry, depending on where they live. When the goods fail to appear the peoples have sometimes projected their advent into the future, but more often assumed that they themselves have yet to perform

Late nineteenth-century votive board from the Nicobar Islands shows (*top to bottom*) European surrounded by his possessions; a native house flanked by native canoe and European ship; pigs—symbol of the native's wealth; sea creatures and what seems to be a drowned European sailor. Museum voor Volkenkunde, Leiden. (*Photo: Werner Forman Archive.*)

the correct ritual to secure them, blaming the white men for witholding its essential secret. Sometimes they have asserted that the white men, or their ancestors, are deliberately changing the labels on crates destined for the natives and diverting them to the whites.

Increased knowledge of Australian life has not so much changed these assumptions as led the more recent cult leaders to reject Christian teaching as the white man's preserve, and to urge their compatriots to return to native religion, their failure to receive cargo now being attributed to neglect of the native gods. Fascinating studies of such cults are Peter Lawrence's *Road Belong Cargo* and Glynn Cochrane's *Big Men and Cargo Cults*.

AUSTRALIA

A dearth of archaeological evidence has so far made it impossible to date the Aborigines' arrival in Australia with any certainty. We do not know exactly where they came from, nor how long they took to spread across the continent and into Tasmania from the coasts of Arnhem Land and Cape York Peninsula, where they probably first set foot on Australian soil.

It was once not uncommon for them to be spoken of as if they were a prehistoric race which, due to its isolation from the rest of humankind, had survived unchanged into the present century. However, although the Aborigines seem to be genetically different from other races, they are not an entirely homogenous people and although their culture is in a sense mesolithic, it has not been static, nor were the Aborigines wholly ignorant of agriculture and such crafts as pottery—they had contacts with peoples who practised both.

The first of these were light-skinned visitors who reputedly came from beyond the Sea of Timor, far to the west. They settled on the north coast and there built stone houses, cultivated gardens and wove and dyed cloth. They were perhaps *Malays*. The Aborigines, who called them *Baniji*, clearly distinguished them from later Indonesian settlers, whom they named *Macassans*. The *Macassans* were potters and apparently the Aborigines helped them in this work, although they did not make pots for themselves, presumably because they had no use for them.

Even in its most fertile north-coast areas, Australia is not a country amenable to primitive arable farming. Probably that is why the *Baniji* and the *Macassans* either moved on or died out. Nor was pastoral farming feasible in a country where the indigenous animals could not be domesticated. Aborigine culture should therefore be seen as an intelligent response to its environment. (In drier areas no system yet devised by Western immigrants has been capable of supporting so many people as the Aborigines' could and did.) The close bond they felt with their environment found expression in the various attitudes and practices that have been given the collective name of totemism.

Totemism

The word *totemism* derives from the North American Ojibwa *ototeman*, meaning 'he is my relative'. Although totemic beliefs and practices have been spoken of as existing among some African tribes, the term is used particularly in relation to North American Indian, Melanesian and Aborigine cultures. Lévi-Strauss, to whose interesting survey, *Totemism*, the reader is referred, suggests that the term is meaningless when applied to a number of very different practices and beliefs. However it is commonly used to signify a metaphorical expression of man's relationship to his fellows and to the rest of the world, in terms of some creature, natural phenomenon or human attribute, with which he identifies himself and other members of his group, or with which he feels he and they are closely associated.

Although various forms of totemism exist, Elkin, the standard Australian authority, suggests they may be divided into two broad categories: social and ritual, or cult, totemism. In the first, the relationship to the totem is determined by one's membership of a particular group and the totem itself is usually thought of as a relative—an 'elder brother' or ancestor. Being of the 'same flesh' it may not be eaten. Social totemism is usually found in groups observing matrilinear descent and members of the same totem may not intermarry. Totemism of this kind is common in parts of Melanesia as well as in some areas of Australia.

Aborigine artist's painting of Indonesian *Macassans* aboard their ship. Private collection. (*Photo: Axel Poignant.*)

Aborigine ritual stones from the Melville Islands and the bag in which they were kept. British Museum. (*Photo: British Museum.*)

Ritual, or cult, totemism is associated with particular sacred sites, which are cared for by the initiate men, who lead or perform the associated rituals and guard the sacred emblems and ritual objects. In this case the totem creature, for example the witchetty-grub, may be eaten and the meal is not usually regarded as being in any way sacramental.

Ritual totemism is usually found in groups which observe patrilinear descent, although the Berndts, in their excellent *World of the First Australians*, quote a report of matrilinear cults in the Cape York Peninsula. In societies practising ritual totemism, totemic exogamy is unusual and may even be thought undesirable.

An individual's totemic affiliation may be inherited or determined in one of various other ways. In many areas of Australia the father 'finds' the unborn child's spirit in a dream, and the infant's totem is determined by the context of this dream. In other cases the totemic association may be decided by the locality in which the mother first realises she is pregnant, or, as among the *Aranda*, by the place in which the baby is actually born—a matter which is to some extent susceptible to the mother's control, but not entirely so. Thus children do not necessarily belong to the same totem as their parents or siblings. In some areas it is moreover common for each person to have several totems, though some will be more important to him than others.

The Dreamtime and Dreamtime Beings

The name Dreamtime or Eternal Dreaming has come to be given to the mythical era in which divine beings and totem ancestors inhabited Australia and roamed the countryside, forming its landscape, establishing human societies, showing men sacred sites, giving them sacred objects and teaching them the rituals by which Aborigine life was governed. In myths these beings may be referred to indifferently as human or animal (see **144–152**) and appear to change from one form to the other as quickly as drawing breath. They were called *wongar* by the *Maurgin* of north-east Arnhem Land, *muramura* in the Lake Eyre region, *djurgurba* in the western desert and *wondjina* in the northern Kimberley area. They may be roughly divided into three kinds, but no clear-cut divisions exist.

Aborigine bark painting of a *wondjina*, from NW Australia. British Museum. (*Photo: Axel Poignant.*)

At the turn of the century, some investigators held that the Aborigines of the south east believed in a supreme All-Father, who lived in the sky and was called Nurundere (Ngurunderi) in the region of the lower Murray Basin, Bunjil in Victoria, Baiame among Queensland tribes west of the Great Dividing Range, and Daramulun along the coast. However, recent scholars believe that these beings were no more than culture-heroes. As no members of the relevant tribes now survive, the question cannot be finally determined.

Among the *Aranda* of central Australia, the chief Dreamtime beings are paternal totemic ancestors such as Lukuru, while along much of the northern coast pre-eminence is given to a third kind of being, the fertility-spirit or Great Mother, Waramurungugju, Imberombera or Kunapipi. At times she is identified with the other great fertility-spirit of Australia, the Rainbow Snake, but in other cases the snake is held to be masculine or androgynous. Both creator and destroyer, it is associated particularly with streams and water-holes, in which it is said to live.

Marinbata bark painting from northern Arnhem Land depicting the Rainbow Snake. Private Collection. (*Photo: Axel Poignant.*)

Arnhem Land Aborigines singing and dancing to the ritual music of a *didjeridu* drone pipe. (*Photo: Axel Poignant.*)

The Dreamtime is believed to be a living part of the present, as well as a mythic past. Man participates in it by observing the ritual the Dreamtime beings established and in which they still manifest themselves, in the human forms of the participating actors. The rituals and their associated myths have therefore been—in some areas still are—a vital part of the Aborigines' daily life.

No one group or dialect-unit is likely to own (in this case synonymous with 'to know') a complete myth, for the Dreamtime beings wandered far and wide, crossing many groups' boundaries, and, although contiguous peoples may own related parts of a myth and come together to perform the associated rites, the whole is never enacted at one time because it would be impossible for all the owners to meet.

Normally the stories were enacted by men, sometimes masked, decked fantastically in blood, ochre, pipe-clay and feathers, and accompanied by chants, drums, bullroarers and the weird music of the *dijeridoo* pipe. A narrative outline of the ritual myth (see **162–167**) can therefore only hope to indicate a faint shadow of the whole.

A NOTE ON SPELLING AND PRONUNCIATION

Names of deities and heroes are spelled phonetically. Among the Oceanic islanders names are standardised, but there is no agreed spelling for many of the Australian names; here, therefore, we have followed the variants used by the authorities quoted in the bibliography.

It will be noticed that many of the Oceanic islanders' gods and heroes have similar names. This is partly due to the fact that isolation of one island people from another led to dialectic variants of common originals, and partly because the names were first written down by missionaries who did not always choose exactly the same spelling to represent similar sounds.

PART 2

Narrative Outlines

INDONESIA

Creation Stories
1–14

(i) THE CREATION OF THE WORLD

1 The complex culture of Indonesia is vividly illustrated in the variety of its creation myths. Here we may trace the immediate origins of many of the stories found in Oceanic islands further to the east. In the Minahassa area of north Sulawesi, the world is said to have evolved, or been created, from a rock in the midst of an otherwise empty, boundless sea, a theme prominent in myths from Polynesian Tonga and Samoa (**25–29**). In some tales from the *Kayan* people in central Kalimantan, the primaeval rock is dropped into the ocean by a creator spider, who seems an ancestor of the Micronesian Na Areau (**87–92**). In Sumatra and parts of New Britain, it is said that sky-beings descended from heaven and created the first animals, plants and men, a theme common in many parts of Melanesia.

2 Perhaps the most distinctive Indonesian stories are those in which Hindu elements have been absorbed into the native tradition, which delights in tales of fabulous birds and beasts, such as those in the following *Dairi Batak* story from Sumatra.

Batara Guru and the Raven

3 The pregnant wife of the great god Batara Guru hankered for venison, so Batara despatched a raven to seek some. Unsuccessful, the bird roamed the heavens, and came eventually to a cave which contained a seemingly bottomless pit. He could hear nothing when he threw down a bamboo cane to sound its depth, so he flew into the pit and at length emerged on the surface of a dark sea, only to realise that he could not find his way back. Fortunately just then the bamboo he had cast down the pit floated by him, so he perched on that and rested.

4 Eventually Batara Guru, attended by several servants, set out to look for the raven. With him the god took a handful of soil, seven pieces of wood, a chisel, a goat and a bumble-bee. Arriving at sea-level, he began to make a raft. Just then up floated the raven on his bamboo stick. Since all was still pitch dark, the bird asked Batara Guru to enlighten the scene, which the great god did. Then Batara Guru ordered the goat, accompanied by the bumble-bee, to go down under the raft and steady it on his horns.

43

Unfortunately, just then the god broke his chisel. Flying from his hand, the pieces hit the goat hard on its head, making it buck wildly, so the raft was badly shaken. Sternly commanding the animal to keep still, Batara Guru spread his handful of soil over the raft and so made the earth, which he gave to the raven for his home.

Batara Guru and Boru deak pordjar

5 Another Batak myth says that Batara Guru's daughter, Boru deak pordjar, the 'All-knowing', seeking to escape from the unwanted attentions of her uncle, the god Mangalubulan, leaped from the heavens into the empty limitless sea. Learning of her plight, Batara Guru sent a swallow to her with a handful of soil. Scattered on the sea this formed the earth, but it also shut out all light from the underworld domain of the great serpent Naga Padoha. Exceedingly annoyed, the serpent rose and drowned the earth, but Batara Guru retaliated and had him fixed to a rock; then he recreated the earth and heaven above the serpent's head. Some say that one day Naga Padoha will break free again and once more drown the world.

Lowalangi and Latura

6 In the beginning there was only a formless chaos. Eventually this parted and the goddess Ina-da Samihara Luwo was born, and created the world. Then a stone split and there came forth Ina-da Samadulo Hose, the mother of men and gods. She gave birth to two pairs of twins, who married each other. The younger son, Lowalangi, rules the skies, living in the uppermost of the nine heavens. The older son, Latura, governs the underworld.

7 After a quarrel lasting nine days, Latura stole his brother Lowalangi's consort, his own older sister, and made her his second wife. She bore him a round limbless child. This was cut into halves and, being of different sexes, the two halves then married and gave birth to the first man, Hulu. (Myth from the southern *Nias*.)

(ii) THE CREATION OF MAN

8 Human beings were sometimes spoken of as the descendants of gods who came down to live on earth, but other stories tell a different tale. The *Ami* of Taiwan said a divinity stuck his staff into the ground, where it grew and sent out two shoots, from which came a man and a woman. In Kalimantan and the Philippines, people were often said to have emerged from eggs, while in Amboina and Buru they were believed to be the offspring of a tree impregnated by a bird. Other tales speak of man's being moulded from earth or carved from wood. In Minahassa, the supreme being made two people from clay and brought them alive by blowing powdered ginger into their ears and nostrils. The following *Dyak* story comes from the Baram and Rejana districts of Kalimantan.

Iri and Ringgon

9 Two birds Iri and Ringgon created the earth, plants and animals. Next they decided to make men. Their first version of a human being was formed from clay, but he was speechless and motionless. Annoyed, they ran at him, frightening him so badly that he fell over backwards and smashed to pieces.

A second prototype, carved from hard wood, proved moronic. After much thought, the birds then took some wood from the Kumpong tree, which has very strong fibres and bright scarlet sap. From this they made a man and a woman and were so delighted with the results that they spent some time gazing in admiration at their handiwork. At last, they returned to the Kumpong tree to fetch more wood, only to realise that they had quite forgotten the design they had used for the successful models. Nor could they recall how these had been executed. Subsequent attempts to repeat their success produced very inferior designs: the ancestors of the orang-utan and the monkeys.

(iii) THE SEPARATION OF EARTH AND HEAVEN
10 The following stories have affinities with those from other parts of Oceania, but they often seem even closer to African myths and perhaps support the theory, held by some scholars, that Indonesian traders early reached not only the eastern but the western coasts of Africa. (See vol. 2: 4.2. 82.)

A *Tagalog* story from the Philippines
11 Originally the sky could be touched and when men were playing they often banged their heads against it. Eventually some men grew very annoyed and pelted the sky with stones. God then withdrew it to its present height.

A *Manoba* story from Mindanao
12 Once the sky was so close to the earth that when women pounded rice they continually thumped it with their pestles. At last the heavens could endure no more and moved away.

An *Ifugao* story from Kiangan in the Philippines
13 Originally the sky was so low that it prevented men from throwing their spears properly, and being a man-eater, it also promised to exterminate the human race, so men went to the gods and begged for their help. One deity, who had previously always remained sitting, then stood up, thrusting the sky up on his head and shoulders, and so men were saved.

The Flood

14 One morning, just as the rice harvest was ready, great areas of the fields were found plundered, but there was no sign of any footprint or track which would indicate the thief, so a night guard was set up. The next night the waiting men saw a huge serpent descend from the heavens and begin eating their rice. One man dashed up to it and cut off its head. Next morning he breakfasted on some of the snake-flesh. Hardly had he finished his meal than there was a cloudburst, and such a flood that only those few who managed to reach the hills survived the inundation. (An *Iban* or *Sea Dyak* myth from Kalimantan.)

Swan Maiden Myths
15–18

15 'Swan maiden' stories are common in both Indonesia and Melanesia. The following example comes from Java.

16 One day a hunter in the forest saw maidens descend from the sky. Laying aside their clothes they bathed in a pool. The huntsman stole one set of these magic garments, so their owner could not return to heaven. However he promised to give the girl new clothes if she would marry him. Having no alternative, she agreed.

17 One day, when setting out for the river to do their laundry, she asked her husband to mind the pot of rice, which she had left cooking, and warned him on no account to raise its lid. Although he had only ever given her a single measure of rice, she had never asked him for more yet always produced good meals, so he was consumed with curiosity and immediately she had gone, lifted the lid of the pot and peered inside. There he saw but a single grain of rice.

18 When she returned the woman knew at once what he had done, for her spell had been destroyed and the rice had not multiplied in the pot. She had to fetch more from the bin and at its bottom came upon her heavenly clothes, which her husband had hidden beneath the rice. At once she put them on and told him she must return home. As their child was too young to accompany her, she must leave that behind. Whenever the baby cried her husband should put it on the roof and burn a rice stalk; then she would come down and feed the child. Taking a stalk of rice she then set it alight and ascended to the heavens on its smoke. (See also vol. 2: 3.3 and vol. 3: 5.3.)

The Legend of Ken Angrok and Prince Dangdang Gendis
19–22

19 This legend tells how Ken Angrok, founder of the last great Hindu-Javanese kingdom of Majapahit, came to power.

20 The whole land of Java was disturbed. Eventually Ken Angrok decided to go to Mount Leyar, the meeting-place of the gods. There he hid himself in a rubbish-heap. Hardly had he done so than seven sounds were heard: rolling peals of thunder and shorter thunderclaps. There came an earthquake, lightning and sheet-lightning, wild gusts of wind, torrential rain—though it was the dry season—and rainbows appeared simultaneously in the eastern and western skies. There came loud voices crying: 'Who shall make Java strong? Who shall be its king?' Then the great god Batara Guru replied, saying he had chosen his son Ken Angrok, born of a woman in Pangkur. At these words Ken Angrok clambered from the rubbish-heap and stood before the gods, who approved Batara Guru's choice and acclaimed Ken Angrok as king, giving him the title Batara Guru.

21 Meanwhile Prince Dangdang Gendis of Daha (Kediri) called all the priests of his city and ordered them to bow down before him, for he was the king, he claimed. With one voice the priests declined, for none had ever bowed down to a mere king. Then Dangdang Gendis stuck his spear, point uppermost, in the ground and sitting on its head created an illusion of himself with three eyes and four arms, like the great Batara Guru himself. Now the priests could hardly deny him homage, yet they were loath to give it, so they fled to Tumapel, Angrok's city, and gave him their allegiance.

22 Before long the story of Ken Angrok's elevation to the kingship reached the ears of Dangdang Gendis, who scoffingly declared that only Batara Guru could defeat him. Hearing of this boast, Ken Angrok publicly claimed the title the gods had given him. Then he marched against Dangdang Gendis, routing his army and killing the prince's gallant brother Raden Mahisa Walungan and his minister Gubar Baleman. Dangdang Gendis himself fled to a temple and there hanged himself high in the air, together with his horse, his shield-bearer, his umbrella-bearer, his betel-carrier, the page who carried his water and the page who carried his mat. When his wives Dewi Amisani, Dewi Hasin and Dewi Paya heard that the prince was now lost in the realm of the gods they disappeared, and the prince's palace and all his goods vanished into thin air. So Ken Angrok became king.

POLYNESIA

Creation Stories
23–55

23 Polynesian creation myths comprise a mixture of elements from different sources but in general they may be divided into two kinds. The first, found predominantly in the Tongan and Samoan islands, envisages a primordial waste of waters into which a sky-god, Tangaroa or Tangaloa, drops, or sends, a stone and so creates land. A variant of this type, found in Hawaii and New Zealand, imagines the world emerging from a cosmic egg, laid in the sea by a primordial bird. This variant is probably a late development influenced by Hindu concepts.

24 A second type of myth envisages an original chaos or void, usually named Po, from which elemental beings slowly evolve and, after aeons of time, give rise to a skyfather, Rangi or Atea, who unites with the earth-mother, Papa, and fathers a host of creatures as well as the great Polynesian gods. This 'evolutionary' form of myth is most common in central and eastern Polynesia, and among the New Zealand *Maoris*.

(i) SAMOAN AND TONGAN STORIES
25 A great octopus emerged from the primaeval cliffs. Its children were Fire and Water. A terrible quarrel which arose among their descendants led to the

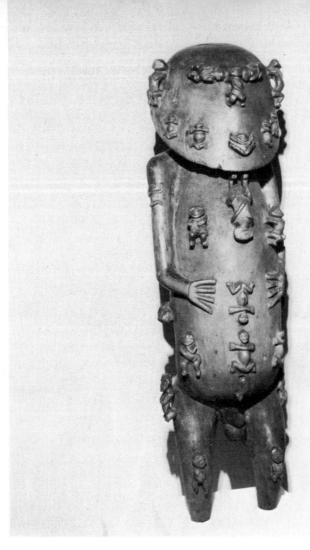

Carving of Tangaroa Upao Vahu (Tangaroa-up-in-the-Sky) in the process of creation. The figure, which comes from the Austral Islands, is hollow and contained further, smaller, humanoid carvings inside it. British Museum. (*Photo: Photoresources.*)

world being engulfed by the sea, so the god Tangaloa had to recreate the universe.

26 Some versions omit all reference to the octopus and say that in the beginning there was nothing but the boundless ocean. Looking down from the heavens, Tangaloa noticed a stone floating in the water below. He descended, took it up and carried it back to heaven. There he carved it into the shape of a woman, gave the form life and took her as his consort. Their offspring was a daughter, the snipe Tuli.

27 Tangaloa threw a boulder down into the sea and commanded Tuli to descend and make her home on this rock. Before long she returned complaining that it offered no shelter. Tangaloa then gave her a vine, which she planted on the boulder. In some versions of the myth, Tuli continues to commute between earth and heaven, reporting each change in the new world. At first she finds the vine flourishes, covering the whole land. On her next visit it has withered and maggots have formed in its rotting tendrils. Later she returns and discovers the maggots have been transformed into men.

Wayang kulit (shadow puppet) figure of Arjuna, hero in the Javanese *Wayang Purwa* plays. Private Collection. (*Photo: Werner Forman Archive.*)

Early nineteenth-century Balinese figures of fertility spirits, made from rice straw. Private Collection. (*Photo: Werner Forman Archive.*)

Carved and painted figures of ancestral spirits from a cult house of the *Abelam* tribe in the Maprik district, New Guinea. (*Photo: Axel Poignant.*)

Rock with figure of the Easter-Island bird-man holding the world egg. He was probably identified, or associated, with the creator Make-make. British Museum. (*Photo: Michael Holford.*)

28 Another version says that Tangaloa took the maggots and gave them each limbs, a heart and a soul and so made them into human beings.

29 In a Tongan version of the myth, four great gods lived in the sky above the formless sea. They were Tama-pouli-alamafo, King of Heaven, Tangaloa-eiki, the Heavenly Chieftain, Tangaloa-tufuga, the Celestial Craftsman and Tangaloa-atu-logo-logo, the Heavenly Messenger. The Messenger was ordered to search the sea for land and he did so, riding on a bird. Eventually he descried a sandbank, but complained it offered no resting-place. The Craftsman therefore threw down woodshavings and chips of stone and formed the island of Eua, where Tangaloa-atu-logo-logo was commanded to live. He was given a seed to sow there. It grew into a great vine and covered the island with vegetation.

(ii) STORIES FROM TAHITI

30 Amidst the dark chaos, Ta'aroa existed within an egg-like shell. Eventually he cracked it open and came and stood on it, calling into the darkness. Nothing replied. He summoned rock and sand but nothing came for there was nothing. So Ta'aroa retreated into a second shell, where for aeons he remained.

31 When for a second time he emerged, Ta'aroa took the first shell, turned it over and lifted it up to form the dome of the sky, which he named *Rumia*, the Overturned. From his second shell he formed rocks and sand. Then, making himself one with Te Tuma, the source of all things, he called the great gods to him from the void.

32 From his own spine and ribs he created mountains. He made clouds from his lungs, liver, heart and kidneys. From his nails he formed shells and fish-scales. He put the richness of his flesh into the earth and created vegetation from his own sacred scarlet feathers. His intestines he transformed into eels and crustacea, and from his hot blood came everything red: the skies of dawn and dusk, the rainbow and all scarlet birds. (Cf. vol. 2: 3.2. **142–145**; vol. 3: 5.2. **47–56** and 6.2. **58–60**).

33 All was yet dark, for Atea the sky-god was clasped to the earth by Tumu-ra'i-feuna, a great octopus, whose name means Foundation-of-Earthly-Heaven. Rua, god of the abyss, killed the creature with a charm, but the octopus's arms still clamped earth and sky together.

34 The demi-god Rû attempted to force them apart, but he could only raise Atea a little and was so damaged in the attempt that his ruptured intestines fell out and floated off, forming a cloudbank. The demi-god Maui (see also **60–61** and **73–80**) quickly pushed in wedges and props to keep Atea and the earth apart; then he sought the help of the great god Tane, whom Ta'aroa had made ruler of the tenth and highest heaven.

35 Tane descended to earth with adzes and, disregarding Atea's yells of pain, gouged holes into him until the god was released from the octopus's grip and rose high above the earth. Then light came into the world. The octopus's arms fell into the sea and formed the island of Tabua'i.

36 Now light had come between earth and sky the gods saw much in the

Carved staff of the
Polynesian creator and
sea-god Tangaroa, from
Rarotonga in the Cook
Islands. Museum für
Völkerkunde, Munich.
(*Photo: Werner Forman
Archive*.)

world that was ugly and misshapen so Tane set stars and planets in the heavens and commanded Tohu, god of the deep, to colour the fish and shells of the sea. Then Tane gave every animal its place and appointed its life-cycle.

37 Since the creator himself had existed within a shell, so do all other things. The sky is the shell of endless space, the land forms the shell of stones, of water and of all vegetation. Man's shell is woman, from whom he emerges, and woman's shell is also woman. The shells of the world are innumerable.

38 Some versions say that Ta'aroa, alone in the darkness of chaos, created the sacred isle of Hawaiki as a body, or shell, for himself. Another story tells how in the darkness Ta'aroa clasped a rock, the foundation of all (a version of Papa, see **45–48**), and fathered sea and land. Then the light-blue and dark-blue skies, heralds of day, came and asked him to give the universe, his child, a soul. Ta'aroa committed this work to his son Rai-taubu, Sky-maker.

39 Rai gazed upon the heavens and they produced the skies, clouds, planets and stars, thunder, lightning, rain and wind. Then Rai gazed down at the formless land and it produced soil, mountains, and all kinds of flora and fauna. Next Rai gazed upon the abyss and it brought forth the ocean, rocks, corals and all sea creatures.

(iii) *MAORI* STORIES

The Evolution of Rangi

40 Te Kore, the Emptiness, brought forth Te Kore-tua-tahi, the First Emptiness, who brought forth Te Kore-tua-rua, the Second Emptiness, who brought forth Te Kore-nui, the Vast Emptiness, who brought forth Te Kore-roa, the Boundless Emptiness, who brought forth Te Kore-para, the Dry Emptiness, who brought forth Te Kore-whinwhia, the Barren Emptiness, who brought forth Te Kore-rawea, the Pleasant Emptiness, who brought forth Te Kore-tamaua, the Restricted Emptiness, who brought forth Darkness, called Po. Te Po brought forth Te Po-teki, who brought forth Te Po-terea, who brought forth Te Po-whawha, who brought forth Hine-maki-moe, the Daughter of Troubled Sleep. Hine-maki-moe brought forth Po and Te Po brought forth Te Ata, the first shimmering Dawn. Te Ata brought forth Te Ao-tu-roa, Constant Light, and Te Ao-tu-roa brought forth Te Ao-marama, Bright Daylight, who brought forth Te Whai-tua, Space.

41 In Te Whai-tua there evolved two amorphous beings: the male Maku, Moisture, and the female Mahora-nui-a-rangi, Wide-spread-out Heavens, and these were the parents of Te Rangi-potiki, the Sky.

42 It seems likely that this chant may have survived only in a composite form, since Po is given as the offspring first of Kore-tamaua and later of Hine-maki-moe. However, the name Po is commonly used not only of the primordial darkness, but also of the darkness of the underworld, and Hine, in another aspect as Hine-nui-te-po, is goddess of the underworld. Possibly, therefore, the myth incorporates these two aspects of Po.

43 In a version from the *Nagi-i-tahu Maoris* of South Island, Po is the origin of all existence. Po produced Ao, Light, Ao produced Ao-marama, which produced Ao-tu-roa, which produced Kore-whiwhia, which produced Kore-rawea, which produced Kore-tamaua, which produced Te Kore-matua, the Unbegotten Void, and Te Kore-matua produced Te Maku, the Dampness, who begat Raki (Rangi) of Ma-hora-nui-a-tea, Great Spread-out Light.

44 Some myths only begin with Rangi's emergence from the primaeval void. Others make no reference at all to his origins, but simply assume his existence. This happens also in the myths of the *Moriori* people of the Chatham Islands, which were colonised by the *Maoris*.

Papa

45 Rangi's consort Papa, the primordial Earth Mother, is sometimes said to have emerged from the sea, but usually no account of her origin is given.

The Separation of Rangi and Papa

46 At first Rangi lay close upon Papa. Their innumerable offspring lay caught in the dark interstices between them. At length five of the six greatest children rebelled. Tu, god of war, suggested killing Rangi and Papa. Tane, god of the forests, proposed that they rather be forcibly separated. After aeons of deliberation the gods agreed to attempt this.

47 Rongo, god of agriculture, Tangaroa the sea-god, and Haumia, god of vegetation (uncultivated plants), each made unsuccessful attempts to push Rangi off their mother. Tu, the war-god, then tried to hack them apart, but the primaeval parents still clung together, although their wounds bled profusely. From this blood was formed the red clay used in sacred rituals.

48 Then Tane tried to lift Rangi off Papa. Finding his arms were too short for this, Tane bent double, placing his feet against his father and his shoulders against his mother. Very slowly, taking many ages of time, he straightened himself, levering his parents apart. Daylight came between them and all their offspring were revealed. These now mated and spread all over the earth, and the children of Tane and his consort Hine became the ancestors of men.

The Flood

49 Rangi was so grieved by his separation from Papa that at first he wept unceasingly. Before long his tears had formed a sea which threatened to overwhelm the whole world. To avert this disaster, Rangi's sons, led by Mataaho, turned their mother Papa over so that Rangi could no longer observe her grief-stricken face. Now he cries less, but his tears can be seen each morning as the dew-drops that have fallen on Papa's back, while her heartbroken sighs rise up as mists.

Ruaumoko, god of the Underworld

50 Papa was suckling Ruaumoko, the youngest of her children, when Mataaho turned her onto her face, and as the infant god still clung to his mother's breast he was carried to the underworld. There he was given fire to warm himself and so he became the god of volcanoes. He causes earthquakes and earth-tremors as he walks about the world below.

Carved barge-board of a *Maori* meeting house near Manutuke, North Island, New Zealand, shows the separation of Rangi and Papa. (*Photo: Axel Poignant.*)

The Clothing of Rangi and Papa

51 Another *Maori* myth says that when Rangi and Papa had been separated, Tane, seeing his parents were naked, decided to beautify them. First he found a red cloak for Rangi; then he fetched the stars and placed them on his father's body. Although these are almost invisible during the day, at night Rangi's full splendour is revealed.

52 Tane planted trees to clothe his mother Papa. Initially he planted them with their branches in the soil and their roots uppermost. Dissatisfied with the effect, he later reversed them.

53 According to some myths, Papa was clothed not by Tane but by Rangi before their union. These stories say the sky-god not only planted trees and other vegetation to cover her, but deposited varieties of insects among their foliage, and crustacea and other living things in various parts of Papa's body.

The War of the Gods

54 Tawhiri had remained silent during his brothers' deliberations and efforts to separate their parents, but he was furious at their treatment of Rangi and rose up into the heavens determined to avenge him. Tawhiri sent his children, the great winds and storms, to attack his brothers and their offspring. They lashed Tane's forests and Tangaroa's seas. Terrified, Tangaroa's children scattered hither and thither, the fish into the depths of the sea and the reptiles into the forests, provoking an eternal quarrel between Tane and Tangaroa, who was furious that any of his children should have sought refuge among his brother's trees. As a result, Tane now gives the offspring of the war-god Tu spears and wood for their canoes, as well as fish-hooks and plant fibres so that they may make nets in which to trap and kill the children of the sea. Tangaroa retaliates by encouraging his monsters of the deep to attack canoes. He shipwrecks sailors and sends tidal waves to flood the shoreline villages, while his waters constantly eat away the land.

55 While, instead of combining against Tawhiri, Tane and Tangaroa were thus set at odds, their gentler brothers Rongo and Haumia sought to evade the storm-god's fury by hiding within their mother, Earth. Tu was therefore left to fight Tawhiri single-handed. Having defeated him, the warrior-god turned on the brothers who had failed to give him their support, and tore up all their plants.

The Great Polynesian Deities
56–72

(i) HINE (*MAORI*), HINA (HAWAII), INA (MANGAIA), SINA (TOKELUA GROUP)

56 Hine, the archetypal woman, goddess of life and death, has many faces. Some *Maori* stories say she was created by Tane and bore him a daughter, Hine-titama or Hine-i-tau-ira. This daughter Tane also took to wife. She became curious about her parentage and when she learned that Tane was her father she killed herself in horror. Descending to the underworld she became the great goddess of death, Hine-nui-te-po.

57 A Tahitian story says that Hina accompanied her brother Ru on voyages of exploration. Then one night she decided to visit the moon by herself and found it so much to her taste that she remained there, as a guide to travellers. At the time of the full moon she may be seen beating tapa cloth from the branches of the moon's huge banyan tree. Once she dropped a branch and it fell to earth near the temple at Opoa Ra'iatea. There it sprouted and became the world's first banyan.

58 Another version of this myth says that Hine was beating tapa one evening when Tana'aroa was suffering from a hangover. Several times he asked her to desist, as the noise was torture to him. At length he told his servant to stun Hine with the tapa mallet. The fellow was too violent and hit her so hard that her spirit left her body and flew to the moon, where she continues to beat her cloth.

59 A number of related stories tell of Hine's marriage to Tinirau, lord of the sea-creatures and of the overwhelming ocean and, like Hine herself, a deity at once creative and destructive. In some *Maori* versions the heroine is called Hina-uri, sister of the hero Maui (73–80); in others her name is Hine-te-iwa Iwa. One story says that after Maui had transformed her husband into a dog, the distraught Hina-uri, seeking to kill herself, jumped into the sea, but was eventually washed ashore and found by two brothers, who shared her as their wife. Tinirau, who in this version is a local chieftain, not a god, heard of her beauty and stole her. His other jealous wives tried to murder her but Hina-uri's superior magical gifts enabled her to kill them.

60 A Tumotuan myth said that Hina was the wife of the great eel Tuna, with whom she lived in a land below the sea. Eventually bored with him and tired of the region's icy climate, she determined to seek a lover elsewhere. She offered herself to the men of the Tane ('Masculinity') clan, to those of the Peka ('Penetrating Embrace') and those of the Tu ('Upright'). Fearing Tuna's

The temple at Opo, Rai'atea, near which, it was said, the first bayan tree grew from a branch dropped by Hina. (*Photo: Axel Poignant.*)

wrath, all refused her, but when she came to the land of Maui, that hero made her his wife.

61 Angered by gossip, Tuna came with companions to reclaim her. Tearing off his stained loincloth, he waved it aloft, causing a tidal wave, but Maui calmed the sea by exposing his penis, so Tuna and Maui compromised and agreed to share Hina. At length however, Tuna said they must fight to the death for her. Maui agreed and accepted the great eel's plan that each should in turn enter the other's body. First Tuna penetrated Maui's and vanished inside him. When he emerged Maui was apparently unshaken. Now he entered Tuna and the eel burst apart, so Tuna died. Maui took the eel's head and buried it and from it there sprang the coconut palm.

62 Another version of this myth, current in Mangaia, Samoa, Tahiti and the Union Islands, says that Ina was seduced by the eel while bathing. Campbell, in his *Primitive Mythology*, interestingly develops the ideas of Kerenyic and Jensen, showing these stories' origins to be of the greatest antiquity, developments of one of the world's earliest mythologems, which, in other areas, gave rise to the myths of Eve and the Serpent and Persephone and Hades. (See vol. 1: 2.2. **111–115**.)

(ii) RONGO (MANGAIA, NEW ZEALAND AND THE CHATHAM ISLANDS), LONO (HAWAII), ONO (MARQUESAS ISLANDS)
63 Rongo was usually held to be one of the sons of the Sky Father and Earth Mother. He was the god of agriculture, although his name means 'sound' and in Mangaia his emblem was a huge triton shell called the *Resounder*.

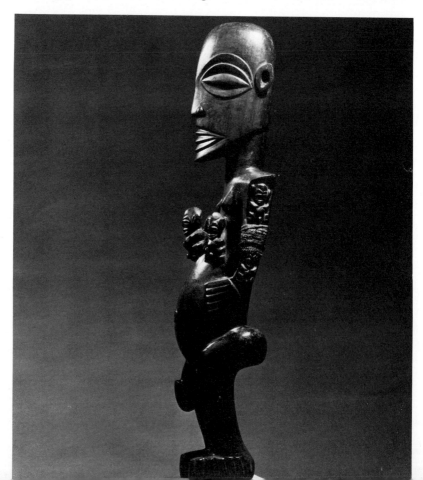

Woodcarving from Rarotonga in the Cook Islands representing either Rongo and his three sons or, possibly, Tangaroa—authorities differ. British Museum. (*Photo: Axel Poignant.*)

Hawaiian islanders sailing out to welcome Captain Cook at Kealakekua Bay. Engraving from a drawing by J. Webber. (*Photo: Axel Poignant.*)

64 The Mangaians said that although Rongo was the second son of Vatea and Papa, his mother favoured him and helped him to win precedence over the firstborn, Tanaroa. Papa suggested that all food which was red, the sacred colour, should be given to Tanaroa, and Rongo should have the remainder. As red food, though precious, is also very scarce, Tanaroa was soon compelled to leave Mangaia and look for sustenance elsewhere. Meanwhile the well-fed Rongo prospered and his three sons became the fathers of mankind.

65 The Hawaiians told how Lono came to earth on a rainbow seeking a human wife. At first the marriage was happy but later, suspecting his wife of infidelity, Lono beat her to death. Then, distraught with grief, he organised a great festival in her honour and went all over Hawaii issuing challenges to wrestling matches. The great Hawaiian harvest rite of Mahkahiki was said to have originated in these funeral games. When the rites were concluded Lono sailed away into the east. It was said he would one day return on a floating island and Captain Cook was welcomed as his reincarnation, for, according to the myths, all the Great Polynesian deities were fair-skinned.

(iii) TANE (HAWAIIAN KANE)

66 Tane's name means 'man' or, more specifically, 'husband'. The god of trees and all forest creatures, he was also associated with all kinds of craftsmanship, particularly canoe-building. Ritual chants emphasise his creative power and refer to him as Tane-the-Living-Water, or Water-of-Life. He it was who brought from heaven the two branches of knowledge called the Upper and Lower Jaws, the upper concerning all knowledge about the gods, the origins of things, astronomy and time-keeping, the lower recording genealogies, the stories of migrations and details of ritual taboos. He also brought the two stones, Foam-of-the-Ocean and White-Sea-Mist, whose replicas stood in every *Maori* Whare; students stood on them to receive *mana* on the day they graduated, a ceremony suggesting something like the Christian rite of confirmation.

67 According to *Maori* myths, Tane not only separated heaven and earth (**48**) and decorated land and sky (**51–52**), but also fathered many plants and animals and created the first woman. Seeking a consort, Tane first approached his mother, Papa, but she advised him that such a union would have an evil outcome and suggested he approach his ancestress Mumuhango. This union resulted in the birth of the *Torara* tree. Disappointed, Tane took a series of other wives, but although they were fruitful they bore no human child, only such offspring as mountain water, reptiles, a stone and a form of reed. At length Papa advised her son to go to the beach at Kura-waka and there model a woman from the sand. This he did, clothing the form and breathing life into its mouth. When the woman grew animate he named her Hine-ahu-one, the Earth-formed-maid, and took her as his wife. Her first offspring was a bird's egg, but her second proved to be a daughter, Hine-titama (**56**).

68 According to another story, Tane modelled the first man, Tiki, from the soil of Hawaiki and then made the first woman, Iowahine, as his companion. Some say the man was formed from clay mixed with Tane's own blood, others that the blood was that which had flowed from Papa and Rangi when Tu tried to cut them apart (**47**).

69 In the Tuamotuan Islands Tane was credited with introducing cannibalism. During a war among the three heavens he took refuge on earth and there men taught him to eat, food being unknown in the sky regions. When Tane eventually returned home he grew hungry and since there was nothing else but wind to swallow, he killed and cooked one of his ancestors.

(iv) TANGAROA (*Maori*) TANAOA (MARQUESAS ISLANDS), TA'AROA (SOCIETY ISLANDS), TANGALOA (SAMOA AND TONGA), KANALOA (HAWAII)

70 In western Polynesia and in the Society Islands Tangaloa was the primordial creator (**25–29**). In the Sandwich or Hawaiian islands it was said that the sea originated from the streams of perspiration that poured from him as he laboured to create Hawaiki, the first, sacred land. In some central Polynesian stories he is said not to have created land, but fished it up from the sea-bed (cf. **75**).

71 A Tahitian story tells how Ta'aroa was the father of Hine, and when she asked him how men might be made he told her to go inland and seek her brother. Then the great god changed his shape and taking the name Tii-maaraatai became Hine's brother-husband. (cf. **56**).

72 In remote Easter Island he and Rongo were the only two Polynesian gods referred to. Here they were held to be ancestors of Hotu-matua, the founder of the people.

Tricksters and Culture-Heroes
73–85

(i) MAUI

73 The greatest of a number of Polynesian Tricksters, the demi-god Maui is the hero of countless stories. In New Zealand and Hawaii he is said to have helped raise the heavens (**34**). *Maori* stories say he caught and imprisoned three of the winds in a cave, though the Samoans aver he enclosed them in a coconut. Only the west wind eluded him. He turned his brother-in-law into a dog and fought and killed the great god Tuna, so winning his wife, the goddess Hine (**60ff.**).

74 In Mangaian stories Maui is an only son, but in Rarotonga he is said to be the youngest of four brothers, and in New Zealand the youngest of seven. The *Maoris* sometimes called him Maui-tikiti-ki-a-Taranga, because his mother, Taranga, cradled him in her hair, but other tales say he was the son of Hine. He had four great adventures: fishing up land, catching the sun, stealing fire and attempting to win man immortality.

75 *Fishing land:* The *Maori* version of this myth says that Maui offered to relieve his brothers of the task of taking food to an aged ancestress. As the brothers had neglected her, Maui found the old woman literally half dead.

Woodcarving from a house at Roturua, New Zealand, shows Maui drawing up North Island in the form of a great fish. National Museum, Wellington. (*Photo: National Museum Wellington.*)

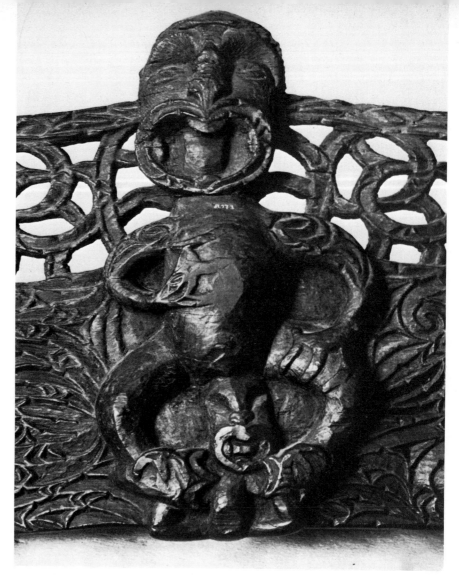

Carved lintel from a *Maori* meeting house is said to depict Maui's fatal attempt to penetrate the body of Hine and so win mankind immortality. Wanganui Museum. (*Photo: Axel Poignant.*)

Tearing off her lower jaw he fashioned it into a fish-hook and next day stowed away on his brothers' canoe. While they were fishing he daubed his hook with blood from his nose, cast his line and caught land in the form of a gigantic fish. Anchoring the line, he went away, warning his brothers not to cut the fish up, but they attempted to do so. Maddened with pain, the fish threshed the water, overturning their canoe and drowning them all. Their superficial wounds left the creature's back very rugged, so the land is mountainous. In some versions the fish is New Zealand itself Te-ika-a-maui, Maui's fish.

76 *Catching the sun:* Hawaiian stories say that Maui's mother found the day too short. Her son therefore decided to amputate the sun's legs and slow him down. His mother gave him strong ropes and from his blind grandmother Maui obtained an enchanted club. Going east he waited for the sun to appear, lassoed six of its legs (rays) and tied the ropes fast to a tree. Then he beat the sun until the crippled god begged for mercy and gladly agreed to run more slowly in future.

77 *Maui captures fire:* Each morning at dawn Maui's mother secretly descended to the underworld. One day, transforming himself into a bird, he followed her and then, revealing himself, asked for food. The fire was out, so his mother accepted Maui's offer to fetch some embers and sent him to Mafuike, guardian of fire. Mafuike gave him a finger, in which fire was hidden. Maui deliberately dropped it into a stream and returned, asking for more. He repeated this stratagem until Mafuike had lost all her fingers and all but one of her toes. Furious, she used this last brand to set the world alight and as Maui fled away she pursued him with huge flames, but summoning hail, rain and snow he succeeded in quenching the fire.

78 In some versions Maui returns to earth with a fireband, in others Mafuike hurled the last of her flames into some trees where it is yet preserved and may be released by friction. Similar stories are told in various parts of Polynesia, but only in New Zealand is the fire deity female. Sometimes birds are involved in the story, as in the Hawaiian account that says Maui obtained fire from the Alae, a wading bird sacred to Hina.

79 *Maui's attempt on immortality:* According to the Tuomotuans, Maui attempted to win immortality by exchanging his own intestines for those of a sea-slug, but abandoned the attempt when his brothers were repelled by it. A New Zealand story says that he decided to obtain everlasting life by overcoming his great ancestress Hine-nui-te-po, the goddess of the dark underworld. His father directed him to the distant horizon, warning him that Hine was not to be tackled lightly: her hair was like tangled seaweed that traps a swimmer, her eyes red as fire, her mouth gaped like a hungry barracuda's and her teeth were sharp as obsidian.

80 Undeterred, Maui set forth accompanied by a flock of small birds. Arriving at Hine's home, they found the great goddess asleep. The hero explained that his plan was to enter Hine's body and creep up through it until he emerged from her mouth. He begged his friends to refrain from laughing while he performed this ungainly trick, for should they wake Hine, all would be lost. However, the sight of Maui wriggling into the goddess's body was so ludicrous that the birds were almost beside themselves. At length the wagtail Tiwa Kawata could no longer contain its mirth and its cry, though hastily stifled, woke the goddess, who crushed Maui inside her, and so the cause was lost.

(ii) TAWHAKI (*MAORI*), TAFA'I (TAHITI), KAHA'I (HAWAII)

81 The other great Polynesian hero was Tawhaki. Unlike Maui he was not a demi-god, but rather the ideal man, and extraordinarily handsome.

82 His mother was early captured by vicious hobgoblins and his father Hema taken prisoner while attempting her rescue. Tawhaki determined to free them. Having successfully rescued his mother and slaughtered all her goblin captors, who were allergic to sunlight, Tawhaki, accompanied by his brother Karihi, sailed off to seek their father.

83 Reaching an island they came there upon their grandmother, the cannibal goddess Whaitiri, now blind and carefully counting her baskets of food. Tawhaki took first one and then another basket until he attracted her attention. Revealing his identity he next restored Whaitiri's sight, either by smearing her eyes with saliva-softened clay, or, some say, by hitting them. Whaitiri then told him that the route to the sky-world was via a spider's web (according to some stories, it was a great vine), and advised the brothers how they might safely ascend. Ignoring her advice, the foolish Karihi fell and was killed, but Tawhaki ascended safely, found his father's bones and then continued to the highest heaven, where he learned many useful charms. These he brought back to earth for mankind's benefit.

84 Some stories say Tawhaki found not his father's bones but Hema himself and rescued him from the cesspit in which he was imprisoned, half-drowned. Tawhaki's journey to heaven is sometimes associated with attempts to persuade his wife, a 'swan maiden' (see **15–18**) from the sky, to return home with him, while a *Maori* version says he stayed in heaven and became the thunder-god. According to other accounts he became the ruler of the dead.

(iii) MATAORA AND NUVARAHU

85 A *Maori* hero Mataora married an underworld *Tutega*, or spirit, called Nuvarahu, but she fled home again when he beat her after jealously imagining she had formed an attachment to his brother. Ashamed, Mataora, who truly loved his wife, pursued her into the underworld, and persuaded her to return home with him. The guardian of the entrance gates refused to allow Nuvarahu to retain her immortal spirit-robe as she passed up into the world above, and once she and her husband were through the gate he closed it firmly behind them. Thenceforward only spirits have been able to pass through into the world below. However, Mataora not only brought back his wife, but also knowledge of tattooing, which he had learned from his father-in-law, Uetonga.

MICRONESIA

Creation Stories
86–101

86 No cosmological myths are known from the Caroline Islands of central Micronesia. There the world is assumed always to have existed much as it is now. In the Marshall Islands to the north-east it was said that the god Lowa summoned land into being by humming. In Truk, Ligoububfanu, wife of the god Anulap, created the land, plants, animals and men, while to the west on Guam, the *Chamorro* people believed that the universe had been made from the body of a primordial god, Puntan, who, as his death approached, ordered his sister to use his corpse to make the world. Some of the most detailed stories so far collected come from the most easterly areas of Micronesia, the Gilbert and Ellice Islands. Here creation myths seem to be of Indonesian origin.

(i) THE CREATOR NA AREAU

87 In Te Bo, the Darkness, and Te Maki, the Cleaving Together, existed only Na Areau te Moa-ni-bai, Sir Spider, the First of All. He walked over heaven's surface feeling and tap-tapping and heaven rang hollow. He penetrated below into the dark cavity between heaven and earth and there called Sand and Water to unite. Their children Na Atibu, Sir Stone, and Nei Teakea, he commanded to unite also and their offspring included Te Nao, the Wave, Na Kika, Sir Octopus, and Te Riiki, the Eel. Last and youngest of their many children came Na Areau the younger, also called Kikinto, the Mischief-maker.

88 Sir Spider gave the world to Na Atibu, commanding him to make it suitable for man; then he himself went away.

89 Na Atibu called his son Na Areau and told him of Sir Spider's final orders. He gave his son authority to do anything he pleased with the world. First therefore Areau went to the innumerable offspring of Sand and Water, who lay supine and motionless. He commanded them to rise, but in obeying him they banged their foreheads on the sky, and fell back stunned. Next therefore Areau called the great eel Riiki and ordered him to raise the skies. Helped by Te Takakea, the Turtle, Na Kika, Sir Octopus, Baka-uaaneku and Te-auanei the Sting Rays, Te Nao, the Wave, and all the children of Sand and Water, Riiki eventually managed to lift the heavens high above and earth sank below the sea. Then Areau summoned four women and sent them to the four corners of the world to hold the sky in its place, which they did, and their feet grew roots like trees', and so they remain, immovable.

90 Next Na Areau sought to furnish the world. He cut off Riiki's countless legs, which fell into the sea and became the eels of the deep; then he ordered Riiki to stretch himself across the sky. There his glittering belly may still be seen, for he became Naiabu, the Milky Way.

91 Now Areau killed his father Na Atibu. He hurled his right eye into the eastern sky, his left into the western and they became the sun and moon. Areau scattered fragments of his father's brain over the skies, forming the stars, and broadcast pieces of his corpse over the sea, forming rocks and stones. Then, on the first land, which was Samoa, Na Areau planted his father's bones and they grew into the great Tree of Samoa, known to initiates as the Tree of Matang, Kai-n-tiku-aba. Its branches stretched from farthest north to farthest south and from them were born both gods and men. Some say that the islands of Beru, Tarawa and Tabuteuea were originally flowers of the tree, which Na Areau took and threw into the ocean.

92 Na Areau married Nei Aro-maiaki and her children were first the Spirits of the South and then many Ancestors, the first of them Te I-Matang, Taburi-tongoun, Kanii and Batiku the skull. Kanii was the first of the Samoan red men, the Men of Matang. He and his brother Batiku were chiefs under the Tree of Samoa and they fed upon the heads of first-born children, the tribute of the *Nuku-maroro* people.

93 One day, a *Nuku-maroro* man, Te-boi, a son of Na Areau, led a rebellion against this barbarous tribute and, having destroyed the canoes Samoa had sent to collect the chiefs' victims, Te-boi made war upon Samoa and conquered it and so the men of Matang were scattered, some to Malin, others to Arorae and Beru.

94 Another version of the story says that the men of Matang were dispersed after one Koura-abi destroyed the Tree of Samoa, being angry with those who lived above his head among the tree's branches, for they insulted him by dropping excrement on his head. (A myth from Beru, Gilbert Islands.)

(ii) AURIARIA

95 In Te Bongi-Ro, the great darkness, the rock of heaven lay upon the earth. They rubbed against each other like two hands and Tabakea and his brother Na Kaa appeared and lived on Baanaba, the navel of the world. They had four younger brothers: Auriaria, Taburima, Tabuaniki and Riiki. Their sister was Tituaabine.

96 From the land of Baanaba came many others, which lay about it in the darkness of Te Bongi-Ro and on each land lived an Ancestor. All these lands were on the farther side of heaven's rock and their people were the *Taukarawa*, the people of heaven.

97 The inhabitants of Baanaba, who lived with Tabakea and Na Kaa, were led by the chief Auriaria (Au-of-the-Rising-Sun), a fair-skinned giant. Noticing that heaven and earth remained clasped together, he asked Tabakea how he might part them. Tabakea gave him Te Rakau, a staff, and with it Auriaria drove a door through heaven; then he pushed the skies from below, lifting them high above earth. He commanded the sting-ray Korereke to cut the bonds which yet held them together and ordered Riiki the eel to push the heavens even higher. Then the skies were high above and earth sank beneath the waters. Auriaria struck heaven with his staff and with a rumbling roar the skies broke asunder and all the lands of Te Bongi-Ro fell into the sea, Baanaba with them. Baanaba itself turned over and fell into the water upside down, so its roots stood up into the air. Auriaria therefore buried Tabakea the great turtle, first of all things, underneath the island, which now rests upon his back. (Myth from Baanaba.)

(iii) MAN'S EXPULSION FROM PARADISE

98 Nakaa, the primordial judge, ruled even the great gods, the Spirits of the Tree of Matang (**91**). He lived below a mountain in the paradisal land of Matang, where he planted two pandannus palms, one in the north for men, the other in the south for women, and all the people lived, each under their own tree, ageless and undying.

99 One day, Nakaa called them all together to tell them he was going on a journey. He ordered them to disperse again, each to their own tree, and they did, but the sight of the others had unsettled them and eventually the men joined the women under their tree, and so their hair began to turn grey. When Nakaa returned and saw this sign of their disobedience, he expelled them from Matang for ever.

100 He said they might take one of the two trees with them. The exiles chose that of the women. Then Nakaa told them they had chosen the Tree of Death,

Canoe figurehead from the Solomon Islands, of carved and painted wood inlaid with mother-of-pearl, in the form of an ancestral spirit. It was believed to help warriors on head-hunting raids. The bird-spirit shown in its hands helped the steersman to keep a true course. Museum für Völkerkunde Basle. (*Photo: Werner Forman Archive.*)

A Dreamtime being of the Arnhem Land Aborigines' *dua* moiety. Yirrkala, Arnhem Land. Artist: Mawalan. (*Photo: Axel Poignant.*)

Mamarangan, the Lightning-man. An Aborigine bark-painting from Oenpelli,
NE Arnhem Land. Artist: Sam. (*Photo: Axel Poignant.*)

so the Tree of Life would stay with him in Matang, while Death would always go with the people. He taught them the ritual, Te Kaetikawai, to perform for the dead and said that their ghosts would always find him sitting at the junction of the lands of the living and dead and all would be judged by him; those who had done well would be allowed to enter the spirits' lands, but those who had committed grave sins would fall into his pit and be forever extinguished. Then, as the people were leaving, Nakaa took the Tree of Death and stripped it of its leaves. In them he parcelled up all kinds of illnesses and these he threw at the people as they departed. So men left the land of Matang, carrying with them sickness and the Tree of Death.

101 This myth from the Gilbert Islands was collected before the advent of Christian missions, and cannot have been influenced by their teaching.

Tricksters and Culture-Heroes
102–114

(i) MOTIKITIK
102 Like the Polynesian Maui, (**73–80**), Motikitik fished up land. The third and youngest son of his mother Lorop, who was herself a daughter of the creator-goddess Liomarar, Motikitik one day followed his mother and spied on her. Muttering a spell she dived into the sea. Transforming himself into a bird, Motikitik did likewise. He discovered his mother collecting baskets full of food in the underworld, and by watching her he unwittingly condemned her to death. Lorop adjured him to tell his brothers nothing of what had happened, but to bury her and then return home with the baskets of food.

103 During the next three days, each time Motikitik went fishing with his brothers he caught not fish, but baskets of food; then on the fourth day he drew up the island of Fais. All three brothers wanted to own it, but eventually their dispute was resolved by Motikitik's living in the centre while his brothers established themselves one at either end. So were founded the three regions of Fais.

104 Some time later, Motikitik lost his fish-hook, which somehow found its way into the hands of the people of Gatschapar on Yap. Since, if the fish-hook were to be lost for good, the island of Fais would sink, its people now have no option but to pay tribute to those of Gatschapar! (A myth from Yap.)

(ii) BUE
105 Bue's mother, Nei Matamona of Tebongiroro (cf. **95**) was impregnated by a sunbeam as she bathed early one morning on the eastern shore. She gave birth to sextuplets but only the two youngest, Bue and his sister Nei Te-raa-iti, survived. The sun took his daughter and built her a rock compound in the east, but Bue remained with his mother until he became a youth and decided to visit his father the sun and ask him for the gift of cleverness and knowledge.

106 At his mother's suggestion he made a canoe from a coconut shell and called it Te Kuo-n-aine. Then his mother gave him two stones of red coral, a fruit of the *non* tree, an old coconut, the first leaf-shoot of a coconut seedling and a strong coconut-palm leaf. She told him to pelt his father with the coral, the *non* fruit and the old coconut, to fan him with the seedling and to bind him with the strong palm-leaf.

107 Bue carefully followed these instructions, so his father the sun floated captive on the sea and Bue told him his desire. The sun gave him cleverness and knowledge as he asked, knowledge of all building crafts, charms for raising and calming winds and making rain. He told him how to make spells to guard children and men and taught him burial rites, the art of composing chants and of overcoming dangerous fish and waterspouts. Then he gave Bue a black and white staff, Te Kai-ni-kamata, and so Bue left him and went to visit his sister, whom he had already seen on his outward journey.

108 Much to the sun's anger, his two children became lovers. He commanded a porpoise to shipwreck them. Bue and his sister fell into the depths, down to the land of Mone. There two Ancestors led Nei Te-raa-iti away to the north. Bue went to the west.

109 He came to the home of the old woman Nei Bairara, Keeper of the Winds, and, overhearing her spells, he was able to steal all her power. Similarly, from Nei Temaing, Guardian of Rain, he stole knowledge of rain-bearing winds and clouds and he pulled up her *Uri* tree, from which fire sticks are made, and ran off with it. Though she pursued him, he called on all the winds he had now learned to command and so escaped her and came to Tarawa, where he met the man Riirongo, who fed him. Later Bue and Riirongo and Riirongo's mother, Nei Te-tauti, Lady Porcupine-fish, went to Beru and Nikunau, where their children remain to this day. (A myth from the Gilbert Islands.)

(iii) OLIFAT

110 Olifat, also known as Yelafath, Iolofath, Orofat, and Wolphat, is the hero of many stories from the Caroline Islands. His mother was a woman, but his father a sky-god, called Lugeiland, Lukelong, Luk, or Great Yelafath, son of Anulap (Analap, Onolap, Enulap). Sometimes Olifat is Anulap's son and Lugeiland is his brother.

111 Born from his mother's head, the hero could run at once. As a lad he went to heaven, rising in a pillar of smoke from a fire he had made of coconut shells. In the sky lands of Lang he was spurned by the children of the first three heavens, so he turned their playthings into malign creatures, giving prickles to the scorpion fish, teeth to the shark and stings to the sting-ray.

112 In the fourth heaven he found his father building a *farmal* house (for spirits). The other workmen, taking Olifat for a stranger, decided to bury him in a post-hole of the *farmal* (cf. Boraspati ni Tano and Teleu), but he foresaw their plan and allowed for it by digging a cavity to the side of the hole, in which he hid and then, helped by ants, bored through the post itself, and so escaped.

113 Olifat was a notorious womaniser, and often changed his shape to attain his desires. On Ifaluk he was said to have turned into a mosquito and contrived to be swallowed by his brother's wife; then he was born as her son, and so gained access to her. The people of Ifaluk also said that he taught them the art of tattooing, which they applied to their genitals.

114 His most outrageous trick was beheading a brother of whose existence he had earlier been ignorant, and then claiming he could not possibly have killed him since he had no brother.

MELANESIA

Creation Stories
115–121

(i) THE CREATION OF THE WORLD

115 Unlike other Oceanic peoples, the Melanesians have no detailed cosmological myths at all. In most cases it seems they assume the universe has always existed much as it is today, although an Admiralty Islands' story says that land was called into being by a primordial serpent who, tired of swimming in the sea, called: 'Let the reef arise!' and so the earth was formed. Other brief creation stories have been collected in New Guinea (**116–117**). In New Guinea also there was, and still is, a widespread belief in pre-existent spiritual beings who came to earth either from the sky or from underground,

Tambaran (spirit) house of the *Abelam* tribe, Maprik District, Papua-New Guinea, decorated with painted sago panels depicting ancestral and other spirits. (*Photo: Axel Poignant.*)

Yi'pon charms, associated with hunting. *Arambak* people, Karawari River, Papua-New Guinea. Philip Goldman Collection, London. (*Photo: Werner Forman Archive.*)

where their world was very like ours. They are usually said to have created particular aspects of the terrestrial landscape and stocked the world with plants, birds and animals. Among the *Dobuan* people such beings were called *kasa soma*; among the *Keraki, gainjin*; among the *Huli, dama*. These spirits were usually thought of as either men's ancestors, or occasionally as their creators. In other Melanesian islands man was usually said to have been created by one or other of the culture-heroes (see **127, 129–131**).

Jugumishanta and Morufonu

116 The great spirit Jugumishanta and her consort Morufonu made the earth from their own faeces. Later they built a domed stone roof over it, so forming the sky, on the far side of which live the great gods.

117 A less common version of the story says that the land is formed from the branches of a huge tree. At its foot sit Jugumishanta and Morufonu, holding the world steady. The tree rests on Morufonu's shoulders, so whenever he eases his position we experience earth tremors. (Myths of *Kamano* and contiguous peoples, eastern highlands, New Guinea.)

(ii) THE SUN AND MOON

The Sun and Moon from Mushrooms

118 The first two beings set trees and created food plants; then they made two mushrooms. The man threw his into the sky, where it became the moon. The woman threw hers aloft after it, and so formed the sun. (Myth from the Admiralty Islands.)

Hana and Ni

119 The story of the *dama* spirits, Hana and Ni, not only refers to the origins of the sun and moon but incorporates details about the seclusion of menstruating women and references to Oceanic peoples' horror of incest. A similar myth was collected by Margaret Mead from the *Arapesh* of the Sepik River area, New Guinea (see bibliography).

120 The fertility-goddess Hana was daughter of the great creative spirit Honabe, first of the *dama*. Secretly she went into the forest and rubbed herself against a tree trunk. Her action was observed by her brother Ni, who later concealed a sharp stone in the trunk, so that when next Hana came she was gashed between the legs. Thus her vulva was formed.

121 Hana remained in the forest until the wound had stopped bleeding and then set out for the women's communal house. Ni intercepted her. When she told him of her accident he asked to see the wound and, aroused by the sight, he seduced her. So ashamed were they of this illicit union that they exiled themselves to the sky. There Hana became the moon and Ni the sun. (*Huli* myth from the southern highlands, New Guinea.)

The Flood
122–124

122 Most Melanesian peoples seem to have stories about a great flood and, as in Indonesia, this is often connected with a serpent or eel.

(i) RAUDALO AND THE FLOOD

123 A great flood covered everything but the summit of the highest mountain, Tauga, to which the people and animals had fled. Still the sea pursued them. Only Raudalo, King of Serpents, was unafraid. He seemed to ignore the rising water, although three times he casually asked his attendants how far it had now reached. On the third occasion, the snakes, Titiko, Dubo and Anauk replied that within a minute the waters would be touching the King. Then Raudalo turned and flicked the waves with his tongue. Immediately they began to retreat. The King of Serpents drove them down the mountainside and across the coastal plain to the shore. So the flood ended. (Myth from Papua-New Guinea.)

(ii) THE OLD WOMAN AND THE WATER-HOLE

124 At first the sea was a tiny water-hole owned by an old woman, who drew salt water from it for her cooking. She refused to tell her two inquisitive sons where she obtained this water, so they spied on her and later went and tore off the water-hole's cloth cover. The further they tore it the wider grew the well until in terror they fled, each still holding a corner of the cover, and so the water rose and spread until only a few rocks remained unsubmerged. Realising that the whole world was in danger of drowning, the old woman hurried to the shore and planted a line of twigs in the sand; so the ocean was confined. (Myth from the *Baining* of New Britain.)

Culture-Heroes and Tricksters
125–137

(i) QUAT

125 Creator, hero and trickster, Quat is the subject of many tales from the Banks Islands. He had eleven brothers, all called Tagaro, including Tagaro the Wise and Tagaro the Foolish. These two are sometimes the protagonists of stories unrelated to Quat himself (see **131**).

126 One tale from Mota says that all eleven Tagaro conspired to kill Quat and steal his canoe and his wife, Ro Lei, but with the help of the spider Marawa, he eluded them.

127 In other tales from Santa Maria, Marawa is Quat's antithesis. It was said that Quat carved the first people from the wood of the *dracaena* tree. Having formed three men and three women he hid them for three days, then brought them out again and by dancing and beating a drum before them, drew them slowly to life. The jealous Marawa decided to imitate Quat's creation, but when his figures began moving he buried them for a week, and when exhumed they were lifeless and decomposing. So death came to man.

128 Sometimes Tagaro the Foolish was held responsible for death. It was said that men at first were immortal, shedding their skins like snakes. Then Quat summoned the man Mate (Death), laid him on a board and covered him. A feast was held and all Mate's property distributed among his relatives. On the fifth day conchs were sounded to drive away Death's spirit, and when Quat removed the covering from the body only its bones remained. Meanwhile, Quat had sent Tagaro to Panoi, the junction of the paths to the underworld and sky world. He ordered Tagaro to ensure that Mate took the upward path, but Tagaro sat in the middle of the road to the sky world, blocking the way, so Mate went below and ever since men have followed him.

(ii) TAGARO

129 Myths from the New Hebrides centre on the hero Tagaro, or Takaro. He created the first ten men from mud, breathed on them to give them life and then ordered them to stand in a row and threw a fruit at them. It stuck on one man's penis and when he pulled it off, the organ came away with it, and so he became the first woman.

130 Tagaro sent the woman away by herself. Later he despatched each man in turn to ask her for fire, water or something similar. She greeted the first eight men as relatives, but the ninth she called 'husband', so Tagaro made them man and wife. (In south Pentecost this story is associated with a sky-hero, Barkulkula and his five brothers.)

131 In a number of myths Tagaro is opposed by the fool Meragbuto or Suquematua. Suquematua wanted the world to be ugly and full of suffering. When Tagaro wished men to walk upright, Suquematua suggested they be made to walk like pigs. However, Tagaro always had the last word, and so saved men from the fool's ignoble schemes.

132 A Lepers' Island myth tells how Tagaro married a *vinmara*, a heavenly 'swan maiden' (see 15–18), whose wings he stole and hid while she was bathing, but promised her others if she became his wife.

133 One day Tagaro took his wife to work in his yam patch. Whenever she touched a vine, ripe yams fell into her hands. Her brothers-in-law, thinking she was digging unripe tubers, for the yam season had not yet come, angrily scolded her. Weeping she ran home and sat in the house doorway, sobbing bitterly. Soon her tears wore away the soil covering her wings, which Tagaro had buried near the doorpost. Hearing a pattering sound as the teardrops fell, she looked down and saw the wings. Taking them up she flew back to the sky.

134 Some versions of the myth say she took her child with her and Tagaro followed them, by climbing a banyan vine. His wife agreed to return with him to earth but craftily cut the ladder, so he fell to the ground while she and the child remained above.

(iii) TO KABINANA AND TO KARVUVU

135 In the beginning a being outlined two men on the ground, sprinkled the figures with blood and covered them with leaves. So he gave them life. They were To Kabinana and his brother To Karvuvu. To Karvuvu became responsible for many of the ills that beset mankind.

136 When To Kabinana told him to fetch two light-coloured coconuts, he perversely picked one light and one dark. The light one he gave to his brother, who transformed it into a fair woman. To Karvuvu then sought to transform his dark nut also, but the result was a dark-skinned woman, and so people became divided into two groups, 'you' and 'us'. Moreover, had both women been light-skinned, mankind would have been immortal, but by creating a dark woman, To Karvuvu brought death to the world.

137 In another story To Karvuvu is credited with introducing cannibalism. When To Kabinana asked him to go and care for their old mother, To Karvuvu killed and roasted her. On another occasion, when To Kabinana created fish for men, by carving a *thum* fish, To Karvuvu made the shark; yet he was not malicious, simply a fool. (Stories from New Britain.)

AUSTRALIA

Myths of the Dreamtime
138–167

(i) NGURUNDERI

138 Ngurunderi paddled down a creek, hunting a giant Murray cod. As it passed, the great fish widened the creek into a river, now the River Murray. Ngurunderi had almost given up hope of catching the fish when he thought of asking his brother-in-law Neple to help him, and between them they succeeded in trapping and killing the cod. They then cut it into pieces and, giving each the name of the species of fish it was to become, threw it back into the water. The last piece they ordered to continue as a Murray cod.

139 Then, leaving Neple, Ngurunderi went on to Bamundang, and from there he walked to Larlangel carrying his canoe. At Larlangel he left two great clumps of freshwater mussels and, having no more use for his boat, lifted it into the sky and made the Milky Way.

140 After various wanderings, during which he fought and killed the evilly-disposed Barambari and created many features of the landscape, Ngurunderi came to the coast opposite Kangaroo Island. At this time he was pursuing his recalcitrant wives and, as they were walking across to the island, which was then still joined to the land by a causeway, Ngurunderi called upon the sea to swallow them. Drowned, the women became the Meralang rocks (the Pages, north-east of Cape Willoughby).

141 Then Ngurunderi himself went to Kangaroo Island, which was called Ngurungaui (Ngurunderi's Path), for this is the route all take on their way to the sky world, Waieruwar.

142 Reaching the island, Ngurunderi made a casuarina tree and rested in its shade; then he went to the western coast, cast his spear into the sea, where it became rocks, and dived into the water after it, to wash away all traces of his former life. Then he ascended to the sky world, to which all dead *Jaraldi* people follow him.

143 This myth was collected from the last surviving initiate member of his tribe. (*Jaraldi* myth, lower Murray Basin.)

(ii) THE KUNIA AND THE LIRU

144 In the centre of the sandy plain of the Gibson desert stands Ayers Rock, a monolith some 1,100 feet high. The myth of which the following story outlines but a small section, incorporates detailed explanations of almost every feature of the landscape around the rock, which is said originally to have been a sandhill, but at the end of the Dreamtime, to have been elevated to its present dominant position. Groups of boulders are held to be the metamorphosed bodies of Dreamtime women and children; nearby scrub and grass, the women's pubic hair. Groups of trees are bands of attacking warriors, a row of small caves the open mouths of the shouting attackers, etc. A detailed account with maps and photographs is given in Mountford's *Ayers Rock.*

Bark painting, by the Aboriginal artist Bunia, shows a man travelling along the pathway of the dead while his tribesmen perform funerary rites (*bottom left*), assisted by the spirit man and his wives (*top right*). The fish represents food for the journey. Private Collection. (*Photo: Axel Poignant.*)

145 In the Dreamtime many non-venomous snakes, the Woma and the Kunia carpet-snakes, left their camp at Pugabuga (probably a waterhole or spring), east of Mount Conner, and journeyed west to a big sandhill in the region of the Uluru (Ayers Rock) water-hole. There they dispersed into a number of camps. The women gathered roots and seeds, the men went hunting. Boulders in the vicinity are the women and children's bodies.

146 Before long, a group of poisonous-snake-people, the Liru, arrived in the area and a party of their younger men soon attacked the Kunia from the south west, armed with spears, spear-throwers, clubs and flint knives. Another band came in from the south. These attackers now have the forms of trees.

147 Meanwhile, the Kunia woman Minma Bula had given birth to a child. Two small adjacent caves have been formed from her uterus, vagina and vulva. Marks on the rock were made by the knees of her midwives. A small, irregular-shaped rock nearby is the baby.

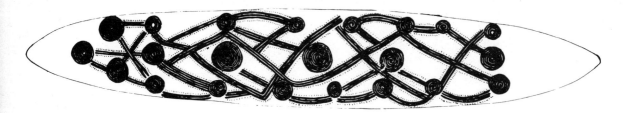

Aborigine engraved *tjuringa* (ritual stone) symbolising the journey of the Kunia carpet-snake women at Ayers Rock. C. P. Mountford Collection, State Library of South Australia.

148 As the enemy approached, Minma Bula took up the infant and walked towards the invaders, spitting at them great quantities of *arukwita* (the spirit of darkness and death). Many of the attacking Liru fell dead, but the rest came on, yelling insults at her and the other defenders, who retreated towards the Mutitjilda gorge. Their tracks can still be seen as strata in the rock.

149 At the gorge, Kulkudjeri, the Liru leader, was engaged in single combat by a young Kunia hero. Both warriors were badly wounded, but at length Kulkudjeri slashed the Kunia youth's leg open and the young hero crawled away to die, his dragging body forming the bed of a stream, whose water comes from his transformed blood.

150 Ingridi, the youth's grief-stricken mother, set upon the victor Kulkudjeri and killed him. Kulkudjeri's brother then avenged his death by slaughtering Ingridi's daughter, Tjinderi–tjinderiba, the Willy-wagtail-woman, as she was resting among her children the Yulanya. She and they are now boulders, she distinguished by the holes of the spear on which she was transfixed.

Aborigine engraved *tjuringa* symbolising the journey of venomous Liru snake-men. The lines indicate the men's tracks, the circles the patterns they had painted on their bodies. C. P. Mountford Collection, State Library of South Australia.

151 Another woman, Minma Mala (the Hare-wallaby), who had gone to collect kindling, was set upon and raped. She and her attacker are now contiguous rocks.

152 When Ingridi learned of the deaths of so many of her relatives, she killed herself, her husband and all the other Kunia people in her camp by chanting the deadly *arukwita* song. (*Pitjandjara* myth, Gibson Desert.)

(iii) THE COMING OF MEN

153 The first men came to the earth in clans through an opening which suddenly appeared in the middle of Lake Perigundi. When they reached the shore they lay in the sunshine for a while, then, having grown strong, they dispersed over the countryside. (*Dieri* myth.)

(iv) THE *MURAMURA* DARANA THE RAINMAKER AND THE DURAULU

154 In the Dreamtime, *muramura* beings wandered over all the lands of the *Dieri* people and neighbouring regions. They included Wariliwulu the Batman, Galadari the Bullfrog, and Gadimargara, a creature like a crocodile. One group of *muramura* girls was pulled up into the sky on a long, hair rope and became the Pleiades; another group was transformed into the stars of Orion's Belt. One of the greatest of all the *muramura* was Darana the Rainmaker, who lived at Pando (Lake Hope).

155 Once, during a long drought, he sang and called the rain until the lake rose and flooded the surrounding land. When it had risen as high as his neck, Darana stuck his boomerang into the ground and the rain stopped, the flood receded, the desert burst into flower and the land was full of witchetty-grubs (a great delicacy to the Aborigine palate). Chanting, Darana drew the grubs together and dried them and stored them in bags hanging from trees. Leaving them there he went away to meet other *muramura*.

156 In his absence there came two youths, the Duraulu, who burst one of the bags with their boomerangs. Dust covered the sun and through the gloom the bags of witchetty-grubs glowed with a strange light. All the *muramura* came hurrying to the spot. They immediately killed the Duraulu and though Darana revived them, the other *muramura* again killed the youths, whose bodies formed two heart-shaped *tjuringa* stones. The *muramura* decided that the next child to be born should be appointed as the guardian of the stones and that if one were so much as scratched there would be a great famine, while if the stones were broken the sky would turn red and dust from Darana's bags of witchetty-grubs would cover the earth, choking everything. The *Dieri* people therefore kept the two sacred Duraulu stones wrapped carefully in a protective covering of feathers and lard.

(v) THE DJANGGAWUL SISTERS

157 The Djanggawul sisters, Bildjiwuraroju and Miralaldu, are sometimes called the Daughters of the Sun, which in north-east Australia is thought of as female. The sisters are a dual manifestation of the fertility-goddess, the Great Mother.

158 Accompanied by their brother Djanggawul and the man Bralbral, they sailed out of the north east in a bark canoe. Pausing at the island of Bralgu in the Carpentaria Gulf, the company then followed the path of the morning star and came to shore at the Place of the Sun (Port Bradshaw) on the mainland coast.

159 As they journeyed inland, Djannggawul made water-holes wherever he thrust his sacred walking-stick, the *rangga mawulan*, into the ground. With their *rangga djuda* poles, the sisters made trees with red parakeets in their branches; with their *rangga ganinjari* sticks they made yams grow in the earth.

160 The sisters carried their *rangga* in the *ngainmara*, a sacred cone-shaped, plaited mat, symbolic of the uterus. Among its contents was the sacred dilly-bag, another uterine symbol decorated with long strings of parakeet feathers, emblems of the sun's rays. From the *ngainmara* the sisters took the first people. They gave them animals and plants, showed them the sacred sites and taught them rituals.

161 One day, leaving all their *rangga* in their camp, Bildjiwuraroju and Miralaldu went out to collect shellfish. Djanggawul and his companions took advantage of the women's absence and stole their sacred objects. Warned by the whistle of a mangrove bird that something was amiss, the sisters hurriedly returned and soon tracked down the thieves, but as they approached them the men began to sing sacred songs and the sisters had to retreat, for their power had been stolen by the men. Now therefore it is the men, not the women, who are guardians of the *rangga* and all the sacred rituals. (*Wulumba* myth, Arnhem Land.)

(vi) JURAWADBAD, GULANUNDOIDJ AND THE MAKING OF THE SACRED *URBAR*

162 The *urbar* is the name now given to a wooden drum formed from a hollow log. Among the *Maung* of Goulburn Island it symbolises both the womb of the Great Mother—who is sometimes identified with the Rainbow Snake Ngalbjod—and also the male Rainbow Snake's penis. In western Arnhem Land the beating of the drum opens the *urbar* ritual, during which the story of Jurawadbad is enacted as part of a rite designed to ensure the coming of the rainy season.

163 The python-man Jurawadbad was engaged to a girl named Gulanundoidj or Mimaliwu, but having a young water-snake Bulugu as her lover, she spurned Jurawadbad. Furious, he made a hollow log and left it on a bush path. Taking python form he then coiled himself inside the *urbar*. Before long Gulanundoidj and her mother came up and, thinking that the log might contain some edible creature, each in turn got down and peered into it, but could see nothing. First one and then the other therefore put a hand inside the log and felt around. Jurawadbad bit them both. As they lay dying from his python venom he emerged from the *urbar* and, assuming his human form, left them. (*Gunwinggu* myth from west Arnhem Land.)

(vii) THE WAWALAG SISTERS AND THE RAINBOW SNAKE

164 Two sisters, Waimariwi and Boaliri, journeyed from the Roper River area with their two children and their bitches Wulngari and Buruwal. At length they stopped to rest by the sacred water-hole Muruwul (Mirara-muinar), home of the great Rainbow Snake Julunggul (Yurlunggur). There they rested in the shade, then collected firewood and began cooking, but their entire meal of goannas, roots, wallaby and snails, leapt from the fire into the water-hole, for, due to its proximity, they had taken on the sacred

character of the well. Unfortunately the elder sister also profaned the well with menstrual blood while fetching water from it. Outraged, Julunggul rose from the water-hole. Water ran flooding over the land. Reaching up to the sky he called down a thunderstorm.

165 Now alive to their peril, the sisters danced and chanted ritual *kunapipi* songs, attempting to halt the python's advance and check the rain. At last the storm abated and they fell asleep. Then the snake put his head into their shelter, wrapping his body round the sacred mound, the *molg*, and swallowed the sisters, their babies and their dogs. He rose again to the sky and all the other pythons rose also from their water-holes and each spoke of what he had eaten. Julunggul boasted of his meal, but just then an ant bit him and jerking involuntarily he vomited up sisters, babies and dogs.

The track of Julunggul outlined on the ground for a ritual enactment of the story of the Wawalag sisters, at Milingimbi, NE Arnhem Land. (*Photo: Axel Poignant.*)

166 Now all the things in the world are divided into two moities or social groups: the *dua* (*dura*) and the *jindja* (*jiridja*). The sisters and the python both belonged to the *dua* group, but the children were *jindja* so, although Julunggul again swallowed the sisters, this time he left the children. Several times he vomited and re-swallowed the women and each time as he rose and fell he made a ceremonial ground where this story's rituals of swallowing and regurgitation are enacted: the rituals of the Djungawon (Djungguan), the Kunapipi, the Great Mother (Gunabibi) and the Ngurlmak (Ulmark).

167 In some versions of the myth the snake is said to be the women's brother, in others it is female. During the *djungawon* circumcision ritual it is symbolised by a trumpet called *Julunggul* (*Yurlunggur*); during the *kunapipi* it is named Muit and its voice is the bullroarer *Mumunaw*. (Mumunaw is also a name given to the Lightning Snake.) In the *ngurlmak* ritual the snake is called Uwar and represented by the *uwar* drum. (Myth from various peoples, north-eastern Arnhem Land.)

PART 3
Index and Glossary

The following abbreviations are used: A: Australia; I: Indonesia; Me: Melanesia; Mi: Micronesia; NG: New Guinea; NZ: New Zealand; P: Polynesia.

Bold numbers refer to the numbered paragraphs of Part 2 unless otherwise indicated.

Adaro (Solomon Is., Me) a sea-spirit.
afterworld the pp. 29–30, 35.
Agunua see *figona.*
Airlangga, King p. 22.
akali semangko (*Kayaka*, W highlands, NG) a fertility cult associated with Komba Ralkingki (q.v.). The name means 'man-spirit'. The cult is also called *kewa kuli.*
Ako (*Mangaia*, Cook Is., P) legendary chief and friend of Tane (q.v.). When Tane tried to suborn his wife, Ako punctured Tane's canoe in revenge.
Alae 78.
Aldjeringa (*Aranda*, N Territory, A) a term for the Dreamtime (q.v.).
Aluluei (Caroline Is., Mi) the great patron of navigators. In *Ifaluk* myths the father of the heroes Longolap and Longorik (qq.v.). In other areas of the Carolines he is said to be their younger brother.
Analap 110.
Anauk 123.
Angoi (*Kalimantan*, I) after the creator had made man, Angoi precipitately gave him breath, and so man was born mortal, instead of immortal, as the creator had intended. In revenge the creator slew Angoi and decimated him. All harmful creatures derive from the scattered fragments of his corpse.
Animism, animistic pp. 24–25, 33—34.
Anulap (Truk Is., Mi) sky-god and husband of Ligougubfanu. See **86, 110.**
Ao see Te Ao.
Argonauts of the Western Pacific p. 32.
Ari (Tahiti, Society Is., P) his companions were turned into porpoises when they unsuccessfully tried to prevent Ari's brother Tafa'i from accompanying them on a cannibal hunt.
Arioi (Tahiti) a special group of talented dancers etc., whose members participated in a fertility cult. At death they were said to go to a special

underworld, whose head was sometimes held to be Urutaetae, at others, Hiro. See p. 27–28.
Arjuna see Pandawa.
Arjunavivaha p. 22.
arukwita **148, 152.**
Atanua (Marquesas Is., P) the dawn-goddess. She rose from the struggles in which Ono destroyed Mutuhei and Atea expelled Tanaoa (qq.v.). Atanua then became Atea's wife. She suffered a miscarriage and the sea was formed from the resulting amniotic fluid.
atea p. 29.
Atea (i) (eastern P) the name usually given to the sky-father. See also Atea Rangi, Rangi and **24, 32–34.**
(ii) (Marquesas Is. P) one myth says that Atea (Light) evolved from Tanaoa and took Atanua (qq.v.) as his bride. He begat the gods and created heaven and earth. His name is cognate with the Cook Islands' Vatea and Hawaiian Wakea (qq.v.).
Atea Rangi (Tuomotuan Is., P) the sky-father. See also Rangi.
Ati Auru (Society Is., P) the place at which Tii (q.v.) made the first woman from earth.
atua p. 29.
Au (Gilbert Is., Mi) the sun-god and lord of the skies. He rose from the sea on the summit of a pandannus tree. Only the initiates of his clan, Karongoa of the Kings, were allowed to know his story. Others knew him only as the culture-hero Auriaria (q.v.).
Auriaria 95–97.
Ava Rei Pua (Easter Is., P) sister of Hotu Matua and wife of Tu'u ko Iho (qq.v.).
Ayers Rock 144–151.
Ayers Rock, by Mountford **144.**

Baanaba 95–97.
Babamik (*Arapesh*, Sepik River, NG, ME) a cannibal ogress. Eventually lured to her death, she then became a crocodile.
Badu (*Walumba*, Arnhem Land, A) mythical island in the Torres Straits to which spirits of dead members of the *jiridja* moiety (q.v.) journeyed.
Baiame p. 40.
Baka-uaaneku 89.

Bakoa (*Nu*, Ellice Is., Mi) on his first wife, Nei Nguiriki, Bakoa fathered all fish; on his second, Nei Nguinaba, the hero Taburimai (q.v.), and the hammer-headed shark Te-anoi.
Baladewa (Baladeva), King cousin to the Pandawa (q.v.).
Balioe (*Nias*, Sumatra, I) after the creator Barasi-Loelo had made man, the great god Lowalangi gave Balioe wind to put in man's mouth and give him a soul.
Bamapama (*Murngin*, NE Arnhem Land, A) trickster-hero.
Bamundang 139.
Banaidja (*Wulumba*, Arnhem Land, A) one of the great Dreamtime beings, son of Laindjung (q.v.).

A wooden figure collected in the Solomon Islands 1890–93 and said to represent a sea-spirit. Its hands and feet are in the forms of dolphins, or sharks, while its face is also that of a great diving shark, whose body and fins form the spirit's headdress. British Museum. (*Photo: Photoresources.*)

Masked Balinese dancers performing the *Barong-Rangda* legend in which the witch Chalonarang (q.v.) is killed by the holy-man Barong. (*Photo: Claire Leimbach.*)

Boraspati ni Tano (*Batak*, Sumatra, I)
earth-spirit. A sacrifice is made to him
when the main pillars of a new house
are rammed home. Formerly the
sacrifice was human, a slave being
buried alive beneath each pillar. Cf.
112 and Teleu.

Boru deak pordjar 5.

Bouru (Gilbert Is., Mi) one of the four
spirit lands below the western horizon.
The others are Marira, Mwaiku and
Neineaba.

Bralbral (*Wulumba*, Arnhem Land, A)
companion of the Djanggawul. See **158**.

Bralgu (*Wulumba*) island home of the
dead of the *dua* moiety (q.v.). Bralbral
and the Djanggawul paused here on
their way to the Australian coast. See
158.

Bu (Torres Straits, Me) once a man, now a
star in the Dolphin constellation, Bu
killed the *dogai* Metakorab (q.v.).

Buddhist pp. 22, 23.

Bue 105–109.

Bugal see *gainjin*.

Bugan (*Ifugao*, Kiangan, Philippines, I)
she and her brother were the only
survivors of a legendary flood.

Bugari (*Nyulunyul*, W Australia) the
Dreamtime.

Bulugu 163

Bunjil p. 40.

Bunosi (*Mon-alu*, Trobiand Is., Me) snake-
man rejected by his human parents but
cared for by his sister Kafisi, for whom
he made fire and coughed up pigs and
various food plants.

Buriskawa see Korawa.

Buruwal 164.

buta see *yang*.

Cananda see Tacabuinji.

Cargo Cults pp. 34–36.

casuarina tree **142.**

Chalonarang (Bali, I) the *Rangda*
(Widow), a legendary sorceress said to
have lived in Girah (E Java) in the time of
King Airlangga (early eleventh
century). She had a beautiful daughter,
Ratna Mangalli, but no suitors dare
approach the girl for fear of her
mother. In anger Chalonarang asked
Durga, goddess of death (see vol. 3:
5.2. **167–169**), for permission to spread
a plague. This was granted and,
gathering her pupils at a crossroads,
Chalonarang cast her spell. Many died,
but eventually a holy man killed the
sorceress, having first tamed her and
taught her the way of redemption. In
the *Barong-Rangda* dramas, the legend
is enacted only to the point of her
contest with the holy man, Barong
(q.v.), her death omitted.

A Balinese carving of the fiendish Chalonarang. British Museum. (*Photo: Axel Poignant.*)

Chupak (Bali) older brother of Grantang (q.v.) with whom he vied to recover the stolen princess Raden Galuh of Daha (q.v.). Being possessed by the demon Kala, Chupak was lazy, boastful and gluttonous and failed in his quest. The story of the brothers' adventures forms one of the most popular subjects of the *Wayang Kulit* (q.v.) dramas.

Cochrane, Glynn p. 36, 109.

Codrington, R. pp. 22, 109.

Conner, Mt. **145.**

Cook, Captain James p. 28 and 65.

Da Duku (*Akar Bale*, S Andaman Is., I) the ancestor Sir Monitor-Lizard. His wife was In Bain, Lady Civet-Cat. He was the first person to tattoo himself. In some ways Da Duku seems to be a variant of the northern Andamanese Tomo (q.v.).

Daeli (*Nias*, Sumatra, I) culture-hero who descended from heaven bringing yams and polished stones (flints?). Some say he also brought men fire.

Dalugeli (*Huli*, S highlands, NG, Me) a heavenly resting-place for the spirits of warriors and others slain in battle.

dama (*Huli*) invisible deities. They control the weather and attack human beings, causing illness, sterility or death. Most of them can also bring good fortune, but a minority are wholly evil. They are both male and female, though the female *dama* are fewer. They sometimes marry and the females practise polyandry. A *dama* may embody part of itself in a stone or fossil, but however many embodiments contain it the god is still also omnipresent. The chief *dama* are Dindiainayi, Helabe, Hone, Lindu and Ni (qq.v.). They are believed to be embodied in stones which are corporately owned and, except on ritual occasions, kept buried. The stones' presence is believed to imbue the district with the gods' power. The *Huli* say they do not know much about the relationships between the various *dama*. They aver there is no hierarchy, but they feel that some of the gods are greater than others.

dama agali duo (*Huli*) the founding ancestors of the people. Their name indicates they were half gods and half ghosts.

dama dagenda (*Huli*) evil forest-spirits. They attack travellers, making their noses bleed and giving them sores. To ward off such attacks the traveller talks to himself in a special language which is believed to puzzle the *dama* and make them think twice before attacking him.

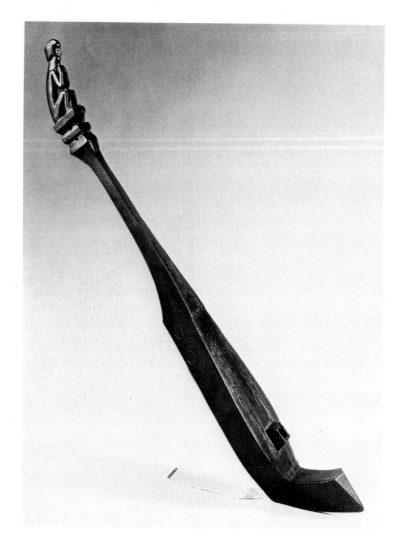

A *Batak* musical instrument decorated with the figure of a *debata*. Museum für Völkerkunde, Munich. (*Photo: Michael Holford.*)

Dangdang Gendis, Prince of Daha **19–22.**

Danhyang Desa (Java, I) one of the most important *yang* (spirits), he lives in a large tree in or near a village and is believed to have settled there before the village was founded. Had he not, it would have disintegrated. All blessings emanate from him. Disasters are signs that he has been neglected.

Daragu boards see *Inma* boards.

Daramulun p. 40.

Darana 154–156.

Datagaliwabe (*Huli*, S highlands, NG, Me) a being described as a giant, standing astride and gazing down on mankind. He punishes all who offend against kinship laws but is uninterested in other crimes. He cannot be propitiated, so no prayers or rituals are offered him. He is never referred to as a god (*dama*) although he shares many of their powers. His punishments take the form of illnesses, fatal accidents and death in battle.

Death, Tree of 99–101.

debata (*Batak*, Sumatra, I) generic term for gods and spirits.

Debata Idup (*Batak*) 'Live Gods', a pair of wooden dolls invoked by childless couples, who tend them as if they were babies.

Debata Natolu (*Batak*) the 'Three Gods', i.e. Batara Guru, Mangalubulan and Soripata (qq.v.), worshipped as a trinity and deriving from the Hindu

Shiva, Brahma, and Vishnu. (See vol. 3:
5.2. **152–162**, **60–64**, and **108–151**,
156–157.)

Devī Shrī p. 25. and 22.

Dewī Amisanī 22.

Dewī Hasīn 22.

Dewī Payā 22.

Dewī Shrī p. 25. and 22.

didjeridu (A) Aborigine drone-pipe played
during ritual ceremonies. See p. 41.

dilly-bag 160.

Dindiainyia see *dama*.

Dinditane (*Huli*, S highlands, NG, Me)
one of the two fertility-gods of
gardening. The other is Wandatilepu.

dinini (*Huli*) a concept roughly
comparable with that of the soul. Cf.
mana.

Djambubarus (*Batak*, Sumatra, I) the
Tree of Life existing in the seventh
(highest) heaven. On each leaf God has
written a word, such as 'wealth'.
Before departing for earth every *tondi*
(soul) must beg a leaf from the tree.
The one it receives determines its
earthly fortunes.

Djanggau see Djanggawul.

Djanggawul (Djanggau) 158–159, 161.

Djanggawul sisters 157–161.

Djata (*Ngadju Dayaks*, Kalimantan, I) god
of the underworld.

djihin (*Minangkabau*, Sumatra, I) good
spirit; the name is derived from
Arabic, under the influence of Islam.

djiibilba boards see *inma* boards.

Djokjokarta, Sultan of see Njai Lora
Kidoul.

Djordjor (Aborigines of W desert, A) the
Night-owl-man, betrothed to Minma
Waiuda, the Possum-woman (q.v.). He
is referred to in stories about the Wadi
Gudjara (q.v.).

djuda 159.

Djuguba (Aborigines of Great Victoria
Desert, A) a term for the Dreamtime
and for Dreamtime beings. It is
sometimes spelled *Djugurba*.

Djumanggani (Aborigines of Balgo area, A)
a term for the Dreamtime.

Djungawon 166.

djungawon 167.

Djungguan 166.

Djunggun (*Ungarinjin*, Kimberley area,
A) the Dreamtime Owl-man.

Djunkgao see Djanggawul.

Djurgurba see *Djubuga* and p. 39.

dogai (Torres Straits, Me) devils, some
male, some female. One, a female is
now a constellation including the star
Altair. Images of the *dogai* were fixed
to canoes and masks of them worn at
seasonal festivals to induce the spirits
to refrain from harming agriculture and
fishing.

dracaena tree 127.

An Arnhem Land Aborigine playing the *didjeridu* pipe. (*Photo: Axel Poignant*.)

Dreamtime pp. 38–41 and **144, 145, 154**.
See also Dreamtime beings and
*Aldjeringa, Dunguba, Djumanggani,
Duma, Gugal, Maradal, Mura,
Ngarunggani, Tjukurapa, Ungud,
Wongar*.

Dreamtime beings p. 38–40. See
also **138–167** and Banaidja, Djordjor,
Djugubar, Djunggun, Gidja, Julana,
Kallin-kallin, Kalwadi, Kulpunya,
Kunapipi, Kunia, Laindjung, Linga,
Liru, Mala, Mali, Mamandabari,
Mamaragur, Metalungana Minma
Mingari, Minma Nganamara, Minma
Wiuda, Mungamunga girls, Ngunung-
ngunnut, Tacabuinji, Tjinimin, Wadi
Baba, Wadi Bera, Wadi Galaia, Wadi
Gulber, Wadi Gudjara, Wadi Malu,
Walangada, Wamolungu, Warana,
Wodi, Wollunqua, *wondjina, wongar*.

dua moiety 166.

Dubo 123.

Dudugera (Massim area, NG, Me) a child
whose father was a huge fish that
rubbed itself against a woman's leg,
causing a swelling. When she asked her
father to lance this Dudugera popped
out. Later he climbed into the sky and
became the sun. In order to prevent
him from destroying the whole world
with his fiery gaze, his mother took a
calabash of lime, climbed a hill on the
eastern horizon and, as Dudugera rose
into the sky, she threw the lime full in
his face. He quickly shut his eyes and
so their heat was dimmed.

Duma (Aborigines of Rawlinson Range area, A) the Dreamtime.

Dunawali (*Huli*, S highlands, NG, Me) a goddess who lodges herself in a woman's internal organs. The innocent victim becomes the involuntary vehicle of Dunawali's evil power and any man she looks at may speedily die. She is said to visit their graves to eat their corpses, so the dead man's brothers keep a secret watch near his grave and shoot any woman who approaches it. The witch may be recognised by her unusually fine complexion and intense gaze. Three other goddesses who bewitch women for similar ends are Kapiano, Pinuwali and Walipolima.

Dunga-Kwab-Dap (Wogeo, Schouten Is., Me) culture-hero. Suspecting that two men from his settlement had stolen his coconuts, Dunga-Kwab-Dap scattered crumbs on their bedding, to attract ants. The victims hurled a flaming log at him and half his body was transformed into the island of Manam, the other half into two active volcanoes on the island of Wogeo itself.

Duraulu 156.

Durga (Bali, I) the goddess of death, a Hindu derivation. See vol. 3: 5.2. **167–169.**

Durna see Korawa.

Durrungna see Mangolu.

Dursasana see Korawa.

Ega kiliapa (*Huli*, S highlands, NG, Me) a vigorous ritual dance performed by two young men while pigs are being cooked in honour of the tribal ghosts. The smell of the roasting meat attracts the ghosts, who then join in the dance, thus loosening their aged joints!

eharo masks see *hevehe*.

Elkin, A. P. p. 32, 109.

Ellis, William pp. 22, 109.

Emakong (*Sulka*, New Britain, Me) a man who descended to the underworld and returned with some darkness, some fire, crickets and birds, all of which had hitherto been unknown on earth.

enda kondapala see *enda semangko*.

enda semangko (*Kyaka*, W highlands, NG, Me) cult of a fertility-goddess. It is also known as *kor enda* or *enda kondapala*. In essence it is the same as a cult of the neighbouring *Metlpa* people, the *kor nganap*, from which the *Kyaka* believe the *enda semangko* developed. The rituals centre on a stone symbolising the fertility-goddess. The whole cycle, which takes some five–six years to work through, symbolises a marriage between the goddess and the participant men of the tribe.

Eneene, husband of Kura (q.v.).

Enulap 110.

epalirai (*Kyaka*) evil forest-demons.

Eua 28.

Eve 62.

Faravai (*Lamotrek*, Caroline Is., Mi) brother of Aluluei (q.v.) whom he treated meanly, but he was forgiven and Aluluei taught him various food taboos and also the art of navigation. This Faravai learned by de-lousing Aluluei's hair, which he found full of staring eyes. His brother explained that these were stars, and so Faravai learned their names and positions in the sky.

farmal house **112.**

figona (San Christoval, Solomon Is., Me) serpent-beings, creative spirits also known as *higona, hi'ona* and *vigona* in other areas of the south-eastern Solomon Islands. They are all manifestations of the supreme *figona*, Agunua, creator of man. Having formed a male infant, Agunua then made a woman to care for it. He also created vegetables, but his brother burned some in his oven, so not all plants are now edible. One of Agunua's most important manifestations is Hatuibwari, a human-headed winged serpent with four eyes and four breasts, with which he suckles his offspring.

Finweigh (*Bilan*, Mindanao, Philippines, I) the god who, with Melu (q.v.), made man.

Foam-of-the-Ocean 66.

Fornander, p. 21.

forso (*Gururumba*, central highlands, NG, Me) ghosts of the dead. They can be harmful, but are more often tiresome, causing accidents, illnesses, bad weather and death. They are not moral agents and attack men only to command their attention, either because their bones need to be cleaned of rotting flesh, or their graves have been disturbed, or simply because they feel a desire for distraction.

Gab'me (*Ngaing*, Rai coast, NG, Me) a god said to have created the bullroarer, which is used in various rituals. A myth says Gab'me first put it into an old woman's bag, but she could not manage to whirl it, so he visited her grandson in a dream and taught him its use. Thenceforth it was used only by men.

Gadimargara 154.

Gadjari see Mamandabari.

gainjin (*Keraki*, Papua, NG, Me) the primal beings. Their name indicates that they were giants. They descended from the sky and all but two later returned there. Bugal the snake and Warger the crocodile stayed behind. The *gainjin's* sky world is supported by a huge rattan and the *Keraki* people fear that this may break during a heavy storm, so when such storms arise they prepare to defend themselves, lest any *gainjin* should fall out of the sky and attack them.

Galadari 154.

Galaru see Galeru.

Galeru (*Ungarinjin*, Kimberley area, A) the Rainbow Snake. His name is sometimes spelled Galaru or Kaleru. An alternative name for him is Ungud (Ungur).

Galwagi (*Wuradjeri*, A) the Dreamtime, which the *Wuradjeri* also call *Maradal*.

ganala (Aborigines of NE coast, A) as part of the *kunapipi* (q.v.) rituals a crescent-shaped trench, the *ganala*, is dug. It is an uterine symbol and in western Arnhem Land one of its walls is decorated with the figure of a snake.

ganinjari **159.**

garirnji see Wondjina.

Gidja (*Wumunkan*, Cape York Peninsula, A) a Dreamtime being who made the first woman by castrating the Dreamtime Eaglehawk, Yalungur. Gidja then formed a baby from bloodwood and inserted it into Yalungur's body. In choosing the Eaglehawk for his wife Gidja broke the marriage laws, which say that people must not marry someone from their own moiety (q.v.). Kallin-kallin, the Dreamtime Chickenhawk, therefore tried to kill Gidja by severing a vine bridge just as Gidja was crossing it. Swept away by the river and out to sea, Gidja then rose into the sky and became the moon.

Gill, W. Wyatt pp. 22, 109.

Gilland p. 21.

Gimigaigai (*Lakalai*, New Britain, Me) the sky world in which the culture-heroes Tauahili and Taio and other godlike beings lived before their descent to earth.

God-Kilibob (Rai cost, NG, Me) Cargo Cult deity. Cf. Jesus-Manup and see also Cargo Cults, p. 34ff.

Grantang (Bali, I) younger brother of Chupak (q.v.). Gentle and refined, he proved the saviour of the Princess Raden Galuh (q.v.).

Grey, Sir George pp. 21, 109.

Grimble, Sir Arthur pp. 21, 30, 109.

Gubar Baleman 22.

Gugal (*Jaraldi*, A) the Dreamtime.

Gulanundoidj 162–163.

Guldana see Kultana.

Gulgabi see Wadi Gudjara.

Gulikiliki-la-mata-La haro (*Lakalai*, New Britain, Me) the 'Children of the sun', said to have been tiny, light-skinned people who long ago invaded *Lakalai* territory, defeated the *Lakalai* in battle and then disappeared.

gwowai (*Gururumba*, central highlands, NG, Me) ambivalent grassland-spirits.

Ha-nui-a-rangi (*Maori*, NZ, P) according to one creation story he was the child of Rangi and Poko-ha-rua-te-po (qq.v.).

Hades 62.

Hafoza (*Jate*, E highlands, NG, Me) god of thunder and lightning.

Hana 119–121.

hantu see ibilih.

Hanua Eepe (Easter Is., P) the 'Heavy-set men' who formed the second wave of Easter Island settlers. Sometimes they are, incorrectly, referred to as the Long-ears. Tradition says it was they who carved the famous stone statues on the island.

Hanua Momoko (Easter Is.) the 'Slender men', the first Easter Island settlers, led by Hotu Matua (q.v.).

Haro see Tauahili.

Hatuibwari see *figona*.

Hau Maka (Easter Is.) legendary seer of Hiva (q.v.), who had a vision of Easter Island and foretold its settlement.

Haumea (i) (Hawaii, P) goddess of procreation and childbirth. Before she taught women otherwise, children were delivered by being cut from their mothers, who died as a result. In other parts of Polynesia this practice was said to have been ended by Hina (q.v.). Like the cognate *Maori* god Haumia, Haumea was also the deity of vegetation.
(ii) (Tahiti, Society Is., P) a goddess who became a cannibal when her husband Ro'o-nui deserted her. She was killed by her son Tuture as she swam after him, trying to prevent his escaping her. Her corpse floated ashore and there revived. Haumea now became Nona (Rona) q.v.

Haumia 47–55. See also Haumea (i).

Hawaiki p. 30 and **67**.

Heke-heke-i-papa (*Maori*, NZ, P) according to one creation myth this goddess was the third of Rangi's (q.v.) six wives and bore him many children, the most important being Tama-nui-a-rangi (q.v.). Her name means 'Coming-down-to-earth'.

Helabe (*Huli*, S highlands, NG, Me) a son of the primaeval goddess Honabe (q.v.).

Helahuli (*Huli*) a son of the goddess Honabe (cf. Helabe). His own four sons

One of the famous Easter Island statues traditionally ascribed to Hanua Eepe. British Museum. (*Photo: British Museum.*)

An *eharo* dance mask worn during the *hevehe* rituals of the *Elema* people. Pitt-Rivers Museum, Oxford. (*Photo: Axel Poignant*.)

were the first men and founders of the four tribes who bear their names: *Huli, Opena, Dugube* and *Duna*.

Hema (i) (Tahiti, Society Is., P) child of the old man who slew Nona (q.v.). Nona's daughter was Hema's mother. (ii) (*Maori*, NZ, P) child of Whaitari and Kai-tangata (qq.v.). His own sons were the heroes Tawhaki and Karihi. See also **82–84**.

Herabe (*Huli*, S highlands, NG, Me) a god who causes insanity, sometimes by working alone, sometimes in consort with two others, Matawali and Podadeli.

hevehe (*Elema*, Orokolo Bay, NG, Me) a ritual cycle in honour of sea-spirits inhabiting the bay. *Eharo* masks worn during part of the rituals symbolise the spirits and other mythical and totem beings.

Heyerdahl, Thor, pp. 22, 109.

Hi-asa (Admiralty Is., Bismarck Archipelago, Me) a solitary woman who cut her finger while slicing pandannus leaves. Collecting the blood from the wound in a mussel shell, she covered it and left it for eleven days, after which she found the blood had become two eggs. From these emerged the parents of mankind.

Hia (*Nias*, Sumatra, I) culture-hero, the father of mankind. As a small child he descended to earth, but returned to the sky when he was adult. Also the moon-god, his name is cognate with that of the Polynesian moon-goddess, Hina (q.v.).

Hian (Kei Is., I) the oldest brother of Parpara (q.v.).

higona see *figona*.

Hina 56–62, 78.

Hina-uri 59.

Hindu(ism) pp. 23, 24, 25–26, and see also **2, 23**.

Hine 40, 42, 48, 56–62, 73, 74, 79–80.

Hine-ahu-one 67.

Hine-i-tau-ira 56.

Hine-maki-moe 40.

Hine-nui-te-po 42, 56.

Hine-te-iwa Iwa see Hina-uri and 59.

Hine-titama 56, 67.

Hine-tu-a-muana (*Maori*, NZ, P) second wife of Tane (q.v.). Her name means 'the Mountain Maid'. Her offspring were rusty mountain water and monstrous reptiles.

hi'ona see *figona*.

Hiro (i) (P) in most of Polynesia, the god of navigation. (ii) (Easter Is., P) the rain-god and probably also a fertility-deity.

Hiva (Easter Is.) the place from which the islanders' ancestors are said to have come. All foreigners are called 'Men of

Hiva'. It possibly refers to an island in the Marquesas group.

hoda debata (*Toba Batak*, Sumatra, I) the horse sacrifice, derived from the Hindu *rājasūya*. (See vol. 3: 5.3.) At a great sacrificial feast, horses are offered to the *debata* (q.v.). Every *Toba Batak* family group has a horse consecrated to one of these gods. It is thought of as the god's throne—the symbol of his presence as their divine father. A black horse is consecrated to Batara Guru (q.v.), a brown to Soripata (q.v.) and a piebald to Manigalubulan (q.v.), the colour of any particular group's horse naturally depending upon which of these three deities it claims as its ancestor. When old the horse is sacrificed and replaced by a young colt of the same hue.

hohao (central highlands, NG, Me) an oval-shaped wooden board carved with a face and painted. Clans kept them in the men's cult houses (*eravao*) and consulted them before any important expedition. Each *hohao* had its own name, personality and sacred character. Cf. the *tjurunga* and *inma* boards of the Aborigines.

Honabe (*Huli*, S highlands, NG) primaeval goddess and first inhabitant of the land. She cooked her food in the heat of her genitals. Seduced by the god Timbu, she bore five deities: Helabe, Helahuli, Korimogo Ni and Piandela were all male, Hana, female. Later Honabe bore seven other gods, and the first bird and first possum grew from her menses. See also **120**.

Hone see *dama*.

Hotu-matua (Easter Is., P) leader of the first Easter Island people, who came from Hiva (q.v.). See also **72**.

Hotu-papa (*Maori*, NZ, P) according to one creation myth Hotu-papa was Rangi's (q.v.) fourth wife. She bore him many children, but none were gods of any importance. Her name means 'Sobbing Earth'.

Houmea (*Maori*) a cannibal who swallowed her two children, but her husband, Uta, made her disgorge them. Later he threw hot stones down her gaping maw and killed her, as she pursued him and the children in the form of a stag.

Hua Lega 61.

Hudog, (*Ifugao*, Kiangan, Philippines, I) the sky world.

Hugenda (*Huli*, S. highlands, NG, Me) a god who attacks pregnant women. Part of him becomes incorporated in the embryo's internal organs and any child born with blood in its mouth is

Carved wooden ancestor figure (cf. Hia) from the *Nias* people, Sumatra. The beard denotes a man of authority, the necklace signifies personal courage. Museum für Völkerkunde, Munich. (*Photo: Michael Holford.*)

believed to be a victim of Hugenda. Various rituals are performed to release the child, for it is a danger to its family and neighbours, inadvertently causing them ill health and bad luck.

Hula p. 27.

Huli (*Huli*) one of the four first men, sons of the god Helahuli (q.v.). He had many children who lived in the Tangari basin area of the southern highlands of New Guinea, but their descendants were killed in a great flood. The gods subsequently created new birds and possums, who produced human offspring, the founding-fathers of the present inhabitants.

Hulu (*Nias*, Sumatra, I) a culture-hero who descended to earth from the heavens. Grass and trees are said to have sprung from his blood. See also **6**.

Humbinianda (*Huli*, S highlands, NG, Me) a hot, arid region inhabited by souls of the dead for an indefinite period.

---

ibilih (*Minangabau*, Sumatra, I) evil spirits also called *setan* or *hantu*.

Ihoiho (Society Is., P) pre-existent god, at first the only living being; then a great expanse of water covered the abyss and the god Timo-tatata appeared floating on its surface.

Iko (Gulf of Papua and Torres Straits, regions, Me) culture-hero also known as Hido or Sido. He is said to have given *kaiaimunu* (q.v.) to the *Namua* people.

Ilara (*Tiwi*, Melville Is., A) the underworld.

Ilkari (*Pitjandjara*, Gibson Desert, A) the sky world and home of the spirits who roamed Australia in the Dreamtime.

Imberombera p. 40.

In Bain see Da Duku.

Ina variant of Hina (q.v.) See also **62**.

Ina-da Samadulo Hose 6.

Ina-da Samihara Luwo 6.

Ina Onian (*Pageh*, Mentawei Is., Sumatra, I) a propitious river-spirit whose name means 'Mother of the water'.

inaptua see Numbakulla.

Ingridi 150–152.

inma boards (Aborigines of Great Victoria Desert, A) a generic term for carved and painted wooden boards used in rituals. They are also known as *djibilba*. Similar boards from the eastern Kimberley region are called *daragu* ('sacred'). They vary from between 1–2in and 18ft in length and include many different types, each with its specific name and ritual function. See also *tjurunga*.

Io (*Maori*, NZ, P) the primordial creator, a concept developed after the *Maoris* had come into contact with Christian teaching.

Iolofath 110.

Iowahine (*Maori*) the first woman. Some stories say she was made by Tane as companion to the first man Tiki. See **68**.

Ipila (*Kiwai*, Papua, NG, Me) the creator of Nugu (q.v.), whom he carved from wood and brought to life by washing his face with sago milk.

Ira (Easter Is., P) one of the seven legendary youths sent from Hiva (q.v.) to reconnoitre Easter Island before its settlement.

Iri 9.

---

jakalabakai see *yang*.

Jari (Wogeo, Schouten Is., Me) culture-heroine, the daughter of a snake. She instituted marriage, not with her first spouse, whom she left when he ignorantly killed her snake-mother, but with her second consort, the wild man Kamarong, for whom she built a house. Jari taught him the use of fire for cooking and how to cultivate the soil. Finally, with a bamboo cane, she pierced him an anus. Before this operation he had been obliged to evacuate through his mouth and smelled foul. When all was done and Kamarong thoroughly civilised, he and Jari became the first married couple.

Javanese shadow puppets, pp. 26, 110.

Jaw, the Lower 66.

Jaw, the Upper 66.

Jesus-Manup (Rai coast, NG, Me) a Cargo Cult deity. Cf. God-Kilibob and see also Cargo Cults, p. 34ff.

jindja moiety **166**.

jiridja moiety **166**.

Jugga see Wadi Gudjara.

Jugumishanta 116–117.

Julana (Aborigines of Western Desert, A) the names Julana and Njirana are used interchangeably for an ancestral Dreamtime man and his personified penis.

Julunggul 164–166.

Julunggul **167**.

Jurawadbad 162–163.

Jutpu (*Aka Bo*, Andaman Is., I) culture-hero, the first man. He grew inside a bamboo joint and hatched from it like a bird from an egg. He made his wife Kot and all the *Aka Bo* ancestors from the clay of an ants' nest and taught them all the useful arts.

Juwuka (*Tiwi*, Melville Is., A) the sky world of the star people. It lies between earth and the upper world of the Tuniruna (q.v.).

Kabigat (*Ifugao*, Kiangan, Philippines, I) the first son of Wigan (q.v.). He changed the earth's original flat surface into hills and valleys by damming up all the estuaries. He married his sister Bugan (q.v.).

Kabo Mandalat (New Caledonia, Me) a female demon in the form of a giant hermit crab. She causes elephantiasis.

kabu ceremony (*Ngaing*, Rai coast, NG, Me) an elaborate ceremony in honour of the spirits of the dead. It once lasted three months but is now limited by the government to one. It involves exchanges of pork and other valuables, fertility rituals designed to ensure large catches of fish, and feasts and dances to the accompaniment of trumpets and slit-gongs. The cult is said to have been founded by the god Yabuling, whose secret name is breathed over a trumpet and this then played above a bowl of pork. From time to time the *kabu* ceremonies have been assimilated to Cargo Cult rites, see p. 34ff.

Kafisi see Bunosi.

Kaha'i 81.

Kaharinganism (Kalimantan, I) generic term for animistic religions.

Kahiki (Hawaiian Is., P) the spirit land. The word is cognate with *Tahiti*.

Kahukura (i) (*Maori*, NZ, P) a war-god. His symbol, the rainbow, was sacred to the descendants of those *Maoris* who reached New Zealand in the canoes *Aotea* and *Takitumu*.

(ii) (Rarotonga, Cook Is., P) possibly a

Woodcarving of an Hawaiian deity, possibly Kane or Ku from the royal temple at Karakakua. British Museum. (*Photo: British Museum.*)

war-god but this is far from certain.

Kai (*Maori*, NZ, Me) a hero who killed the pet whale belonging to Tinirau (q.v.). Tinirau had lent him the whale as a steed to carry him home after the baptism of Tinirau's son Tu-huru-huru. Disregarding his friend's instructions, Kai beached the whale, killed it, cut it up and cooked it. Tinirau later took his revenge.

Kai-n-tiku-aba 91.

Kai-tangata (*Maori*, NZ, P) a great warrior, whose name 'Man-eater', misled the cannibal goddess Whaitari, who took him as her husband. One of their children was Hema (q.v.).

kai vera (*Tikopia*, Solomon Is., Me) fertility ceremony connected with the yam harvest. Its name means 'hot food'. It involves men trying to eat burning hot yams. The first man to swallow a morsel is believed to be especially favoured during the coming year by the great god-culture-hero Te Atua Fakamataku (q.v.).

kaiaimunu (*Vaimuru* and *Namua* peoples, Purarui delta, Papua, NG, Me) wickerwork of figures of monstrous animals with gaping mouths. Used in male initiation ceremonies, each represents a different, named, spirit. The *Vaimuru* people say Iko (q.v.) gave them to the *Namua*.

Ka'ioi p. 27.

Kalakua, King of Hawaii p. 22.

Kaleru see Galeru.

Kallin-kallin (*Wumunkan*, Cape York Pen., A) the Dreamtime Chickenhawk-man. He married Yalungur, the first woman. See also Gidja.

Kalwadi (*Murinbata*, N Territory, A) a Dreamtime being, the 'Old Woman', whose name was Mutjingga. She is the most important figure associated with the *Murinbata* fertility rituals. These enact the myth of her swallowing her grandchildren, who were later cut alive from her womb.

Kamarong see Jari.

Kambel (*Keraki*, SW coast, W Irian, I) a sky-being who felled a palm tree and so released mankind, who were trapped within it. In the evening his son, the moon, floated up from the tree. Kambel and his family eventually returned to the sky after the son, Moon, had committed incest with his mother. Kambel slew the youth secretly, but the moon's dog saw him and protested at the deed. To prevent it from betraying him, Kambel pinned its tongue with a feather, since when dogs have only been able to howl.

Kameian (*Pageh*, Menawei Is., Sumatra, I) a malevolent river-spirit. Its name means 'Father's sister'.

Kanaloa see Tanaloa.

Kane (Hawaii, P) one of the three great gods, the others being Lono and Ku. Lono made man from red earth in the shape of Kane himself. See also **66–69.**

Kangaroo Island 140–142.

Kanii 92.

Kapiano see Dunawali.

Kapo (Hawaii) fertility-god.

Karapeli (*Arapesh*, Sepik River, NG, Me) rain-spirit.

Karia (Aborigines of South-east A) the Rainbow Snake.

Karihi 82–83.

Kasa soma (*Dobu*, D'Entrecasteaux Is.,

Me) ageless creative spirits born with the sun, moon and earth. They once lived here but now dwell in the sky.

Kawelu (Hawaii, P) heroine who died of grief during her husband's absence from home. He descended to the underworld, trapped her spirit in a hollow coconut shell and forced it to re-enter her body through a hole in her left big toe. So he restored her to life.

Kayai (*Aeta*, Luzon, Philippines, I) the supreme being, also called Bayagaw. He lives in heaven in a stone house or cave. The thunder is his voice and storms manifest his anger.

Kelana Tunjung Seta (Bali and Java,

A shadow puppet from the Javanese *Wayang Gedog* (q.v.) represents the Kelana Tunjung Seta. British Museum. (*Photo: British Museum.*)

l) the adversary of Panji (q.v.).

Ken Angrok 19–20.

kepa (*Huli*, S highlands, NG, Me) the very powerful ghosts of female ancestors.

Kepei (*Huli*) a very powerful male god. He lacks a penis and only continent men may safely enter his shrine.

kewa kuli (*Kyaka*, W highlands, NG, Me) a fertility cult associated with Komba Ralkingki (q.v.). Its title means 'stranger bone'. An alternative name is *akali semangko*.

Kii (Hawaii, P) the ancestor of man. His mother was the daughter of the great gods Bright Light and Pleasant Quiet. His name is cognate with those of Tii and Tiki (qq.v.).

Kikinto 87.

kilyakai (*Kyaka*, W highlands, NG, Me) small, ugly, nature-demons, believed to steal pigs and infect men with malaria by shooting poisoned arrows at them. They also steal babies and cause boils.

kina (*Mentawei*, Sumatra, I) the soul, which all things possess.

Kirata-n-te-rerei (*Nui*, Ellice Is., Mi) the son of Te-ariki-n-tarawa (q.v.) and Nei Te-reere. He was so beautiful that he caused the spontaneous creation of two men from inanimate objects. The first, Beia, sprang from the spot where Kirata had had a meal; the second, Te-kai,

grew from his discarded coconut-leaf body scraper.

ko hau [motu mo] rongorongo (Easter Is., P) wooden tablets inscribed with hieroglyphs. Only a few examples survive and no one knows how to read them. Tradition says Hotu Matua (q.v.) brought sixty-seven of them with him from Hiva. There were schools which taught the art of writing and the tablets are said to have fallen into three classes, one of which included hymns.

Kobine (Gilbert Is., Mi) in some myths the daughter of Na Areau (q.v.) and his assistant in creating the earth.

Koevasi (Solomon Is., Me) snake-mother of the Florida-islanders.

Komba Ralingki (*Kyaka*, W highlands, NG, Me) a 'foreigner' who it is said was large and fair-skinned. He travelled across the *Kyaka* territory, resting at several places known as *imbwünda*, from which powerful fertility stones are said to have come. He is reputed to have taught the *Kyaka* to build with latticed cane and introduced them to particular varieties of banana, taro and sugar-cane. One of his bones is said to have been found wrapped in a blanket or bag of European make. This bone now forms the ritual object of the *Kyakas'* chief cult and fertility rite, performed at Kamenispa and known as *kewa kuli* ('stranger bone') or *akali*

semangko ('male spirit'). It is the only cult now performed by the whole tribe, whose ancestor is said to have found the abandoned bone.

Konori (Geelwink Bay area, NG, Me) the creator of the earth.

kor enda see *enda semangko*.

kor nganap (*Metlapa*, NG, Me) a ritual essentially the same as the *enda semangko* (q.v.) of the *Kyaka*.

Korawar, the One Hundred (Java, I) the Kaurava (see vol. 3: 5.2. **197–246**), opponents of the five Pandawa (q.v.).

Korereke 97.

Korimogo (*Huli*, S highlands, NG, Me) an evil god, son of Honabe and Timbu (qq.v.). Unlike most of the *Huli's* major gods he is not associated with any particular cult object or locality, but the corpses of those he has slain are believed to exude his dangerous power. They are therefore buried with extra care, their finger and toe nails being removed and substituted for each other so as to confuse Korimogo and safeguard local people from his attacks.

Korwar (W Irian, Me) sacred statues of the gods.

Kot see Jutpu.

Koura-abi 94.

kovave (*Parevavo*, NG, Me) an initiation festival in which youths don the *kovave* mask. 'Power' is transferred to

A *ko hau rongorongo* tablet from Easter Island. British Museum. (*Photo: Axel Poignant.*)

the younger men by their maternal uncles during this rite.

Kreshna, King (Java, I) Krishna (see vol. 3 : 5.2. **142–151**), mentor of the Pandawa (q.v.).

Ku see Kane.

Kui (Tahiti, P) blind old woman, the grandmother of Tafa'i and Ari (qq.v.).

Kukailimoku (Hawaii, P) war-god.

Kula p. 32.

Kulkudjeri 149–150.

Kulpunya (*Pitjandjara*, Gibson Desert, A) the spirit-dingo.

Kultana (*Wulumba*, Arnhem Land, A) the spirit who lights fires to guide dead souls to Badju (q.v.). He is also referred to as Guldana.

Kumlimpo Chant of Creation, the p. 22.

kumpong tree.

Kunapipi (Aborigines, S Arnhem Land, A) mother of the Mungamunga girls (q.v.). A man-eater, she was killed by the Dreamtime Eaglehawk and is a central figure in the *kunapipi-kalwadi-kadjari* fertility and initiation rituals. See also Ganala, p. 40 and **165, 167.**

kunapipi see Kunapipi.

Kunia (*Pitjandjara*, Gibson Desert, A) the Dreamtime totem carpet-snake people. See **145–152.**

Kunmanggur (*Murinbata*, N Territory, A) the Rainbow Snake.

Kura (*Mangaia*, Cook Is., P) wife of Eneene. While she was gathering flowers with her sister the earth opened and she fell through into the underworld, where she was imprisoned, guarded by a blind gaoler. Eneene eventually rescued her.

Kura-waka 67.

Lai (E Torajas, Sulawesi, I) a sky-god, though less well-known than Poeempalaburu (q.v.).

La'i-la'i (Hawaii, P) the first female being, which existed in the darkness of Po (q.v.). The sky-god took her as his wife and she bore him the ancestors of mankind.

Laindjung (*Wulumba*, Arnhem Land, A) one of the great Dreamtime beings, father of Banaidja (q.v.).

Langal (N and NW Territories, A) the Rainbow Snake.

Larlangel 139.

Latoere (*Nias*, Sumatra, I) the god who made the first, unsuccessful, attempt at creating man.

Latura 6–7.

lau (Andaman Is., I) generic term for spirits, also applied to all foreigners on the assumption that, since they were evidently not Andamanese, they must be spirits.

Figure of the Hawaiian war-god Kukailimoku, made from scarlet feathers on a reed trellis. The teeth are dogs' teeth, the eyes made of shells. British Museum. (*Photo: Axel Poignant.*)

Laulaati (*Lifu*, Loyalty Is., New Caledonia, Me) creator of the earth.

Laval, Père pp. 22, 109.

Lawrence, Peter p. 22, 109.

Lévi-Strauss, Claude pp. 37, 110.

Life, Tree of 98–101.

Lightning Snake 167.

Ligoububfanu 86.

Lilavatu (Nandi district, Viti Levu, Fiji, Me) goddess, wife of the chief god. She caused swollen necks and those who failed to observe her rites were killed in battle, or simply died. The Fijians gave the name *lila* to an epidemic brought by their first European visitors.

Wooden figure of a man wearing a bird mask. Carvings of similar figures are found on rocks at Easter Island and possibly refer to rituals associated with the god Make-make. British Museum.)*Photo: Axel Poignant.*)

Elaborately carved and painted head of a *malanggan* figure from New Ireland.
The Australian Museum. (*Photo: Axel Poignant.*)

93

Aborigine bark painting of the Mamarangan spirit. Private Collection. (*Photo: Axel Poignant.*)

the moon Gidja (q.v.) and therefore flies ahead of him.

Malinowski, Bronislaw, pp. 32, 109.

Mamandabari (*Walbiri*, N Territory, A) the two chief Dreamtime beings, sometimes referred to as brothers, sometimes as father and son. They instituted the *gadjari* ('senior woman') fertility ritual.

Mamarangan (Aborigines, Arnhem Land, A) the Lightning-man.

mana (i) pp. 31, 32, and **66.**
   (ii) (*Huli*, S highlands, NG, Me) the name for their myths.

Mande Rubiah (*Minangkabau*, Sumatra, I) the oldest of the female *djihin* (good spirits), she is consulted in a trance by doctors.

Mangalubulan (*Batak*, Sumatra, I) p. 24 and **5.** The third of the three great gods, sons of Mula djada na bolon (q.v.), living in the sixth heaven. He blesses and helps mankind in general, but is also the special patron of thieves. The word *bulan* means 'moon' and possibly Mangalubulan was once thought of as a lunar god.

Mangolu (*Murngin*, NE Arnhem Land, A) the father of all. He lives in the sky and resembles an ordinary man in appearance, except for his great size. After eating he puts the bones from his meat in a neat pile, taking great care that none drop from the sky to earth. Mangolu is also known as Durrungna and Lilpilna. Concepts of him have possibly been influenced by Christian teaching. He is said to have fathered the children of the Wawalag sisters (q.v.).

Manual (Admiralty Is., Me) a culture-hero. Feeling lonely he created the first woman from a tree trunk.

Manuk-manuk (*Batak*, Sumatra, I) the fabulous Blue-chicken, wife of Mula djadi na bolon (q.v.). She is almost certainly an indigenous goddess, introduced into a myth of Hindu provenance to account for the appearance of the three eggs from which Mula djadi na bolon's sons, the Debata Natolu (q.v.), were born.

Maradal (*Wuradjeri*, A) the Dreamtime, which was also called *Galwagi*.

maraiin (Aborigines, W Arnhem Land, A) ceremony involving a variety of *maraiii* (ritual objects): also called *muraian*.

Marama Kai see Nuku Kehu.

Marawa 126–127.

Marelulu (S Pentecost, New Hebrides, Me) the most important of Barkulkula's (q.v.) five brothers. He seduced Barkulkula's wife and was killed in revenge. After five days he revived but some of his brothers shunned him, for he stank of corruption. Furious, he returned to the sky, accompanied by Barkulkula and the two friendly brothers. They all became immortal. The two brothers who remained on earth lost their immortality and became the first people.

Marira see Bouru.

Marruni (Medina, New Ireland, Me) the spirit of the earthquake. He had a man's body but a snake's tail. When his wives accidentally caught sight of the tail he cut it into pieces. These grew into people, animals and fish. He named them and gave the people their *malanggan*, mortuary rituals.

Marsaba (Truk Is., Mi) probably once a god of the underworld, but now thought of simply as a demon.

marsalai (*Arapesh*, Sepik River, NG, Me) bush-spirits. Each has a definite form, the preferred ones being of double-headed, two-tailed, multicoloured snakes or lizards. Less commonly the *marsalai* assume the shape of deformed animals and trees.

Mataaho 49.

Matang, Men of 92–94.

Matang, paradise of p. 30 and **98–101.**

Matang, Tree of 91, **98.** See also Samoa, Tree of.

Mataora 85.

Matawali see Herabe.

Mate 128.

Matuku (*Maori*, NZ, P) a cannibal giant who, some stories say, killed Wahieroa, son of Tawhaki (q.v.), but was himself destroyed by Wahieroa's son Rata. See also Matu'u-ta'u-ta'uo.

Matu'u-ta'u-ta'uo (Tahiti, Society Is., P) a giant bird who, according to one story, swallowed Wahieroa and carried off his wife and child, Rata. See also Matuku.

Mau-Tiki (*Efate*, New Hebrides, Me) the creator of the world, according to some stories.

Maui 34, 59, 60–61, 73–80, 81, 102.

Maui-tikiti-ki-a-Taranga 74.

mawulan **159.**

Meanderi (*Ngaing*, Rai coast, NG, Me) originally a woman. She invented sugar-cane and other staple foods. An important myth accounts for her distribution of the red and white taro plants and she is now a taro goddess. Her shrine is near Maibang.

Meenod (*Kapauku*, W Irian, Me) a ghoul who takes possession of women, inducing them to devour corpses. Cf. Dunawali.

Melu see Finweigh.

Mentek (Java, I) rice disease is believed to

An Aborigine named Mangordja, from Arnhem Land, singing a sacred *marain* song. (*Photo: Axel Poignant.*)

be caused by the evil spirit Mentek, who behaves like a thoughtless child and ruins the crop.

Meragbuto 131.

Meralang rocks 140.

Metakorab (Torres Straits, Me) a *dogai* (q.v.) killed by the man Bu.

Metalungana (*Pitjandjara*, Gibson Desert, A) Dreamtime Sleepy-lizard totem beings, who made part of the south face of Ayers Rock (q.v.)

Milbali see Wadi Gudjara.

Milky Way, the 90, 139.

Mimaliwu 162.

mimi (Aborigines, W Arnhem Land, A) very thin spirits living in rock crevices. Their main food is yams, but they also eat men. They fear to emerge on windy days lest their threadlike necks should break.

Minanag Kabau (*Minangkabau*, Sumatra, I) the name of a fourteenth-century *Malay* kingdom in central Sumatra. Legend says that when it was attacked by the Javanese Madjaphit it was agreed that the war should be settled by a combat between two *karabau* (buffalo). The Javanese chose a mature animal, the *Malays* a starting calf, to whose nose they attached an iron stake. Desperate for milk the calf rushed at the other animal, which was mortally wounded by the stake. So the *Malays* won the war and named their saved kingdom and people after the calf.

Mindi (*Kurnai*, Victoria, A) the Rainbow Snake.

Minma Bula 147, 148.

Minma Mala 151.

Minma Mingari (*Pitjandjara*, Gibson Desert, A) the Mountain-devil-woman, a Dreamtime being.

Minma Nganamara (*Pitjandjara*) the Mallee-hen-woman, named Djugurba, a Dreamtime being.

Minma Waiuda (*Pitjandjara*) the Dreamtime Possum-woman.

Miraldaldu 157–161.

Miraramuinar 164.

Miru (i) (*Maori*, NZ, P) a goddess, who, in some myths, rules the lowest three of the nine levels of the underworld, the other six being divided between Rohe and Hine-nui-te-po (qq.v.).

(ii) (Hawaii, P) lord of the underworld.

Moa'ri (*Kamano* and contiguous peoples, E highlands, NG, Me) the goddess of a special type of highly-prized red stone. She is the wife of the sun-god Wainako' (q.v.).

moai kavakava (Easter Is. P) unique wooden figures of people. The ribs are carved in detail, hence the figures' name, 'statue with ribs'.

Bark painting of *mimi* spirits by the Aborigine artist Yirawala of Yirrkala. The Australian Museum. (*Photo: Axel Poignant.*)

moiety (Aborigine, A) term used for a widespread type of Aborigine social system of classification, all people and things being divided between two moieties. The term is also used more specifically to refer to an exogamous social unit. The Aborigines of northern Arnhem land are divided into two such moieties, the *dura* (*dua*) and *jiridja* (*jindja*). See **166**.

molg **165**.

Morufonu 116–117.

Moslem p. 24.

Mother, the Great pp. 24–25, 40 and 157, 162.

Motikitik 102–104.

Mpu Kanwa p. 22.

Muit (Aborigine, N Territory, A) in the north west of this region Muit is the name of the Rainbow Snake. See **167**.

Mula djadi na bolon (*Toba Batak*, Sumatra, I) the supreme being, living in the highest of the seven heavens. See also Manuk-manuk, Debata Natolu.

Mumba'an (*Ifugao*, Kiangan, Philippines, I) the sun-god.

Mumuhango 67.

Mumumanu Gara see Wollunqua.

Mumunaw 167.

Mumunaw 167.

Mungamunga girls (*Mara*, Roper River area, A) daughters of Kunapipi (q.v.) who used them to entice youths, whom she then swallowed. The girls are sometimes identified with the Wawalag sisters (q.v.).

Mura (*Dieri*, Lake Eyre region, A) the Dreamtime.

muraian see *maraiin*.

muramura p. 39 and 154–156.

Murray River 138.

Muruwuil 164.

Mutitjilda Gorge 148–149.

Mutjingga see Kalwadi.

Mutuhei (Marquesas Is., P) 'Silence', which reigned in Po with Tanaoa (qq.v.) and was eventually destroyed by Ono—'Sound'.

Mwaiku see Bouru.

Mwanubwa see Mafofo.

Na Areau 1, 87–93.

Na Areau te Moa-ni-bai 87–88.

Na Atibu 87–89, 91.

Na Kaa 95, 97, 98–101.

Na Kauvandra (Fiji, Me) traditional home of the Fijian people.

Na Kika 87, 89.

Nabaeo (Ruk Is., New Britain, Me) originally a good spirit but now regarded as malevolent.

Naga Padoha 5.

Naiabu 90.

Nakula see Pandawa.

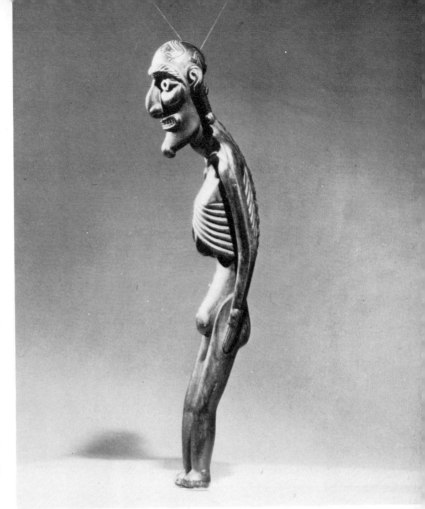

A *moai kavakava* figure from Easter Island. The significance of such figures is unknown but they probably represent ancestors. The owner wore his *moai kavakava* dangling from his waist at dances and ritual feasts. British Museum. (*Photo: Axel Poignant.*)

Nanga (*Mangaia*, Cook Is., P) a notorious thief who could only work when the sky was overcast. He stole the family ornaments Ina (q.v.) was guarding.

nara (*Wulumba*, Arnhem Land, A) rituals enacting the story of the Djanggawul.

Naraka (*Minangkabau*, Sumatra, I) hell fire. The word is Sanskrit in origin. Souls have to run along a wire stretched over Naraka. The evil fall in, the good cross to Sirugo (q.v.).

Ndara (E Torajas, Sulawesi, I) god of the underworld.

Ndengei (Fiji, Me) a great serpent who hatched the first people from two bird's-eggs. She is also known as the Old Woman of Na Kauvandra, a fertility-goddess inhabiting a cave in the Na Kauvandra mountains.

Nei Aro-maiaki 92.

Nei Bairara 109.

Nei Matamona 105–106.

Nei Nguinaba see Bakoa.

Nei Nguiriki see Bakoa.

Nei Te-arei-n-tarawa (Ellice Is., Mi) the second wife of Taburimai (q.v.) and mother of his son Te-ariki-n-tarawa.

Nei Te-raa-iti 105, 107–108.

Nei Te-tauti 109.

Nei Teakea 87.

Nei Temaing 109.

Neineaba see Bouru.

Neple 138–139.

Ngahue (*Maori*, NZ, P) according to some myths, the ruler of the underworld.

Ngaina-buaka (*Nui*, Ellice Is., Mi) the sky-country.

ngainmara 160.

Ngalbjod 162.

Nganaoa (Cook Is., P) a man who stowed away on Rata's (q.v.) boat during a

Painting by the New Guinea artist Mea Idei shows ancestral crocodile men, cf. Nugu. (*Photo: Axel Poignant.*)

monster-killing expedition. He slew a giant clam, an enormous octopus and finally the whale that had swallowed his parents. This he destroyed by leaping down its throat and kindling a fire inside its belly, so that in its agony it ran itself ashore and all its victims escaped.

Nganug (*Walumba*, Arnhem Land, A) the 'Paddlemaker', He ferries dead souls to Bralgu (q.v.).

Ngaore (*Maori*, NZ, P) 'the Tender One'. According to some myths she was the fourth wife of Tane (q.v.), and bore him the rush-like grass *toetoe*.

Ngarunggani (Aborigines, E Kimberley area, A) the Dreamtime.

Ngendi (Fiji, Me) a fertility-god, who showed men the use of fire. Some say he rules the dead. He is also said to support the world, so earth tremors and quakes are attributed to his

moving. His mother was a stone. Some stories say he created the world and hatched mankind from an egg. He is half snake and half rock.

Ngerganbu (*Wuradjeri*, A) a term meaning 'the beginning of all things', that is, before the Dreamtime.

Ngunung-ngunnut (*Wotjobaluk*, Victoria, A) the Dreamtime Bat, who turned his companion into the first woman.

Ngurlmak 166.

ngurlmak **167.**

Ngurlungaui 141.

Ngurunderi p. 40 and **138–143.**

Ni (*Huli*, S highlands, NG, Me) according to one version of the *Huli* ancestor myth, he seduced the wife of his brother Helahuli (q.v.) and so he, not Helahuli was the father of man. He is also the sole cause of leprosy. See **119–121.**

Niaas (Amboina, I) the first man. He emerged from a tree fructified by a bird.

Njai Lora Kidoul (Java, I) the goddess of the Indian Ocean. She lives on the rocky coast of south Java and rules countless spirits. Her oracle is consulted at the famous grotto of Karang, the hub of an extensive cult involving the collection of birds'-nests. The Susuhunan (prince) of Surakata is believed to be the goddess's lover. He and the Sultan of Djokjokarta are said to send her an annual gift of their cloaks.

Njirana see Julana.

Nobu (*Eromanga*, New Hebrides, Me) the creator of the earth.

Nogamain (*Murinbata*, N Territory, A) a primordial spirit and giver of spirit children. The *Murinbata* were vague about him though they obviously felt him to be important.

nokondisi (*Gururumba*, central highlands, NG, Me) ambivalent forest-spirits.

Nona (Tahiti, Society Is., P) the name of the revivified Haumea (q.v.). A cannibal, she was killed by the old man with whom her daughter took refuge.

noso (*Nias*, Sumatra, I) the soul. After death it returns to the gods. Lowalangi (q.v.) keeps all *noso* in large pots. Before a person is born, Si Barasi-ja-Noso takes some from a pot and gives it to the unborn baby, while Ture Luluwo sees that each individual receives exactly the amount of *noso* that Lowalangi wishes it to.

Nugu (*Kiwai*, Papua, NG, Me) a crocodile-man made by Ipila (q.v.), who also created three companions for him. Two of these grew bored with their diet of sago and began to kill animals. So they turned into crocodiles. Nugu and the remaining companion tried to make themselves new comrades, but Ipila altered their work so that all they produced was men, the ancestors of the *Kiwai's* crocodile clan. Nugu annoyed Ipila and was condemned to bear the world on his shoulders.

Nuku Kehu (Easter Is., P) Hotu Matua's (q.v.) master builder. He was unhappy on Easter Island, grieving for his wife Marama Kai, who had been left behind in Hiva (q.v.).

Numbakulla (*Aranda*, A) two primordial sky-beings who descended to earth and made the first people from the shadowy, amorphous *inaptua*.

Nurundere p. 40. See also Ngurunderi.

Nuvarahu 85.

Olifat 110–114.

Oma Rumufa (*Siane*, E highlands, NG, Me) 'the Black Way', the pre-existent deity and only god of the *Siane*. He is not spoken of as a creator—these people seem to have no creation myths—but controls certain natural events, such as the course of the sun, and is ruler of the dead.

Ono (*Maori*, NZ, and Marquesa Is., P) 'Sound' which, according to one myth, evolved from Atea ('Light'). See also 63.

Onolap 110.

Opoa Ra'iatea 57.

Orion's Belt 154.

Orofat 110.

Orsmond, J. M. p. 22.

Oteka (Easter Is., P) the canoe in which Hotu Matua (q.v.) reached the island. See also *Oua*.

ototeman p. 37

Oua (Easter Is., P) the second boat in which the first settlers travelled to the island. See *Oteka*.

Ove (Fiji, Me) according to some stories, the world's creator.

Pakoti (*Maori*, NZ; P) the fifth wife of Tane (q.v.) to whom she bore *harekeke* (*Phormium tenax*).

Pälülp (Caroline Is., Mi) the father of Rongerik, Rongelap and Aluluei (qq.v.). Some stories say he was Aluluei's son.

Pandawa, the five (Java and Bali, I) the five sons of King Pandu, heroes of the Hindu epic the *Mahābhārata* (see vol. 3: 5.2. **197–246**). The princes are named Yudhishthira, Bhīma, Arjuna, Nakula and Sahedewa (Sahadeva). Their story forms a central theme of the Balinese and Javanese *Wayang Purwa* (q.v.).

Pando 154.

Panji (Bali and Java, I) East Javanese prince, hero of many legends which form the basis of the Balinese *Wayang Gambuh* and the Javanese *Wayang Gedog* (qq.v.).

Panoi (Banks Is., Me) the spot where paths to the underworld and sky-world diverge.

Papa 45–53, 54, 64, 67, 68.

Papa-tu-a-nuki (*Maori*, NZ, P) according to some myths, this goddess 'Flat-like-the earth' was the second of Rangi's (q.v.) six wives and bore him Paia, Rehua, Rongo, Ru, Tane and other, minor deities. Originally she was wife to Tangaroa (q.v.) but deserted him in his absence. When he heard of this he attacked Rangi, wounding him in the thigh.

Parakaton, the pp. 22, 109.

Parambik (*Ngiang*, Rai Coast, NG, Me) immanent but transcendent creator-god. He formed the world, but now takes no interest in it so no rituals are performed for him.

Parpara (Kei Is., I) the youngest of three brothers who, with their two sisters, lived in the sky-world.

Pasiko (*Lakalai*, New Britain, Me) a relative of Sumua (q.v.). He was given fire by this great god and passed it on to man, although he had no authority to do so.

Peka 60.

Pele (Hawaii, P) great goddess of volcanoes and death.

Perjido (*Aka Kede*, N Andaman Is., I) the son of Biliku (q.v.), Perjido was the first man to find and catch a pig. This original animal had neither ears, eyes nor mouth. Perjido placed it whole upon a fire to roast it. Its skin eventually split in the heat, forming holes for the missing organs. Now realising that it was being burned, the pig leaped from the fire and ran away, pursued by Perjido, who threw a leaf at it. The pig jumped into the sea, where it was transformed into a dugong, the leaf becoming its flipper. Perjido was also the first person to discover honey, which the *Aka Kede*, like other primitive peoples, greatly value.

Persephone 62.

Piandael see Honabe.

Pinuwali see Dunawali.

Pisiwa (*Kamano* and contiguous peoples, E highlands, NG, Me) the Bird-of-Paradise-god, a variant of the sun-god, Wainako' (q.v.).

Pleiades, the 154.

Po (*Maori*, NZ, P) (i) the underworld or land of darkness. See 42.
(ii) the original void of chaos. See 24, 40, 42–43.

Podadeli see Herabe.

Poeempalaburu (E Torojas, Sulawesi, I) sky-god. He is sometimes identified with the sun, but usually the sun is said to be his eye. All souls originate in him.

Poko-ha-rua-te-po (*Maori*, NZ, P) according to one myth she was the first of Rangi's (q.v.) six wives. She bore him Ha-nui-a-rangi (q.v.), Ta-whiri-ma-tea and a series of personified winds, rites and incantations.

Polynesian Mythology pp. 21, 109.

Port Bradshaw 158.

Poutan (Mariana Is., Mi) the night breeze, an inventive man (sic) who, long before heaven and earth existed, dwelt in empty space.

Pugabuga 145.

Puimi (*Kyaka*, W highlands, NG, Me) a female spirit associated with the *sandalu* (q.v.) initiation cult. She is represented in its ceremonies by ten containers of sacred liquid. See also Puiwa.

Puiwa (*Kyaka*) male spirit associated with the *sandalu* (q.v.) cult and represented in its ceremonies by two containers of sacred liquid. See also Puimi.

Pulotu p. 30.

Puluga (S Andaman Is., I) the chief god. Being all-seeing, he is omniscient in daylight but not at night. He has the form of a spider. See also Biliku.

Puna (*Pitjandjara*, Gibson Desert, A) the earth, the lower level of the universe, the upper being the heavenly Ilkari.

punj (*Murinbata*, N Territory, A) the chief ceremony of these people. It is associated with the *kalwadi*

Figure of a deity from the Hawaiian royal temple at Karakakua. It possibly represents the volcano deity Pele. British Museum. (*Photo: Werner Forman Archive.*)

fertility cult. See Kalwadi.

Puntan 86.

Pwiya (*Kyaka*, W highlands, NG, Me) the rainbow, a great serpent that lives in the forest.

Quat 125–128.

Raden Galuh (Bali, I) legendary princess of Daha in East Java. She was kidnapped by a giant, Limandaru. The princes Chupak and Grantang (qq.v.) sought to rescue her. Grantang succeeded.

Raden Mahisa Walungan 22.

Raffles, Sir Thomas Stamford, p. 21.

Rainbow Snake see p. 40 and 162, 164–167, and also Galeru, Karia,

Kunmanggw, Langal, Mindi, Muit, Pwiya, Taipan, Wonungur, Yero, and Yulunggu.

Rai-taubu 38–39.

Raja Guru (*Batak*, Sumatra, I) the gods' huntsman. He catches souls with his hounds Sordaudau and Auto Porburu, who can be heard in the rustling wind that precedes a storm. When they catch a soul the person dies suddenly. Raja Guru lives in one of the lowest of the seven heavens.

Raja Indainda (*Batak*) the messenger and spy of the other gods, Raja Indainda is also the thunder-god. He lives immediately above the sky, in the first heaven.

Raja Moget Pinajingan (*Batak*) the high god. It is thought his name may be translated as 'All Spirit', 'World Spirit'

or 'World Power'.

Raka (Cook Is., P) 'Trouble', one of the six offspring of Vari-ma-te-takere (q.v.).

Raki (Maori, NZ, P) according to one creation story, the child of Maku (q.v.) and Ma-hora-nui-a-tea. His name is a variant of Rangi (q.v.). See also **43**.

Rangahore (*Maori*) according to one myth the third wife of Rangi (q.v.). She bore him a stone.

Rangda (Bali) see Chalonarang.

rangga (Aborigines, Arnhem Land, A) sacred objects. Those belonging to the *dua* moiety (q.v.) are mostly associated with the Djanggawul (**157–161**) and are used in the *nara* rituals (q.v.). Those belonging to the *jiridja* moiety (q.v.) are more varied. They include a pole symbolising the fire which, during the Dreamtime, destroyed a hut built on the sacred ground. The *jiridja rangga* are used during the *laindjung* and *banaidja* (qq.v.) rituals.

Rangi (*Maori*, NZ, P) the sky-father and one of the primaeval parents. Cf. Atea and see also p. 29 and **24, 43, 44, 45, 46–49, 51–54, 68.**

ranguma p. 23.

Rata (*Maori*, NZ and Tahiti, Society Is., P) son of Wahieroa. He killed the cannibal Matuku (q.v.).

Rati-mbati-ndua (Fiji, Me) the 'One-toothed-Man', god of the underworld, who devours the dead. He lacks arms but has great wings, on which he flies like a meteor.

Ratna Mangalli (Bali, I) the beautiful daughter of Chalonarang (q.v.). She remained a spinster as would-be suitors feared her mother.

Rato-ngkasimmpo (E Torajas, Sulawesi, I) the underworld plain, temporary home of the dead, while they await their recall to earth during the great mortuary feast. After it they are led to heaven.

Ratou Adil (Java, I) legendary religious leader of pre-Islamic times.

ratu demit see *yang*.

Raudalo, King of Serpents 123.

Raven 3–4.

Rehua (*Maori*, NZ, P) the daughter of Rangi and Papa (qq.v.). She was the ancestress of Rupe, Maui and Hina-uri (qq.v.).

Reinga p. 29.

Rice Mother pp. 24–25.

Riiki see Te Riiki and **95, 97.**

Riirongo 109.

Ringgon 9.

Ro Lei 126.

Road Belong Cargo pp. 36, 109.

Rohe see Miru.

Rona (*Maori*, NZ, P) she cursed the moon because it clouded over while she was fetching water and she missed her footing in the dark. Angry at her insult, the moon seized her. She clung to a tree but the moon tore that up too and carried them both away to the sky, where they are still visible on the moon's surface.

Rongelap see Rongerik.

Rongerik (Marshall and Caroline Is., Mi) 'Small-cheeks', brother of Rongelap ('Big-cheeks'). In the Caroline Islands these heroes are also known as Longorik and Longolap (qq.v.).

Rongo 47, 49, 55, 63–65, 72.

Ro'o-nui (Tahiti, Society Is., P) a man who rose from the underworld and married the goddess Haumea. She bore him Tuture. After a quarrel Ro'o-nui deserted his wife and went home.

Roper River 164.

Rû 33, 57.

Rua 32.

Ruaumoko 50.

Ruku-tia (*Maori*, NZ, P) wife of Tama-nui-a-rangi, whom she deserted for Tu-te-koro-punga.

Rumia 30.

Rupe (*Maori*, NZ, P) younger brother of Maui and Hina-uri (qq.v.). In one version of the story of Hine and Tinirau (see Hine and Tinirau, 59–62), he sought the help of their great ancestor Rehua (q.v.) who told him where Hina-uri could be found. Changing himself into a pigeon Rupe flew to her. Evading Tiniurau's men he took up his sister and her child and carried them to Rehua. Another myth says that, again in pigeon form, he helped Maui to fish up land. See **75**.

Sadewa see Pandawa.

sadjaratu'l-muntaha see Sirugo.

sambaon (*Batak*, Sumatra, I) nature-spirits. The fortunes of living people are held to depend upon the goodwill of their dead, the position of the dead on the wealth of sacrifices made to them by the living. Feasts are given in honour of deceased relatives and in this way the *begu* (q.v.) is transformed into a *sambaon*. If the descendants of the dead person are numerous and rich they dig up their ancestor's bones and feast them. The dead person then becomes a *sumangot*, a spirit almost on the level with the gods.

Samoa, Tree of 91, 92, 94.

sandalu (*Kyaka*, W highlands, NG, Me) male initiation cult. See Puimi and Puiwa.

Sankuni see Korawa.

Scott-Kemball pp. 26, 110.

Sebuwa (*Nias*, Sumatra, I) culture-hero who descended from the heavens carrying a sacred drum.

semangat p. 24.

Semar (*Java*, I) shadow-puppet character in the *Wayang Purwa* (q.v.) dramas. He is an embodiment of natural goodness and considered sacred. If water he has touched is later sprinkled on rice seedlings it is believed an abundant crop will ensue. In the Balinese *Wayang Purwa* his counterpart is Twalen.

setan see ibilih.

Shaliom (*Arapesh*, Sepik River, NG, Me) a 'swan maiden' (q.v.). The cassowary bird-woman who married a human husband after he had stolen her heavenly feather-apron. See also *vinmara*.

Si Baja (*Nias*, Sumatra, I) the sun-god.

si baja (*Nias*) the soul.

Sido see Iko.

Sina a variant of Hina (q.v.)

Singa Tandang (*Lubu*, Sumatra, I) the first tribal chief. His spirit is specially honoured by the *Lubu* who, although nominally Moslem, retain many of their earlier animistic beliefs and practices.

Sirugo (*Minangkabau*, Sumatra, I) the Paradisal home of the good souls. It contains the Tree of Mankind, *sadjaratu'l-muntaha*. Here the souls wait for the day of resurrection, when they will inherit the earth.

Soripata (*Batak*, Sumatra, I) one of the trinity of great gods, sons of Mula djada na bolon (q.v.), who live in the sixth heaven. His name derives from the Sanskrit Shripāta, one of Vishnu's names (see vol. 3: 5.2. **108–151**).

South, Spirits of the 92.

sumangat p. 24.

sumange p. 24.

sumangot see sambaon.

Sumua (*Lakalai*, New Britain, Me) the chief god. Unlike other *Lakalai* deities he is never depicted in animal form.

A fish *rangga* from Cape Stewart in NE Arnhem Land. (*Photo: Axel Poignant.*)

There are various stories of his origins, but all agree he was born of a human mother in most unusual circumstances. One story says he was born to her ghost in the land of the dead. He gave men taro, yams, pigs, fowls, fire and the *valuku* (q.v.) rituals. He controls natural phenomena, and though now Christian missions have had powerful influence in the area he is less important to the people than formerly, he is still held to live on the summit of Mt. Pago and to be aware of all that happens.

Suquematua 131.

Surakarta, Susuhunan of, See Najai Lora Kidoul.

'Swan Maiden' 15–18, 84. See also Shaliom and *vinmara*.

Ta'aroa 30–32, 34, 38.

Tabakea 95, 97.

Taboeja (*Sulawesi*, I) the supreme being gave men fire, but they let it die. Taboeja went to the sky world and fetched some more.

Tabua'i 34.

Tabuaniki 95.

Taburi-tongoun 92.

Taburima 95.

Taburimai (*Nui*, Ellice Is., Mi) son of Bakoa (q.v.). His older half-brothers, the fish, hated him and determined to eat him, but his brother·Te-anoi, the hammer-headed shark, carried him to safety in Samoa. One of his descendants, Te-nti-nti, founded the people of Nui.

Tacabuinji (*Wardaman*, Daly River area, N Territory, A) the older of the two Lightning Brothers portrayed in rock paintings at Delamere. The younger, Wagtjadbulla, was killed in a fight over Tacabuinji's wife, Cananda.

Tafa'i (Tahiti, Society Is, P) Tahitian variant of Tawhaki (q.v.). See also Ari and Kui, and 81.

Tagaro 125–126, 128, 129–134.

Tagaro the Foolish 125, 128.

Tagaro the Wise 125.

Tagaro-mbiti (New Hebrides, Me) cleverest son of Tagaro (q.v.).

Tagisomenaja (*Kamano* and contiguous peoples, E highlands, NG, Me) goddess of the evening star, wife of the moon-god Wajubu (q.v.).

tai-ka-baga-koat (*Mentawei*, Sumatra, I) sea-spirits.

tai-ka-baga-polak (*Mentawei*) spirits of the earth.

tai-ka-leleu (*Mentawei*) jungle-spirits.

tai-ka-manua (*Mentawei*) sky-spirits, the most important of all spirits, who are thought of as living lives like human beings, in villages, with children, animals, etc. The sky-spirits are the guardians of all the best seers and often invoked for help with banana and taro crops because they control the rain.

Taio (*Lakalai*, New Hebrides, Me) moon-goddess, wife of Tauahili (q.v.).

Taipan (*Wumunkan*, Cape York Peninsula, A) the Rainbow Snake.

Takaro 129.

Take (*Mangaia*, Cook Is., P) the root of all being. It subsists in the stem of the universal coconut, sustaining all things.

Takume (*Wogeo*, Schouten Is., Me) the first hero to have two wives.

Talking Chiefs, the p. 27

Tamakaia (*Efate*, New Hebrides, Me) he was so ugly that his wife deserted him for Te-te-kor-punga. He pursued her in the form of a crane and when he found her she begged him to take her back. He agreed to, but killed her and buried her head. In the spring, hearing a faint buzzing from the grave, he opened it and his wife was restored to him.

Tama-nui-ate-Ra (*Maori*, NZ, P) 'Great-child-of-the Sun' a name of the sun-god.

Tama-pouli-alamafo 28.

Tamate (Banks Is., Me) a secret society in which masked men wearing cloaks of leaves, assumed the roles of *tamate* (ghosts) and in this guise raided the gardens of the uninitiated. The society was said to have been founded when a ghost sitting in a tree gave a village woman a present of a cloaked and hatted image—in fact a *tamate* spirit. She invited men to come and see it. They killed her and stole the *tamate*, which taught them how to establish their secret society.

tamate see *Tamate*.

Tamberan (*Arapesh*, Sepik River, NG, Me) guardian spirit of the male cult organisation. He 'speaks' in the music of such instruments as the bullroarer, flute and drum.

Tanaoa (Marquesas Is., P) together with Mutuhei (q.v.) he reigned supreme in Po (q.v.) until Atea (q.v.) emerged and drove him away.

Tana'aroa 58, 71. See also Ta'aroa, Tanaroa, Tangaloa, Tangaroa.

A *tamate* mask from Banks Island. University of Cambridge Museum of Archaeology and Ethnography. (*Photo: Axel Poignant.*)

Tanaroa 64.

Tane 33–35, 46, 48, 49, 50–55, 56, 66–69.

Tane 60.

Tangaloa 23, 25–27, 70–72.

Tangaloa-atu-logo-logo 28.

Tangaloa-eiki 28.

Tangaloa-tufuga 28.

Tangaroa (i) (*Maori*, NZ, P) sea-god, ruler of fish and reptiles, patron of fishermen. His name is cognate with that of Tangaloa (q.v.). See also 23, 47, 49, 54–55, 70–77.
(ii) (Cook Is., P) one of the five great children of Vatea and Papa (qq.v.).
(iii) (*Beru*, Gilbert Is., Mi) leader of the Spirits of the South (q.v.) who fought the Spirits of the North, led by Auriaria (q.v.), for possession of Samoa.

Tangiia (Cook Is., P) one of the five great gods, children of Vatea and Papa (qq.v.).

Tango (Cook Is.) one of the six offspring of the primaeval goddess Vari-ma-te-takere (q.v.). His name means 'Support'.

Tarai see Biliku.

Taranga 74.

Taringa nui (*Rarotonga*, Cook Is., P) god of fishermen.

Tasu (New Hebrides, Me) cannibal who killed a pregnant woman. Discovering her condition, instead of eating her, he dumped her body in a thicket. Twins were born and miraculously survived. Later, while wandering in the forest they met their maternal uncle, Quatu. When they were adult he told them of their mother's fate and they avenged her, killing Tasu.

Tau-Marawa (Gilbert Is., Mi) 'Holder-of-the-Ocean', a title given to Tabakea (q.v.).

Tauahili (*Lakalai*, New Britain, Me) this god is also known as Haro ('Sun') and his wife Taio is the moon-goddess. Tauahili, the founding-father of the Hailili clan, is sometimes said to have created both men and the universe, but it is thought these higher roles have only recently been assigned to him, possibly under the influence of Christian teaching or of Cargo Cult doctrines.

Taukarawa 96.

Tautobitatmo (N Andaman Is., I) a sky-being. Each evening he shuts the day under a stone, so darkness falls.

Tawhaki 81–84.

Tawhiri 54–55.

Te-anoi (*Nui*, Ellice Is., Mi) see Taburimai. Te-anoi eventually fixed himself in the sky and became a star.

Te Ao (*Maori*, NZ, P) according to one myth the offspring of Te Ata (40). He is sometimes referred to as Te-ao-tu-roa.

Wooden figure of a god, probably Taringa nui, from the Cook Islands. British Museum. (*Photo: Axel Poignant.*)

See also 40, 42, 43.

Te Ao-marama 40, 42.

Te-ariki-n-tarawa (*Nui*, Ellice Is., Mi) the son of Taburimai (q.v.) he took Nei Te-reere, child of the *uekera* tree, as his wife. Their son was Kirata-n-te-rerei (q.v.).

Te Ata 40.

Te Atua Fakamataku (Tikopia, Solomon Is., Me) one of the most common titles of the Tikopians' chief god and culture-hero, a superhuman being who once lived on earth. He is especially the protector of yams and is believed to possess the body of the tribal chief and watch the first fruits ceremony of *kai vera* (q.v.) through his eyes. Te Atua Fakamataku means 'Fearsome God'.

Te-auanei 89.

Te Bo 87.

Te boi 93.

Te Bongi-Ro 95, 96, 97.

Te I-Matang 92.

Te-ika-a-Maui 75.

Te Kaetikawai 100.

Te Kai-ni-kamata 107.

Te Kore 40.

Te Kore-nui 40.

Te Kore-para 40.

Te Kore-rawea 40.

Te Kore-roa 40.

Te Kore-te-matua 43.

Te Kore-te-tamaua 40–43.

Te Kore tua-rua 40.

Te Kore-tua-tahi 40.

Te Kore-whiwhia 40, 43.

A skull-bone *tiki*. British Museum. (*Photo: British Museum.*)

Opposite: Tjuringa stones from the central Australian desert. (*Photo: Axel Poignant.*)

The upper part of a *Batak Tunggal Panaluan*. Museum für Völkerkunde, Munich. (*Photo: Michael Holford*.)

Uetonga 85.

Ugatame (*Kapauku*, W Irian, Me) the creator, who lives beyond the sky, which is solid, and manifests himself in the dual, androgynous forms of the sun and moon. While the conception of this god seems old, the name is thought to be recent, probably developed under mission influence. The *Kapauku* assert that although Ugatame is omniscient and omnipotent, he cannot himself be said to exist since all existence was created by him.

Ui (Tahiti, Society Is., P) a blind old woman, a variant of Kui (q.v.).

uli (New Ireland, Me) bisexual spirits depicted in *uli* carvings.

Ulmark 168.

Uluru 145.

Uma see Teteu.

Ungud (*Ugarinjin*, Kimberley area, A) the Dreamtime. See also Galeru.

Ungur see Galeru.

Uoke (Easter Is., P) a mythical being who came from Hiva (q.v.) and travelled the Pacific, prising up the islands from the seabed. In the vicinity of Easter Island the rocks were so hard that he could not remove them all, so the island remains to this day.

urbar see *ubar*.

Ure (*Murngin*, NE Arnhem Land, A) a trickster-hero exactly like Bamapama (q.v.). He was leader of a band of underground people, but came up to earth to hunt. One day, mistaking the sun for a kangaroo, he began to chase it. Overtaken by nightfall, which was unknown below, he was at first afraid, but next morning decided that earth's night and day were preferable to the underworld's unvaried light, so he brought his people up to earth to live.

Uri tree

Uritoy p. 28.

Uta (*Maori*, NZ, P) hero, husband of Houmea (q.v.).

uwar see *ubar* and 162–163.

Vakai a Heva (Easter Is., P) wife of Hotu-matua (q.v.).

valuku (*Lakalai*, New Britain, Me) a men's cult society, also a collective noun for the society's masks. According to one group the *valuku* was instigated by ancestral spirits who now live in the River Doge and rise from it each year to indicate the time for the ritual cycle to begin. Another group says it was initiated by Sumua (q.v.), who ordered rites to be performed annually by both the living and the dead. The designs of the cult's masks are revealed to their makers by ghosts, either in dreams or to those who have eaten charmed ginger. It is believed that each mask has a shadow soul which comes to it from the River Doge and returns there when the masks are destroyed at the end of each annual celebration.

Vari-ma-te-takere (Mangaia, Cook Is., P) 'The Beginning-and-Bottom', the primaeval parent who tore from her side six children: Raka, Tango, Tinirau, Tu-metua Tu-mute-anaoa and Vatea. An uncreated being, she lives at the very bottom of the great coconut shell of the universe. *Vari* also means 'primaeval mud'.

varua p. 29.

Vatea (Mangaia) lived in the Thin Land and took Papa, daughter of Tima-te-more as his wife. Their children were the five great gods Rongo, Tane, Tangaroa, Tangia and Tonga-iti. Although his name is a variant of Atea (q.v.) in the Cook Islands he is neither the sky-god nor the primordial parent, but one of the six children of the primaeval mother Vari-ma-te-takere (q.v.). He was half fish, half man. See also Atea, Wakea and 64.

vigona see *figona*.

vinmara 132, 134. See also Shaliom and Swan Maiden.

Wadi Baba (Aborigines of Western Desert, A) the Dreamtime Dog-man.

Wadi Bera (Aborigines of Western Desert, A) the Dreamtime Moon-man.

Wadi Galaia (Aborigines of Western Desert) the Dreamtime Emu-man.

Wadi Gudjara (Aborigines of Western Desert) the two most important Dreamtime beings of this region, the Two Men. They were Wadi Guigabi or Milbali, the White-goanna-man and Wadi Jungga, the Black-goanna-man. (A goanna is a species of lizard.)

Wadi Gulber (Aborigines of Western Desert) the Dreamtime 'Blue' kangaroo-man.

Wadi Malu (Aborigines of Western Desert) the Dreamtime Kangaroo-man.

Wagtjadbulla see Tacabuinji.

Wahieroa (*Maori*, NZ, P) son of Tawhaki (q.v.).

Waieruwar 141, 142.

Waimariwi 164–167.

Wainako' (*Kamano* and contiguous peoples, E highlands, NG, Me) the younger son of Jugumishanta and Morufonu (qq.v.). He was the sun-god. He was also known by the title Pisiwa, 'the Bird-of-Paradise'. He married Moar'ri (q.v.).

Wajubu (*Kamano* et al.) the moon-god and older son of Jugumishanta and Morufonu (qq.v.). He married Tagisomenaja (q.v.).

Wakea (Hawaii, P) a variant of the names Atea and Vatea (qq.v.).

Walangada (*Ungarinjin*, Kimberley area, A) an amorphous Dreamtime being whose name means 'Belonging-to-the-sky'. Unlike other Dreamtime beings of the *Ungarinjin*, he ascended to the sky and now forms the Milky Way. (The others were all transformed into rock paintings.)

Waliporlimia see Dunawali.

Wamolungu (*Murngin*, Arnhem Land, A) the father of the Wawilka (Wawalag) sisters. His name means 'Stone-spear'. He is also called Burpaloma, 'Stone-headed spear'.

Wandatilepu see Dinditane.

wanigi (Aborigines, Arnhem Land, A) a ceremonial headdress, conical in shape and topped with feathers. It is also called *waninga*.

waninga see *wanigi*.

Waramurungugju p. 40.

Warana (*Ungarinjin*, Kimberley area, A) the Dreamtime Eaglehawk.

Warger see *gainjin*.

Warilliwulu 154.

Wawalag sisters 164–167. See also Wamolungu.

Wayang Gambuh (Bali, I) plays enacting the feats of the legendary Panji (q.v.). Cf. *Wayang Gedog*.

Wayang Gedog (Java, I) shadow-plays enacting the feats of the legendary Panji (q.v.). Cf. *Wayang Gambuh*.

Wayang Golek (Java) puppet drama based on the feats of the legendary Prince Dama Wulan. The puppets are three-dimensional and made entirely of wood.

Wayang Kulit (Bali and Java) parchment shadow puppets used in the *Wayang Purwa* (q.v.) drama.

Wayang Purwa (Java and Bali) shadow-puppet plays based on the adventures of Rāma and the five Pandawas, ultimately derived from the Hindu *Rāmāyana* and *Mahābhārata* epics. See pp. 22, 25–26 and vol. 3: 5.2. **115–141, 197–246.**

Wayang Topeng (Java) masked dance-drama comparable with the Balinese *Barong-rangda* (q.v.).

Wetar (Amboina, I) the first woman. She emerged from a tree that had been fructified by a bird. See also Niaas.

Whaitari (*Maori*, NZ, P) the thunder, a cannibal sky-goddess. Her name is sometimes spelled Whaitiri. See also Kai-tangata and 83.

Whare p. 27.

Whare Wananga, the *Lore of the* p. 22.

Javanese *Wayang Golek* puppets. British Museum. (*Photo: British Museum.*)

White-sea-mist 66.

Wigan (*Ifuago*, Kiangan, Philippines, I) a youth who was one of the only two human beings to survive a great flood. His sister Bugan was the other.

Winia (Ceram-Laut and Gorrom Is., I) the first woman. She was strikingly beautiful.

Wodoi (*Ungarinjin*, Kimberley area, A) the Dreamtime Rock-pigeon.

Wollunqua (Warramunga, N Territory, A) the Great Snake, which rose from the Thapauerla water-hole in the Murchinson Ranges and, while keeping its tail in the hole, journeyed far overland depositing spirit children and performing other creative feats. The man Mumumanugara, the Snake's companion, emerged from his body. He struck Wollunqua in an attempt to drive him back into the water-hole. Wollunqua wrapped himself round his son and descended into the hole, taking Mumumanugara with him.

Wolphat 110.

Woma 145.

wondjina (*Ungarinjin*, Kimerley area, A) the Dreamtime beings. Eventually their bodies were transformed into rock-paintings while their spirits entered a sacred water-hole. The paintings were touched-up annually at the end of the dry season. The figures lack mouths, for, it is said, if they had them incessant rain would fall. One group of *wondjina*, the *garirnji*, are believed to control tornadoes. See also p. 39.

Wongar (*Wulumba*, Arnhem Land, A) the Dreamtime.

wongar (*Murngin*, Arnhem Land, A)

Dreamtime beings. See p. 39.

Wonungur (Aborigines, N and NW Territories, A) the Rainbow Snake, also called Worombi and Wollunqua in some areas. See Wollunqua.

World of the First Australians pp. 38, 109.

Worombi see Wonungur.

Wulngari 164–165.

Wurake (E Torajas, Sulawesi, I) a spirit living in a village of the fifth heaven. It attends on *shamans* and comes to their call.

wuramu (Aborigines, Arnhem Land, A) wooden figures, sometimes simply posts, sometimes carved to represent human figures (these are probably a late development). They are used (a) on graves and in mortuary rituals; (b) during certain other religious ceremonies; (c) in 'collection' ceremonies, when a *wuramu* is carried through a camp and 'seizes' any goods that have not been carefully hidden.

Wutmara the human wife of Takume (q.v.).

Yabuling (*Ngaing*, Rai coast, NG, Me) the god who created pigs and instituted the pig exchange, which is part of the *kabu* (q.v.) ceremony. He made the first gourd trumpets, used to invoke spirits during the harvest-festival rites and the *kabu* ceremony. It is said his trumpets were found by women, but as they defiled the instruments these were passed into men's keeping. Women and children are never allowed to see them now, though adult women may know of their existence. Some Christian

evangelists have encouraged converts to display the sacred trumpets publicly as part of their renunciation of the native religion.

yakirai (*Kyaka*, W highlands, NG, Me) the sky-gods. One is responsible for storms, thunder and lightning and kills men whose ancestral spirits have left them unprotected.

Yalungur see Gidja.

Yama Enda (*Kyaka*) the goddess of ill health. A forest spirit, she appears to a man as a beautiful woman and seduces and kills him. She has special authority over all forest creatures.

yang (Java, I) generic term for spirits, of which there are several classes: *danhyang*—protectors of villages; *ratu demit*—generally protective spirits; *jakalabakai*—spirits of the founders of villages; *buta*—giants who devour the sun and moon, causing eclipses.

Yelafath 110.

Yero (Aborigines, Queensland, A) the Rainbow Snake.

Yudhishtira see Pandawa.

Yulanya 150.

yulanyar 150.

Yulunggul (Aborigines, Arnhem Land, A) the Rainbow Snake.

Yurlunggur 164.

Yurlunggur 167.

PART 4

Bibliography

AGONCILLO, TEODORO A *et al. South-East Asia: An Introduction. Essays . . . reprinted from The Far East and Australia.* Europa Publications. 1973.

ALPERS, ANTONY *Maori Myths and Tribal Legends.* John Murray. 1964.

*—— *Legends of the South Sea.* John Murray. 1970.

BATESON, GREGORY 'An Old Temple and a New Myth' in *Traditional Balinese Culture.* Essays selected and edited by J. B. Belo. New York and London: Columbia University Press. 1970.

BENDA, HARRY J. and LARKIN, JOHN A. *The World of Southeast Asia: Selected Historical Readings.* New York: Harper & Row. 1967.

*BERNDT, R. M. and BERNDT, C. H. *The World of the First Australians; an introduction to the traditional life of the Australian Aborigines.* Angus & Robertson, 1964.

*BUCK, PETER H. *Vikings of the Pacific.* New York and London: University of Chicago Press, 4th. impression. 1967.

BUHLER, ALFRED, *et al. Oceania and Australia, the Art of the South Seas.* Methuen. 1962.

BURRIDGE, KENELM *Tangu Traditions. A Study of the Way of Life, Mythology and Developing Experience of a New Guinea People.* Oxford: the Clarendon Press. 1969.

*COCHRANE, GLYNN *Big Men and Cargo Cults.* Oxford University Press. 1970.

CODRINGTON, R. *The Melanesians. Studies in their History, Anthropology and Folklore.* Oxford: the Clarendon Press. 1891.

*CRANSTONE, B. A. L. *The Australian Aborigines.* British Museum. 1973.

DIXON, ROLAND B. *Oceania.* Vol. 9 of *The Mythology of All Races.* Editors Louis Herbert Gray and George Foot Moore. New York: Cooper Square Publications Inc. 1917/64.

ELIADE, MIRCEA *Australian Religions: An Introduction.* Ithaca and London: Cornell University Press. 1973.

ELKIN, A. P. *Studies in Australian Totemism: The Nature of Australian Totemism.* Sydney: Australian National Research Council. Oceania Monographs No. 2. 1933.

—— *Studies in Australian Totemism: Sub-section, Section and Moiety Totemism.* Oceania 4. vol. 1. 1933.

ELLIS, WILLIAM *Polynesian Researches.* 4 vols. Fisher, Son and Jackson. 1839–42.

ENGLERT, FATHER SEBASTIAN *Island at the Centre of the World: New Light on Easter Island.* Translated and edited by William Mulloy. New York: Charles Scribner's Sons. 1970.

FAGG, WILLIAM *The Tribal Image.* British Museum. 1970.

FIRTH, RAYMOND *Social Change in Tikopia.* George Allen & Unwin. 1959.

GILL, W. WYATT *Life in the Southern Isles.* Religious Tract Society. 1876.

—— *Myths and Songs from the South Pacific.* H. S. King. 1876.

—— *Historical Sketches of Savage Life in Polynesia.* Wellington: G. Didsbury. 1880.

*GLUCKMAN, MAX *Politics, Law and Ritual in Tribal Societies.* Oxford: Basil Blackwell. 1965.

*GOULD, RICHARD A. *Yiwara: Foragers of the Australian Desert.* Collins. 1970.

GREY, SIR GEORGE *Polynesian Mythology.* Whitcombe & Tombs, 1855/1965.

GRIMBLE, SIR ARTHUR *Migrations, Myth and Magic from the Gilbert Islands.* Early writings of Sir Arthur Grimble arranged and illustrated by Rosemary Grimble. Routledge & Kegan Paul. 1972.

—— *A Pattern of Islands.* John Murray. 1952.

*HALL, D. G. E. *A History of South-East Asia.* Macmillan, 3rd. ed. 1968.

HARRISON, BRIAN *South East Asia.* Macmillan. 1968.

HENRY, T. *Ancient Tahiti.* Honolulu: Berenice P. Bishop Museum Bulletin 48. 1928.

*HEYERDAHL, THOR *American Indians in the Pacific.* George Allen & Unwin. 1952.

HOGBIN, IAN *The Island of Menstruating Men: Religion in Wogeo, New Guinea.* Chandler Publishing Co. 1970.

HUDSON, A. B. *Padju Epat—The Ma'ayan of Indonesian Borneo.* New York: Holt, Rhinehart & Winston. 1972.

KROM, N. J. (ed.) *Parakaton, the Book of the Kings of Tumapel and Majapahit.* Batavia. 1920.

LANDTMAN *The Kiwai Papuans of British New Guinea.* Macmillan. 1927.

LANGER, SUSANNE *Philosophy in a New Key.* Cambridge, Mass: Harvard University Press. 1942/60.

LAVAL, PÈRE HONORÉ *Mangareva.* Belgium: Braine-le-Comté. 1937.

*LAWRENCE, PETER *Road Belong Cargo.* Manchester: the University Press. 1968. With a new preface and postscript, 1971.

*LAWRENCE, P. and MEGGIT, M. J. (eds.) *Gods, Ghosts and Men in Melanesia. Some Religions of Australian New Guinea and the New Hebrides.* Melbourne: Oxford University Press. 1965.

LÉVI-STRAUSS, CLAUDE *Totemism.* Translated by Rodney Needham. Merlin Press. 1964.

LOEB, EDWIN M. *Sumatra its History and People.* Kuala-Lumpur: Oxford University Press and Toku Buku Deli. 1972.

LUOMOLA, K. *Voices on the Wind.* Honolulu: Berenice P. Bishop Museum. 1955.

MALINOWSKI, BRONISLAW *Argonauts of the Western Pacific.* Routledge & Kegan Paul. 1922/66.

MEAD, MARGARET *The Mountain Arapesh.* Vol. 2: *Arts and Supernaturalism.* Garden City, New York: The Natural History Press; London: Frederick Muller. 1970.

MERSHON, KATHARINE EDSON 'The Five Elementals.' in *Traditional Balinese Culture.* Essays selected and edited by J. B. Belo. New York and London: Columbia University Press. 1970.

METRAUX, A. *Easter Island.* André Deutsch. 1957.

MCCONNEL, URSULA *Myths of the Muŋkan.* Melbourne: Melbourne University Press. 1957.

*MCPHEE, COLIN 'The Balinese "Wayang Kulit" and its Music' in *Traditional Balinese Culture.* Essays selected and edited by J. B. Belo. New York and London: Columbia University Press. 1970.

*MOUNTFORD, CHARLES P. *Ayers Rock: Its People, Their Beliefs and Their Art.* Angus and Robertson. 1965.

NEWMAN, PHILIP L. 'Religious Belief and Ritual in a New Guinea Society', *American Anthropologist* Part 2 Vol. 6 No. 4. August 1964.

*PALMER, LESLIE H. *Indonesia*. Thames & Hudson. 1965.

*POIGNANT, ROSLYN *Oceanic Mythology*. Paul Hamlyn. 1967.

POSPISIL, LEOPOLD. *The Kapuku Papuans of West New Guinea*. New York: Holt Rhinehart & Winston. 1963.

PRICE, A. GRENFELL (ed.) *The Explorations of Captain James Cook in the Pacific as told by a selection of his own Journals 1768/1779*. New York: Dover Publications. 1971.

RADCLIFFE-BROWN, A. R. *The Andaman Islanders*. New York: The Free Press, reprint (1964) of Cambridge University Press ed. 1922.

RAFFLES, SIR THOMAS STAMFORD *History of Java*. Oxford University Press 1969 reprint of 1817 ed.

RASSERS, DR W. H. *Pañji, the Culture Hero. A structural study in the religion of Java*. The Hague: Martinus Nijhoff. 1959.

*SCOTT-KEMBALL, JEUNE *Javanese shadow puppets*. British Museum. 1970.

SIMPSON, COLIN *Adam in Ochre. Inside Aboriginal Australia*. Angus & Robertson. 4th ed. rev. 1962.

—— *Adam in Plumes* Angus & Robertson. 1955.

SOUTH SEA ASSOCIATION *The South Seas Studied Economically, Culturally, etc.* Tokyo: South Sea Association. 1940.

STARZECKA, DOROTA CZARKOWSKA and CRANSTONE, B. A. L. *The Solomon Islanders*. British Museum. 1974.

STRATHERN, ANDREW *The Rope of Moka: Big Men and Ceremonial Exchange in Mount Hagen New Guinea*. Cambridge: the University Press. 1971.

SUGGS, ROBERT C. *The hidden world of Polynesia*. The Cresset Press. 1963.

—— *Island Civilisations of Polynesia*. Mentor Books. 1960.

SYME, RONALD *The Travels of Captain Cook*. Michael Joseph. 1972.

WALES, H. G. QUARITCH *Prehistory and Religion in South-East Asia*. Bernard Quaritch Ltd. 1957.

WARNER, W. LLOYD *A Black Civilization. A Social Study of an Australian Tribe*. New York: Harper Brothers. rev. ed. 1958.

*Books with useful, detailed bibliographies.

CHAPTER 8

The Americas

PART 1

Introduction

The civilisations whose myths and legends are the subject of this chapter vary considerably in sophistication, ranging from the primitive hunting cultures of the Arctic wastes and Amazonian forests, to the splendour of *Inca* Peru and the scholarly erudition of the *Maya*.

There has been—and remains—much controversy about the origins of the American peoples; but the consensus of scholarly opinion is that they derive from Palaeolithic hunters who, in successive waves, crossed the Bering Strait from Siberia at some time between about 23 000 and 20 000 B.C., before the ice-cap melted. Dispersing slowly south and eastwards they had reached Tierra del Fuego by *c.* 5 000 B.C.

The immigrants were of Mongoloid stock and like their Asian relatives had a *shamanistic* religion, that is, one based on the belief that spirits can be controlled by certain gifted initiates (see vol. 2: 3.1), and *shamanism* plays an important part in the myths and legends of the whole area.

Carved head of a rattle used in shamanistic ritual dances by *Haida* Indians of the North West Coast. James Hooper Collection, Watersfield. (*Photo: Werner Forman Archive.*)

An Eskimo *shaman's* magical necklace. Ottawa Museum. (*Photo: Werner Forman Archive.*)

As they dispersed over the American continents, the Indians' cultures were, naturally, modified by the environments in which they found themselves. In the western Great Plains of Canada and the U.S.A. they remained nomadic hunters until, and even after, the advent of the white man. Further south, in Mexico, they became settled farmers and by *c.* 3000 B.C. were growing the staple foods of maize, beans and squash. At about the same time, or rather earlier, agricultural settlements had developed on the Peruvian coast.

In considering these vast areas it is helpful to divide them into more manageable units.

THE ESKIMO

Inhabiting the Arctic coasts from Alaska to Greenland, the Eskimo, until the recent influx of oil prospectors, had remained semi-nomadic hunters, living upon whale, walrus and caribou in summer, fish and seal in winter.

Their imaginative and religious life was dominated by the concept of all-pervasive spirits, *inue*, with whom their *shaman*-priests were able to communicate, and which they professed to control.

THE NORTH AMERICAN INDIANS

The Indians of Canada and the U.S.A. are usually divided into four or more groups according to their habitat. Here we shall use four divisions: the Woodlands, the Great Plains, the North West Coast and the South West.

Mica figure of a snake, found in the Turner Mound, Hamilton County, Ohio. It dates from the ancient Indian Hopewell culture (200–300 A.D.). Peabody Museum of Archaeology and Ethnology, Harvard University. (*Photo: Peabody Museum, Harvard University.*)

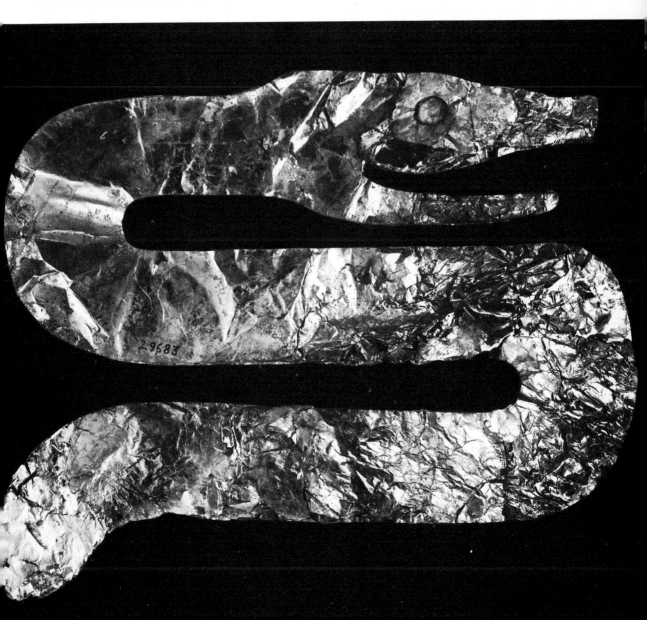

Regions inhabited by the *Eskimo* and the North American Indians.

The Woodlands

Stretching from Alaska across northern Canada to Labrador, from the Great Lakes south to Florida, the Woodlands ranged from coniferous forests in the north, through birchwood and hardwood forests to the swamps of the Everglades. Dependent upon a mixture of hunting and agriculture, the Indians of this great region expressed their vivid sense of the natural powers in elaborate ceremonies of thanksgiving, commonly called 'dances'.

Linguistically they are divided into three main groups: the *Algonquian*-speakers of the north, the *Iroquoian* of the Great Lakes region and the *Muskhogean* of the south. Among these broad groupings there are of course many tribal variations, just as there are among, say, the different Romance languages of Europe. The *Algonquian*-speakers included the *Algonquin, Chippewa, Cree, Delaware, Menominee, Montagnais* and *Potowatomi*. Among the *Iroquoian* were the *Cherokee, Huron, Mohawk, Oneida* and *Seneca*. The chief *Muskhogean* tribes were the *Creek* (*Muskhogee*) and *Chicksaw*.

Physical prowess was, naturally, highly valued among all the tribes, but the *Algonquin* and *Muskhogean* were generally fairly peaceable, by contrast to the ferocious and internecine *Iroquois*—hence the importance of the establishment of the *Iroquoian* confederacy in the sixteenth century, and the considerable opposition with which its promoters had to contend, as is recalled in the legend of Hiawatha **174–178)**

The Great Plains

Before the coming of the white man, from whom they obtained horses and guns, the Indians of the eastern Plains supplemented hunting by agriculture. From *c.* A.D. 800 *Sioux* immigrants had entered the region from the north-east, *Caddoan* from the south and south-east, bringing knowledge of agricultural techniques.

The Indians of the more arid 'far west' were more dependent upon hunting. From the middle of the sixteenth century, when the first white explorers appeared, the acquisition of horses and guns made all these peoples more mobile and hunting, at least initially, offered greater rewards than farming.

As all the Plains Indians were nomadic or semi-nomadic they were, of necessity, highly disciplined and their rituals centre on hunter and warrior fraternities.

Linguistically they are divided among the *Athapascans*, who occupied the region from Alaska to Alberta, but also included the southern *Apache* tribe; *Algonquian*-speaking *Arapaho, Blackfoot, Cheyenne* and *Cree*; the *Shoshonean*-speaking *Comanche* of Texas. Between these were the numerous *Siouan* and *Caddoan* tribes, the first including the *Assinaboin, Crow, Dakota (Sioux), Mandan, Omaha, Osage* and *Winnebago*; the second the *Arika, Caddo* and *Pawnee*.

North West Coast

Between Puget Sound and Yukatat Bay a warm offshore ocean current gives the American North West Coast a mild climate. The land is fertile and rich.

Assured of easy subsistence, the hunter-fishermen of the region had ample leisure and in their settled communities developed a complex social life. Here, as in Melanesia (7.1.), social status depended upon ritual feasting and the presentation of gifts, of which the most valuable were blankets and 'Coppers' (sheets of beaten copper). The settled nature of their lives made the Indians of this region particularly sensitive to history and lineage, which they expressed in elaborate ceremonies and works of art. The most famous of these are, perhaps, the spectacular *totem* poles, symbolising the clan's mythic theriomorphic ancestors.

The tribes of the region speak six different languages. They include the *Bella Coola, Chinook, Haida, Kwakiutl, Nootka, Salish* and *Tsimshian* Indians.

Tlingit headdress of copper inlaid with abalone shell. Masks of this type were worn by chiefs and *shamans* at *potlach* ritual exchanges. Portland Art Museum. (*Photo: Werner Forman Archive.*)

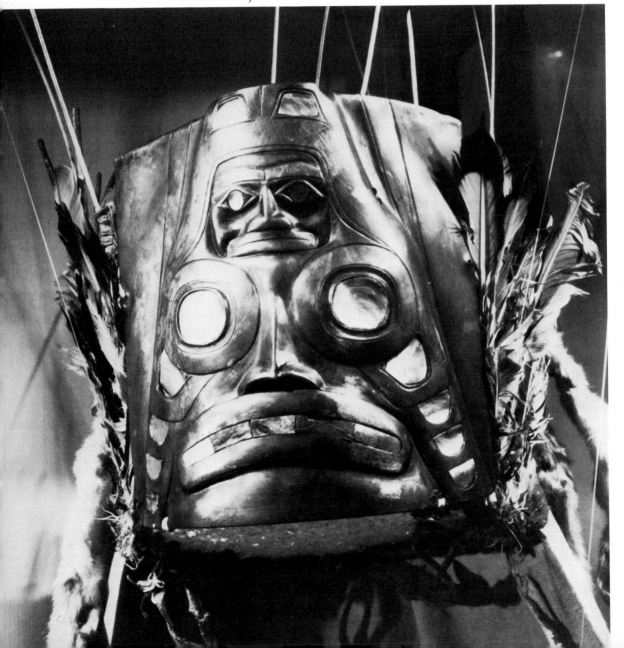

Tsimshian totem pole at Skeena River, British Columbia. (*Photo: Werner Forman Archive.*)

The South West

The practice of agriculture in the South West led to settlement in closely-knit villages of cliff and cave dwellings and the adobe houses known as *pueblos*. The arid nature of the region makes its people especially dependent upon careful use of water resources and hence fosters close-knit communities. These are also encouraged by the isolation of one valley from another, especially along the coast, and it is almost certainly due to the cohesive independence of their lives that the Pueblo Indians have been able to preserve so much of their traditional culture to the present day. Like other

Pueblo cliff dwellings in the Mesa Verde National Park, SW Columbia. (*Photo: Werner Forman Archive.*)

agricultural communities they have a close and intimate sense of relationship with their immediate environment and a conservative sense of history, expressed in their myths and legends by precise references to local geographical features: the mountain homes of the spirits, and the caves and islands from which it is said their ancestors emerged from the subterranean regions, which are the source of all life and fertility.

Common Themes and Concepts

Common to all North American Indian peoples is a belief in pervasive spirits with whom the *shaman* can communicate. Many tribes, especially among the Woodlands Indians, conceived of a more or less vaguely-defined Great Spirit. Often, but not always, he was thought of as expressing himself in the sun. At times, but again not invariably, he is identified with the Sky Father. He is not often spoken of as the creator of the world as a whole, though sometimes as the creator of the heavens. The creation of the earth and its peoples is usually assigned to a hero or to the Trickster (see below).

More clearly defined than the Great Spirit is the archetypal Earth Mother, Grandmother Earth, as she is usually called, for her grandsons are the twin heroes who play a particularly important rôle in the myths. Among south-western tribes the twins are war-gods (see **91–102**). Further north they personify the age-old conflict between good and evil, benevolent and malign powers (see **83–90**).

The concept of the Trickster is related to that of the twin heroes, either or both of whom embody some of his aspects. A protean figure, Trickster is a creator, but also cunningly devious and sometimes spiteful, sometimes 'too clever by half' as in **129–132**. He appears in both myth and folktale, forming the first world, recreating the earth after the flood, obtaining fire, creating man, causing his death and loss of immortality, defeating monsters. Where the creative rôle is assigned to some other figure, Trickster's rôle as an adventurer is predominant, but even where he is the creative demi-urge he is also a joker. He is usually conceived of in theriomorphic terms, on the North West Coast as Raven (Yetl)—see **103–114**—or Crow; on the Great Plains and in the South West as Coyote—a species of wolf—(see glossary), in the Woodlands as the Great White Hare or Rabbit, a figure who reappears in the folklore of the southern Negro as Brer Rabbit—an amalgam of the Indian Trickster and West African animal heroes.

Tlingit rattle with a raven's head and figure of a man lying along the bird's back. The beak of another raven lies parallel with his knees, while a third bird's head forms the lower side of the rattle. British Museum. (*Photo: British Museum.*)

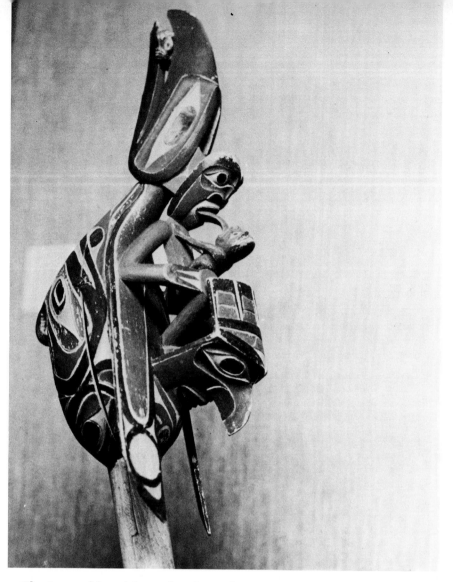

Kwakiutl rattle carved to represent the Thunderbird carrying a pair of human beings *in copulo* on its back. Royal Scottish Museum, Edinburgh. (*Photo: Photoresources.*)

Theriomorphic spirits and gods predominate in many of the myths and legends. Apart from Trickster, one of the most important of these figures is the Thunderbird (q.v.) or Thunderer. Like the thunder-gods of Āryan myth (Indra, vol. 3: 5.2. **94–100**; Thórr, vol. 2: 3.2. **176–202**; Zeus, vol. 1: 2.2. **6–11, 23–28**), the North American Thunderbird is an embodiment of the life force that strikes down the man-eating monster or serpent. He also acts as the guardian of fire.

As will be seen from the narrative outlines in Part 2, the Indians thought of the universe as comprising several storeys of which the earth and visible sky form the centre. The sky has to be supported at each of its corners, a task often performed by Trickster. The present earth is usually thought of as the second, created by Trickster or a hero following the drowning of the first.

Among tribes of the South West, however, the present earth is the highest of a series, men and animals having ascended from below, emerging on an island, which parallels the concept of the raft upon which survivors of the flood float across its waters (see **45–47; 121–122**).

The Sources of Eskimo and North American Tales

Knowledge of these myths and legends derives from two sources: the accounts of early explorers and settlers and reports from the Indians themselves. Although their long, and in some respects continuing, exploitation by the white man is a subject of scandal and concern, members of many Eskimo and North American Indian tribes yet survive and preserve something of their forefathers' traditions. In a few areas, especially in the pueblo villages of the South West, age-old rituals are still observed.

The most important collections of material are those published by the Canadian Department of Mines, the Canadian National Museum and the Bureau of American Ethnology.

CENTRAL AMERICA

By contrast with those of the North American Indians, the myths and legends of Meso America are those of long-extinct civilisations, known to us partly from archaeological research, more especially from the records of the Spanish *conquistadores*, priests and their converts.

The first of these civilisations, the *Olmec* and *Teotihuacan*, were already history when the *conquistadores* arrived. Neither left written records, so far as we know. Archaeologists date the early *Olmec* finds between 800 and 400 B.C. They include pyramidal structures obviously the precursors of the *Maya* and *Aztec* pyramids, and sculptures embodying many representations of jaguars and jaguar-men, suggesting that these had an important religious significance, but of this we cannot be certain.

Olmec jadeite axe head carved in the figure of a god decorated with jaguar motifs. Dallas Museum of Fine Art. (*Photo: Werner Forman Archive.*)

The civilisation of Teotihuacan reached its zenith in *c.* A.D. 200. By then the city included the two great structures known to the *Aztecs* as the Pyramid of the Sun, the Pyramid of the Moon (see **282**), and a third, the Temple of the Feathered Serpent, whose sculptures include symbols characteristic of the *Aztec* rain-god Tláloc and the fire-god Huehuetéotl. It is uncertain whether the feathered-serpent *motifs* relate to an early cult of the god later known as Quetzalcóatl.

Teotihuacan dominated the Mexican plateau for several hundred years, but after *c.* A.D. 200 its power was on the wane. In *c.* 650–750 the city was abandoned and partly destroyed by fire and violence.

The Maya

The history of the *Maya* presents many unsolved problems. Their civilisation spread over three areas: to the south the highlands and coast of modern Guatemala, to the north the peninsula of Yucatán and inbetween over a region now long buried by dense tropical forests. It was in this third, unpropitious zone that their civilisation reached its peak.

The cities seem to have been predominantly centres of religion and learning confined to a priestly class; but this is not certainly established. The first large building so far excavated dates from *c.* 300 B.C. It is in Guatemala. The great centres of the lowland region fell into desuetude between A.D. 750 and 900.

The intellectual achievements of these people were extraordinary, including a most complex calendar, mathematical and astronomical knowledge. Potentially theirs are the most interesting of all the central American civilisations for the student of myth and legend, but as yet understanding of their script eludes us. Most of their manuscripts were burned by their Spanish conquerors. Of the three that remain—known from

Late seventh-century lintel from a *Maya* ceremonial centre at Yaxchilán, Guatemala, shows a worshipper kneeling to a double-headed snake-god. British Museum. (*Photo: British Museum.*)

their present homes as the Paris, Dresden and Madrid codices—we can understand little. Nor are the many stone inscriptions as yet more meaningful. In so far as we can understand either, interpretation depends mainly upon the information collected by Diego de Landa. The first Bishop of Yucatán and one of the most enthusiastic destroyers of *Maya* texts, he was, nonetheless, very interested in understanding their hieroglyphs and asked their scholars to explain them.

Our knowledge of *Maya* myths and legends therefore derives partly from tentative interpretations of their surviving books and inscriptions, and partly from three very late works written after the Spanish conquest. Two of these, the *Popul Vuh* and the *Annals of Cakchiquel*, were compiled by southern *Maya* peoples in Guatemala and may reflect more of the *Toltec* than the *Maya* tradition. By the time of the Spanish conquest the southern *Maya* seem to have known very little if anything about the builders of their ancient cities, and their tradition of exile from the legendary Tollan resembles that found among the central Mexican *Toltec*, who certainly penetrated as far south as Guatemala.

A further pointer to possible *Toltec* influence is the marked similarity between the concepts in the stories of the *Popul Vuh* and those of *Toltec*, *Aztec* and North American Indian myth. Here, as in the *Toltec* and *Aztec* stories we have a series of creations each destroyed by flood, and, as in North American Indian myth, an emphasis upon the adventures of twin heroes, grandchildren of the Earth Mother and Sky Father. On the other hand, it is possible that these themes were common to the classical *Maya* myths as they were to those of the neighbouring and succeeding civilisations.

The third sixteenth-century source of fragmentary knowledge comes from Yucatán, which was, again, conquered by the *Toltec*. It is the work known as the *Book of Chilam Balam [Jaguar Priest] of Chumayel*, a collection of chronicles and miscellaneous information.

The People of the Aztec Empire

From about the end of the eighth or beginning of the ninth century to the beginning of the twelfth, successive bands of warlike *Nahuatlan* tribes entered central Mexico from the north. The first of these were the *Toltecs*. They were followed by the *Chichimecs*, and the *Mexica* or *Aztecs*. The *Toltecs'* god was the Sky Father, Mixcóatl, Cloud Serpent, with whom they seem to have identified the great war-leader under whom they conquered central Mexico. Even more important was his son, the god, culture-hero, *shaman*, priest-king, Quetzalcóatl—Green-Feathered-Serpent.

It is impossible to disentangle history from myth in the accounts of these people's arrival in Mexico. We may however note that their pantheon seems to have resembled that of the North American Indians in so far as chief importance was given to the son of the Sky Father and Earth Mother, who, like the heroes of the northern myths, was credited with the re-establishment of culture. According to one myth Quetzalcóatl recreated the earth after a flood (**236–237**). He was also credited with restoring *Toltec* civilisation by establishing the legendary city of Tollan (possibly modern Tula) and introducing all the arts of living.

Mosaic of mother-of-pearl on stone shows a warrior in a coyote helmet. Found at Tula it is sometimes called Quetzalcóatl of Tula. Instituto Nacional de Antropología e Historia, Mexico City. (*Photo: Werner Forman Archive.*)

Tollan fell to the *Chichimecs*, who established themselves in the lakeside city of Tetzcoco, their fortunes made by their dominance of the lake's salt pans.

Finally came the *Aztecs*, who may have been poor vassals of the *Toltecs*. After being expelled from various cities they settled on the marshy island of Tenochtitlan (the centre of modern Mexico City), from which they gradually came to dominate the entire region.

Problems of Aztec Myth and Legend

Any study of the myths and legends of this empire is complicated by the fact that, like those of the Ancient Egyptians (vol. 1), *Aztec* myths expressed highly syncretistic religious and cultural beliefs in which gods of the subject peoples were assimilated to those of the dominant group and city. Indeed *Aztec* Tenochtitlan contained a special temple housing statues of the deities of all their subject peoples, perhaps symbolising their inferiority to the great *Aztec* sun-god Huitzilopochtli—a subjection gruesomely expressed by the ritual sacrifice of prisoners to this god. (Human sacrifices were also made to the fertility deities, but here the purpose was, it seems, not so much to feed and honour the deities as to enact their annual death and resurrection.)

On the other hand, as the importance of the cult of the great *Toltec* god Quetzalcóatl indicates, the *Aztecs* saw themselves as the heirs and in some ways the upholders of *Toltec* culture—rather as the Romans admired and imitated the Greeks. It is therefore very difficult—often impossible—to disentangle the various religious and mythical traditions.

Aztec greenstone figure of Quetzalcóatl between the jaws of the feathered serpent. British Museum. (*Photo: Werner Forman Archive.*)

A not dissimilar problem presents itself in the study of the legends of the *Aztecs* and their *Nahuatlan* cousins, because, like the Romans (see vol. 1), they tended to interweave myth, legend and history and we at present lack the knowledge necessary to unravel the resulting tissues.

THE CARIBBEAN ISLANDS

The indigenous cultures of these islands have been so damaged by the effects of their European exploiters and by the slave trade that, apart from brief accounts made by priests accompanying Columbus's two expeditions, we have little knowledge of the myths and legends of the indigenous peoples: the *Arawakian*-speaking *Taïno*, and the *Caribs*. Such information as does exist suggests that their beliefs resembled those of the North American Indians of the South West.

More recently, an amalgam of native, West African and Christian lore has given rise to the *Voodoo* cults, which are especially important in Haiti. The cultists seem to have developed few myths. Details of their gods and spirits are included in Part 3. Two particularly interesting studies of the cults are Francis Huxley's *The Invisibles* (1966) and parts of William Sargant's *The Mind Possessed* (1973).

SOUTH AMERICA

Our knowledge of early South American civilisations is very limited and entirely dependent upon archaeological evidence. So far as we know these cultures left no written records or did so in forms that have since perished. Certainly writing did not exist at the time of the Spanish conquest.

The Chavin Culture

After the gradual development of fishing and agricultural villages along the Peruvian coast from *c.* 4000 B.C., quite suddenly, in *c.* 1000 B.C., there arose a highly-developed culture including great temple buildings. It seems to have been peaceable rather than warlike, but spread over much of the Andean region. Known as the *Chavin* from one of their greatest temples, Chavin de Huántor, the peoples of this civilisation seem to have worshipped a jaguar-god, for jaguar motifs predominate in their temple carvings. Two representations of an anthropomorphic god have also been found, the El Lanzón and the Raimondi stele, both of which show a man with snaky locks and feline features.

The origin of this civilisation is a mystery. Some scholars believe it to be associated with the *Olmec* culture of Central America. A few suggest even a Chinese origin. Its disappearance in *c.* 300 B.C., was as sudden as its rise and equally puzzling.

Mochica

The next classic civilisation, the Mochica, developed gradually in the valleys
of the north Peruvian coast. It depended on a highly-organised system of
irrigation canals and centred on the valleys of Chicama and Moche. Its most
important public buildings are the great temple pyramids of the sun and
moon in Mohic valley. Both sun- and moon-gods seem to have been
important, but it is believed that the moon-god was the chief. The many
subordinate deities included a jaguar-god whose worship seems to have
involved human sacrifices, or possibly he was a war-god.

Tiahuanaco

The first great civilisation of the Andean highlands seems to have been
centred on Tiahuanaco near Lake Titicaca on the Bolivian plateau.
Radiocarbon tests have indicated that its main buildings date from about the
early first century A.D. They include four pyramids and the great complex
known as the Kalasasaya, a huge platform containing a patio entered through
the monolithic Gateway of the Sun. At its centre is a head surrounded by

sun-rays, some of which begin as pumas. Attendant deities hold staffs, possibly sun-ray emblems, terminating in condor heads. These subordinate gods themselves wear animal and bird masks, of jaguar, condor and other predators.

Art in the Tiahuanaco style seems to have been disseminated gradually across the whole Andean region up to A.D. 600–1000, but whether by conquest or trade we do not know. Again the civilisation's end is a mystery. No signs of either conquest or emigration have been discovered. To the peoples of the Inca empire, Tiahuanaco was a legendary city, its origins unknown, its buildings already in ruins.

Chimor, Chuicuito and Other Pre-Inca States

Of the several states which succeeded the dissolution of Tiahuanaco the most important and extensive was the great kingdom of Chimor (Chimu), founded in the early fourteenth century and centred on the coastal valleys of northern and central Peru. Its capital was Chan-Chan in Moche valley. According to legend, Chimor was founded by an overseas' prince, either Tancanaymo or Naymlap (329–334) who, it is now thought, probably came from the region of Ecuador.

Chimor was highly centralised and its ruler worshipped as a god. Other deities included the moon- and sea-gods and ancestral totem stones called *alec pong*.

Painted stirrup vase from Chimor decorated with a sea-god. Private Collection. (*Photo: Werner Forman Archive.*)

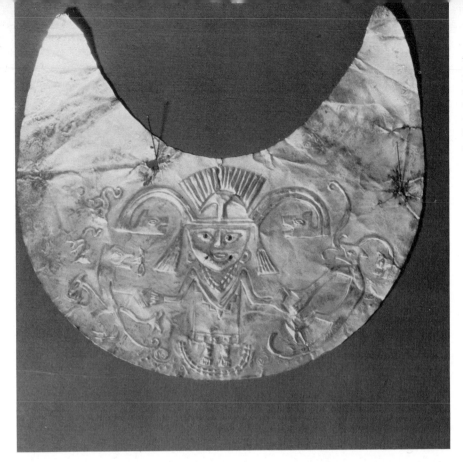

Beaten silver pectoral from Chimor showing god or god-king wearing solar or lunar headdress and attended by stylised monsters, possibly sea-gods. Museum of the American Indian, New York. (*Photo: Werner Forman Archive.*)

In the northern highlands, by contrast to the centralised might of lowland Chimor, there existed a loosely-knit federation of villages, each divided into two moities and centred on the scarcely larger village of Chuicuito which was ruled by two equipotent chiefs. Further south were smaller village-states, which seem to have been constantly at war with each other.

Of the beliefs of these areas we know little for certain because they were to be assimilated to those of the *Incas*.

The Inca Empire

Whether, as their legends asserted, the *Incas* originated in the area of Lake Titicaca, or from near Cuzco, we do not know, but it is generally agreed they settled in the Cuzco Valley in *c.* 1250. At first they encountered considerable opposition from neighbouring settlers and in the middle of the fifteenth century were all but vanquished by a confederation of these neighbours, the *Chancas*. Under the inspired leadership of one Pachacuti, they turned near defeat into resounding victory and embarked upon a campaign of aggressive warfare that, within thirty years, gave them an empire covering most of Ecuador, Bolivia, Peru and parts of Argentina and Chile.

Throughout the *Inca* empire, myth, legend, folklore and history were orally preserved. Both among the *Inca* themselves, and among the *Aymará*-speaking peoples of Bolivia, a special class of learned man was entrusted with their transmission.

131

Like the *Aztecs*, the *Incas* assimilated the beliefs and traditions of conquered peoples to their own; but, unlike the *Aztecs*, they seem to have had an overwhelming—and, in view of their meteoric rise to power, understandable—need to emphasise their own superiority. They therefore adapted and suppressed others' stories, the better to enhance the prestige of their own theocratic rulers. Such myths and legends as have come down to us have therefore survived in what seem to be highly edited forms.

After the Spanish conquest a number of *Inca* converts recorded what they knew of these traditions, but in some cases they seem to have selected or emphasised those aspects of the stories which were most akin to the Christian beliefs to which they had been converted. Two of the most important of these records are the illustrated codex *Nueva coronica y buen gobierno* by Don Felipe Guamara Poma de Ayala, who claimed *Inca* royal descent through his mother, and the *Comentarios réales de los Incas* by the *metzio* Garsilasco de la Vega, also of royal descent but brought up in Spain. Unlike de Ayala he was highly educated.

Detail from an *Inca* painted and lacquered wooden beaker (*keru*) showing *conquistadores* and a Peruvian, with birds flying above. British Museum. (*Photo: Photoresources.*)

The second source of records is that of the Spanish *conquistadores* and their missionary followers. Again, their perspectives were biased, on the one hand by the desire to emphasise the glory of the state they had conquered, on the other by their own religious beliefs and dogmas. Nevertheless from both *Inca* and Spanish sources, sufficient evidence is available to enable us to see that there existed no organised pantheon of gods amongst the *Incas* or their subject peoples. The state cult of the sun-god, Inti, from whom the *Inca* claimed divine descent, predominated. Various personified natural powers, the moon-goddess, the rain-god and similar deities were of some importance; but amongst the people as a whole, apart from various nature-spirits and individual clan heroes, the most widely acknowledged deity seems to have been the creator Vivacocha, whose cult was developed by the *Inca* Pachacuti, but combined aspects of long-worshipped culture-heroes. The multifarious nature of these origins of the god is well illustrated in the confusion of surviving stories about him.

Other South American Peoples

Among the various less sophisticated peoples of the South American continent, animism seems to remain the predominant religious form. Explorers, missionaries, and more recently, anthropologists, have collected details of individual peoples' myths and legends. Notes on some of these are included in Part 3.

A NOTE ON SPELLING AND PRONUNCIATION

The spelling of Eskimo and North American Indian names is phonetic.
    Central and South American names should be pronounced:
vowels: a as c*a*rt; e as s*ay*; i as ch*ie*f; o as g*no*me; u as m*oo*n;
consonants; g as in En*g*lish, except if followed by an i or e, when it becomes
    h; j as *h*; tl as in ket*tl*e; x as *sh*ed.
    In *Nahuatlan* (*Toltec, Chichimec, Aztec*) names the accent falls on the penultimate syllable. In others, it falls on the penultimate syllable of words ending in vowels or in 'n' or 's', on the final syllable of those ending in different consonants.

PART 2

Narrative Outlines

ESKIMO STORIES
Creation Myths
1–8

(i) THE FIRST PEOPLE
1 Long ago the earth dropped down from the skies. Babies were born from the earth and lay about among its willow trees until they were discovered by a man and a woman. She made clothes for them. He stamped in the ground and from the spots where he stamped there sprang forth the dogs upon which human kind are dependent.

2 The first people were immortal, but as there was no sun or moon they lived in perpetual darkness. At length two women began to discuss whether or not it would be better to go on living under these conditions or to change them. The first woman thought it would be better to keep things as they were, preferring to remain without light rather than to lose her immortality; but the second thought it would be better to have light even though that meant people would die—and that is what happened.

(ii) MOON, SUN AND STARS
3 The moon and sun were a brother and sister. In the darkness they lay together; then they lit torches so that they could look at each other. When the girl realised she had been lying with her brother, she tore off her breasts and threw them at him, crying, 'You liked my body. Taste these too!' Then, still clutching her fiery torch, she ran away, pursued by her brother, who chased her right up into the sky.

4 As she ran, the girl's torch flared brighter and brighter; but her brother's died down to a mere spark: so she became the *inua* (ruling spirit) of the sun, he of the moon.

5 One day hunters and their dogs chased a bear far out onto the ice floes. Even when they saw it begin to rise into the air they still did not falter in their pursuit and can yet be seen in the skies as the shining Pleiades chasing the Great Bear.

6 A similar story accounts for the origin of the constellation Orion, while the planet Venus, seen low in the western sky as spring approaches, is an old man who was chased into the air by parents of the children he had killed by imprisoning them in a cleft of rock, after they had disturbed him when he was hunting seals.

(iii) THE FLOOD AND THE CREATION OF WHITE MEN

7 At first there were no people other than the *Eskimo*, but then there came a great flood and when the waters subsided a girl bore white children, fathered by a dog.

8 Putting them in the sole of a boot, the mother sent these children off to find their own country, and when, long after, they returned to the *Eskimo* lands they came in ships which still resembled the sole of a boot!

The Old Woman of the Sea
9–15

9 Whereas for most peoples the archetypal Great Goddess is the Earth Mother, for the *Eskimo*, who are primarily dependent upon the sea for their food, the Great Goddess is a water spirit. Like her earthly counterparts she has an ambivalent nature, being the ruler of the dead as well as the source of life. She has various names, being known in eastern Greenland as Nerrivik (Food-dish), by the Alaskan *Eskimo* as Sedna and also as Arnarkusuagsak or Arnakuagsak (Old Woman) and Nuliajoq.

Detail from a nineteenth-century engraved walrus tusk, showing Eskimo hunting caribou. British Museum. (*Photo: Photoresources.*)

10 Long ago two giants bore a daughter, Sedna, who had a terrifying appetite. One night, as they lay sleeping, she even began to chew at her parents. Starting up, they grabbed Sedna, and carrying her to their *umiak* (hunting canoe), paddled far out to sea. There they threw her overboard. She clung to the boat's side, trying to climb in again, but her parents cut off her fingers and so she sank into the waters' depths. There she remains, governing both the sea and all its creatures, who were born from her severed fingers.

11 According to Greenland peoples the goddess was not originally a cannibal giantess, but an ordinary *Eskimo* woman named Nerrivik. Wooed by a petrel, she allowed him to carry her off to his home far across the sea, but there she discovered he had tricked her.

12 Nerrivik's kinsfolk rescued her, but the angry petrel raised such a terrible storm that, in order to save their own lives, her relatives eventually decided they must abandon Nerrivik; so they threw her overboard, cutting off her fingers when she clung to the boat's side.

13 All published versions of the myth agree that the goddess now dwells in the ocean's depths. When *Eskimo* hunters are unable to find any prey their *angakok* (*shaman*, see vol. 2: 3.1.) sends his spirit down to plead with Sedna-Nerrivik.

14 To reach her home the *angakok* must pass through the land of the dead, which Sedna rules; then over an icy whirlpool, which threatens to engulf him. Next he must pass by an enormous cauldron full of boiling seals, evade the great goddess's fearsome guard-dog and cross an abyss on a knife-edge path, before at last arriving at Sedna's beautifully-appointed home.

15 There the *angakok* dances, chanting before the goddess, to induce her to help his people. At last she tells him either that the *Eskimo* must move and build a new settlement—otherwise they will all die—or she agrees again to send them seals and other prey.

Detail of nineteenth-century engraved walrus tusk showing Eskimo hunters in kayaks and canoes. British Museum. (*Photo: British Museum.*)

STORIES OF THE NORTH AMERICAN INDIANS

Creation Myths
16–81

(i) THE OLD MAN OF THE ANCIENTS

16 Long ago, the Morning Star called to Kemush from the ashes of the Aurora Borealis, commanding him to create the world. The Old Man of the Ancients began by making the earth as a flat, bare plain. On this he built the hills and mountains and scooped out valleys and rivers. In the valleys he set grass, ferns and other plants, on the hills and mountains, conifers.

17 Now Kemush peopled the world, setting the white-tailed deer Mushmush in the forests, together with the red and grey foxes Wan and Ketchkatch. On the mountain sides he put the sheep Koil and Luk the grizzly bear and on Mt. Shasta he placed Grey Wolf.

18 As yet there were no Indians in the world, but it was now ready for them, everything in it newly created, except for the crescent-shaped rock in Klamath Lake where the sun and moon had long had their lodge.

19 After finishing his work, Kemush, the Old Man of the Ancients, went to rest in the lodge of the north wind. There he remained fast asleep until he was summoned by Sun Halo to follow the trail of Shel (the sun).

20 Kemush and Sun Halo trailed Shel right to the edge of the dark; then the creator and his daughter Evening Sky went to the lodges of the spirits who lived in the Place of the Dark.

21 For five nights Kemush and Evening Sky danced with the spirits in a circle round their fire, until at last Shel called to the world; then the spirits in the Place of the Dark—who were as numerous as leaves or as the stars of the Milky Way—all turned into dry bones.

22 Kemush collected a sackful of these spirit bones and taking it on his back, followed Shel's trail to the world's edge. As he went he scattered pairs of spirit bones over the mountains, valleys and seashore and the bones turned into Indians—*Chipmunks, Maidu, Maklak* and *Klamath* and the earth was peopled.

23 His work finished, Kemush followed Shel's trail to its very summit in the sky and there built himself a lodge, in which he yet lives with his daughter, Evening Star, and Sun Halo. (*Klamath* myth from North West Coast.)

24 In an interesting variant of this story, from the neighbouring *Modoc* Indians, Kemush, here called Kumush, travels down a very steep hill to the underground world of the spirits and, because he has felt lonely in the world above, decides to bring some spirit bones back with him. His first two attempts to do so are foiled when he misses his footing as he reaches the top of the hill on his return journey. The basket of spirit bones falls from his back and as they tumble onto the ground the bones are once more transformed into spirit people and run home to their lodge.

25 As he reaches the hill-top on his third attempt, Kumush throws the basket over the edge of the world onto flat ground crying, 'Indian bones', and so this time the bones are transformed into people.

26 The creator-spirit then creates animals, fish and food plants for the Indians by naming their names, and organises his people's lives, telling them that the men should be hunters, fishermen and warriors; the women should collect wood, draw water, gather berries and edible roots and do the family's cooking.

27 Having now completed his work Kumush, accompanied by his daughter, went to the eastern edge of the world, where the sun rises, and travelled along the sun's path until he reached the middle of the sky. There he built a lodge for himself and his daughter and there they live still. (*Modoc* myth from North West Coast.)

28 In these stories we see that the Indians of the North West coastal region conceived of the universe as comprising several layers—an idea common to many of the American Indian peoples, as to others. It is given more elaborate expression in myths from the southern part of the continent of which the following *Navajo* creation story is an example.

(ii) THE ASCENT OF THE *NAVAJO*
29 In the Age of Beginnings in the Red World four streams flowed from the earth's centre to the four cardinal points and into the surrounding seas.

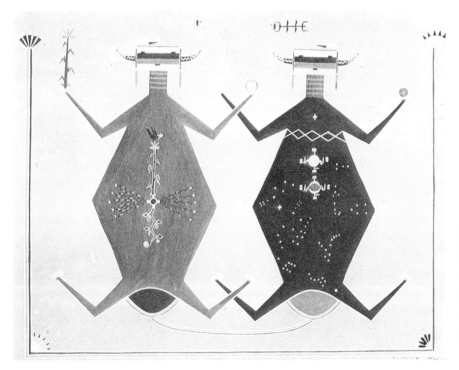

Navajo ritual sandpainting shows the Earth-Mother and Sky-Father. On her body are symbols of the four sacred plants, growing from the 'place of emergence', on his symbols of the sun, moon and Milky Way. Museum of *Navajo* Ceremonial Art, Santa Fé.

30 The people who began life in this world were mostly in insect form, though they also included bats and, according to some versions of the myth, Atse Hastin (First Man), Atse Estsan (First Woman) and the trickster Coyote.

31 Because the inhabitants of the Red World committed adultery, their gods punished them by sending a great flood. As they fled upwards, seeking a way of escape from drowning, a blue head poked through the sky and told them to come up into the Blue World of the Swallow People.

32 On the twenty-fourth night after their arrival in this upper world, one of the refugees committed adultery with the Swallow chief's wife and all the refugees were consequently expelled from the Blue World also.

33 As they once more flew upwards, seeking a new refuge, the voice of the wind Niltshi guided them to an opening in the sky through which they passed into the Yellow World of the Grasshopper people.

34 From this too they were expelled for making free with their hosts' women and so, helped again by Niltshi, came into the next, multicoloured world.

35 The cardinal points of this fourth world were marked by snow-capped mountains. Much bigger than the three lower ones, it was inhabited both by the *Kisani* (Pueblo Indians) and the *Mirage* people. They had four gods, White Body, Blue Body, Yellow Body and Black Body.

36 The *Kisani*, who were farmers, fed the refugees on maize and pumpkins, and now, from ears of white and yellow maize the four gods of this world created Atse Hastin and Atse Estsan—First Man and First Woman.

37 This couple bore five pairs of twins. The oldest pair, who were androgynous, invented pottery and wicker water-bottles. Their younger siblings intermarried with the *Kisani* and *Mirage* peoples and so the tribe of Atse Hastin multiplied.

38 One day they saw the sky bending down towards the earth, which rose to meet it. As they touched, Badger and Coyote came down from the world above. Badger continued his descent through to the Yellow World; but Coyote remained among the people of Atse Hastin.

39 At this time men and women were living apart, having quarrelled; but, finding themselves short of food, the women decided to rejoin their menfolk. As they crossed the stream that divided their territories, the last two women were caught by the water-monster Tieholtsodi and dragged down to his realm.

40 Advised by the four gods, a man and woman went down to the rescue. Unbeknown to them Coyote secretly followed and abducted two of Tieholtsodi's children.

41 The enraged monster flooded the world. Desperately Atse Hastin's people fled uphill and the animals made trees sprout higher and higher in a vain attempt to outgrow the rising waters. At last two men appeared with a little soil and in this was grown a mighty hollow reed in which everyone took refuge. Hardly was the bunghole closed than they heard the waters surging over it.

Navajo ritual sandpainting shows the fourth world into which the people ascended (45). From the 'place of emergence' grow the four sacred plants, between the mountains of the cardinal points, which have tiered clouds beneath them, birds on their summits. Arching round the world is the body of the rainbow-goddess. Museum of *Navajo* Ceremonial Art, Santa Fé.

42 Though temporarily safe the refugees were prisoners for, although the reed reached right up to the sky, there was no opening through which they might escape into the world above.

43 Great Hawk flew up and clawed at the heavens until he glimpsed light filtering through from the upper world; then Locust made a tiny hole and climbed out.

44 He was met by four grebes, guardians of the upper world's four quarters, who engaged him in a contest of power (i.e. as between rival *shamans*). At length, Locust managed to win half their world from them.

45 Badger now enlarged the tiny hole in the sky and all the people climbed through to their new home. So they came to our world, the earth, arriving on an island in the middle of a lake.

46 The gods gave them safe passage to the lake's shore and there they assembled to discover their fate in this new home. Throwing a hide scraper into the water they watched intently to see whether it would float or sink. It floated. That meant they would live; but then Coyote threw a large stone into the scraper, making it sink. Everyone was furious with him. However Coyote explained it was better that their lives should be limited by death, otherwise the world would become overpopulated.

Navajo blanket, *c.* 1880, shows two spirits invoked in the Shooting Chant ritual flanking the sacred maize plant. The body of the rainbow-goddess frames them. Schindler Collection New York. (*Photo: Werner Forman Archive.*)

47 It seemed that a speedy death was very near for everyone when flood-waters were seen surging through the hole by which they had escaped from the world below; but Coyote's abduction of Tieholtsodi's children was now discovered. They were immediately seized and thrown back into the lower world. Roaring, the waters receded.

48 Atse Hastin and Atse Estsan, Black Body and Blue Body now fashioned the *Navajo* land, beginning with its seven mountains, which they anchored firmly to the earth with such things as a lightning bolt, a sunbeam, a rainbow and a huge stone knife. They decorated each with various kinds of weather, light, crops, shells and semi-precious stones and upon each summit placed a nest of eggs, so that the mountains might have feathers to wear.

49 In the eastern mountain, Pelado Peak, they set Rock-Crystal Boy and Girl; in the western, Mt. San Francisco, White-Corn Boy and Yellow-Corn Girl; in the northern, Mt. San Juan, Pollen Boy and Grasshopper Girl and in the southern, Mt. Taylor, Turquoise Boy and Corn Girl.

50 Next Atse Hastin and Atse Estsan made the sun, moon and stars, appointing as Sun-Bearer and Moon-Bearer the two men who had found the soil and grown the reed that had enabled them all to escape from the water monster. They are called Tshohanoai and Klehanoai.

51 At the time men and women had quarrelled and separated in the multicoloured fourth world, some women had engaged in evil practices. They now gave birth to man-eating monsters, the *anaye* (alien gods), who included the hairy, headless Theelgeth, the feathered Tshanahale, a terrible pair of limbless twins, the Binaye Ahani, who killed men with a single glance, Yeitso, a fearsome giant and Delgeth, the flesh-eating antelope.

52 People also fell victims to a celestial gambler, He-Who-Wins-Men, who tricked them into staking and losing their freedom. Two powerful kindly beings, the great *yei* (q.v.) Hastseyalti and Hastshehogan (qq.v.) came to the rescue and, assisted by animal deities and the spirits of wind and darkness, enabled a young brave to overcome the gambler. With a magic bow the youth shot He-Who-Wins-Men back into the sky (from which he later again descended, to rule over the Mexicans).

53 Led by Hastseyalti the *yei* now created two goddesses, Estanatlehi (the Woman-Who-Changes) and Yolkai Estsan (White-Shell Woman), forming the first from turquoise, the second from white shell.

54 Next were born the twin heroes Nayanezgani and Thobadzistshini. According to some versions of the myth they were both sons of Estanatlehi and Tshohanoai the Sun-Bearer. According to others, these deities were the parents of Nayanezgani while Thobadzistshini's mother and father were Yolkai Estsan and Water.

55 Helped by the Spider-Woman and the wind-spirit Niltshi, Nayanezgani and Thobadzistshini made a perilous journey to the *hogan* (home) of the Sun-Bearer, Tshohanoai, and, by surviving many trials, won his confidence (**91–102**). He gave them magical weapons: arrows of lightning, sunbeams and rainbow, a huge stone knife (thunderbolt?) and armour whose every joint flashed lightning.

56 Returning to earth, Nayanezgani and Thobadzistshini battled with the monstrous *anaye*, killing very many of them, but were unable to overcome them all, so once more sought help from Tshohanoai. This time the Sun-Bearer gave them four magic hoops. With these the goddess Estanatlehi raised a terrible storm in which not only were almost all the remaining *anaye* destroyed but the form of the earth itself reshaped.

57 Now, of all the *anaye* only four remained: Old Age, Cold, Poverty and Hunger. They were allowed to live because they convinced Estanatlehi that, if she killed them, men would no longer prize the good things of life or even life itself.

58 Their task being done, the young warrior-gods Nayanezgani and Thobadzistshini went to their mountain home. There *Navajo* braves go to ask for success in battle.

59 Now Tshohanoai peopled the reshaped earth with animals; then he went away to the far west, where he built himself a lodge beyond the waters. With him went Estanatlehi, goddess of rain and fertility.

60 Yolkai Estsan, Estanatlehi's sister, was now left alone on earth until the good *yei* Hastsheyalti came to her and together they decided to create new people. They made a man from an ear of white corn, a woman from an ear of yellow. Niltshi, the wind-spirit, breathed life into them. Rock-Crystal Boy gave them minds. Grasshopper Girl gave them speech. Yolkai Estsan gave them gifts of fire and maize and then she married the man to Ground-Heat Girl, the woman to Mirage Boy and their children became the first *Navajo* of today.

61 When her work was done Yolkai Estsan also went away and became the wife of the Moon-Bearer, Klehanoai. (*Navajo* myth, Arizona.)

62 Neighbouring peoples such as the Pueblo-dwelling *Sia* and *Hopi* Indians of New Mexico and Arizona have similar myths of an ascent through several lower worlds to emerge upon an earthly island. The following striking account of the earth's creation by star spirits comes from further north, from the great plains of Nebraska.

(iii) THE CREATOR STARS
63 In the beginning Tirawa, Chief of Tirawahut (the heavens' circle), and his wife Atira (Sky-Vault) sat in council with the spirits and Tirawa appointed the great spirits to their places in the sky, giving them each special powers that would enable them to help and care for the people he proposed to create.

64 He set Sakuru, the sun-spirit, in the eastern sky, to give light and warmth and Pah, the moon-spirit, in the west, to shine at night. In the west also Tirawa set Bright Star (Venus the evening star), the Mother-of-All-Things; in

Pawnee buckskin chart of the night sky. Field Museum of Natural History, Chicago. (*Photo: Werner Forman Archive.*)

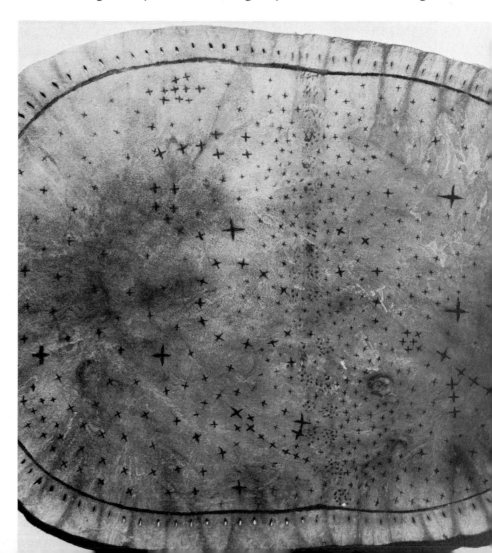

the east the warrior Great Star (Venus the morning star). In the south he placed Spirit Star, who would be seen irregularly on earth, and in the north the Star-That-Does-Not-Move, whom he made chief of all the star-spirits.

65 Four other star-spirits he appointed as the guardians of the four quarters, to support the heavens, and to these four spirits Tirawa gave the power to create people and to bestow upon them holy bundles (see sacred bundles).

66 Now Tirawa told Bright Star he was going to send her wind, lightning and thunder spirits, whom she was to set between herself and her garden. They would then be transformed into people, each wearing in his hair a downy feather (symbolising the breath of life), a buffalo robe, a robe of buffalo hair and moccasins. Each would hold in his right hand a rattle symbolising Bright Star's garden and to these spirits would be given the work of creating the earth.

67 The Wind-spirits blew, Clouds came together and Thunders and Lightnings entered into them and so the space of the sky was covered by a great storm. Into its midst Tirawa dropped a pebble, which rolled hither and thither among the spirits until the storm ended. The Cloud-spirits moved apart, revealing a waste of waters.

68 On Tirawa's orders, Bright Star now commanded the Upholders-of-the-Heavens to strike these waters with their clubs. As they did so, the waters divided and earth appeared among them.

69 Now Bright Star told the Upholders-of-the-Heavens to sing of earth's shaping. As they did so, Winds, Clouds, Lightnings and Thunders again came together in a great storm, forming the earth into hills and valleys. In similar fashion the earth was next clothed with trees and grass, its waters purified and seeds germinated.

70 Tirawa now summoned Sakuru, the sun-spirit, and Pah, the moon-spirit, and told them to come together. From their union was born a son. Bright Star and Great Star came together and from their union was born a daughter who, together with the boy, was set upon the newly-created earth.

71 The children as yet lacked understanding, so Tirawa told Bright Star to order the Upholders-of-the-Heavens to sing about putting life into the pair. As the stars sang the elemental spirits again came together in a great storm. As rain poured down upon the children, Lightnings played about them and the Thunders roared, it seemed that the boy and girl woke. So they received understanding.

72 The couple bore a son and worked hard to feed and clothe him. Tirawa cared for them, sending spirits to help them with gifts and teaching. The woman was given seeds and moisture to make them germinate, the spirits also gave her the lodge house and its holy place, a fireplace and the power of speech. They taught her how to use and guard the fire and gave her charge over the land immediately around the lodge as well as over the materials from which sacred pipes are made.

73 To the man the spirits gave a warrior's dress and a war-club so that he might remember that it had been with war-clubs that the Upholders-of-the-Heavens had divided the waters from the earth. The spirits taught the man how to use paints and bow and arrows, told him the names of plants and animals and showed him which tobacco pipes were to be holy.

74 Bright Star herself now came to the man in visions, teaching him how to make sacrifices and to prepare the sacred bundle which must hang in his lodge.

75 Other people were meanwhile being created by the Upholders-of-the-Heavens and all of them were given bundles, but as yet no one knew how they should be used.

76 Bright Star explained to the first man, who was named Closed Man, that each of the other peoples' bundles contained a species of corn: white for the south-western people, yellow for the north-western, red for the south-eastern and black for the north-eastern. She said someone would come to tell them how the bundles should be used.

77 Closed Man therefore summoned the peoples together and a man who, in a vision, had been taught the proper rituals instructed them in the songs and ceremonies appropriate to each bundle.

78 When at length Closed Man died, his skull was placed on top of a sacred bundle, according to the instructions Tirawa had given him, through Bright Star. So his spirit remains with the *Skidi* people. (Myth of the *Skidi Pawnee* from Nebraska.)

(iv) AN *OMAHA* STORY
79 Finally, in the following priestly myth from the *Pawnee*'s neighbours, the *Sioux*-speaking *Omaha*, we have an account of the Great Spirit creating the earth in order to give a home to lesser beings.

80 In the beginning all things had their existence in the mind of Wakonda, the Great Spirit. Man and all other creatures came into being as disembodied spirits. Wandering through space they sought a home where they would be able to take bodily forms. Finding that both the sun and moon were unsuited to their needs they next descended to earth, but, much to their distress, search as they might, they could find no land. All was water.

81 Suddenly a huge rock rose from the depths and burst into flames. The waters rose in clouds into the air and dry land appeared on which sprouted grass and trees. The spirits descended and, taking bodily forms, fed on the grasses' seeds and trees' fruits. The whole earth reverberated with their happiness and gratitude to Wakonda. (Myth of the Pebble Society priests of the *Omaha* Indians.)

The Two Heroes
82–102

82 The exploits of two related heroes are an important feature of myths from many parts of North America. In some cases the heroes are twins, in others brothers or cousins. They are more or less sharply contrasted in character—

the elder usually an active leader, the younger often a seer *shaman*. Sometimes the elder is presented as beneficent, the younger malevolent, as in the story of Yoskeha and Taswiscana.

(i) YOSKEHA AND TASWISCANA

83 Sons of the goddess Gusts-of-Wind and the Wind-Ruler, Yoskeha (Sapling) and Taswiscana (Flint) were enemies even in the womb and their ante-natal quarrelling was so fierce that they killed their mother.

84 Taswiscana persuaded their grandmother, the great earth-goddess Ataentsic, that Yoskeha was wholly responsible for their mother's death. Ataentsic therefore expelled Yoskeha from the earth and he went to seek his father, the Wind-Ruler, who presented him with a bow and arrows and some maize, signifying Yoskeha's lordship over the animals and plants.

85 When the good youth first prepared the maize so that mankind, who were about to be born, might live happily on earth, his grandmother Ataentsic spoiled it by scattering ashes over it. Yoskeha's good work was therefore made imperfect. He rebuked his grandmother.

86 Yoskeha now created the animals but again his good intentions were frustrated for his wicked twin Taswiscana imprisoned all the beasts in a cave. Yoskeha managed to free the majority. Those who remained were transformed into the evil creatures of the underworld.

87 Next Yoskeha had to fight his brother's evil ally Haidu, the humpbacked source of disease and decay. Overcoming this monster, Yoskeha wrested from him the secret lore of medicine and of the tobacco ceremony which he later taught mankind.

88 Now Yoskeha sought the sun and moon which his grandmother had created from his mother's body but, helped by Taswiscana, had buried in the earth. Helped by the animals of the four quarters, Yoskeha uncovered and stole the sun, evading his pursuing relatives by passing it to the animals, who handed it from one to another in relay and so saved it to light the earth.

89 Now the world was illuminated and stocked with plants and animals, Yoskeha created man. Again Taswiscana tried to spoil his twin's good work and attempted to imitate his creation but all he could produce were monsters, whom the good Yoskeha banished to the underworld together with Taswiscana himself.

90 When he grew old Yoskeha transformed his body, becoming once more a youth in the first vigour of manhood and so he has done again and again from that day to this, and his *orenda* (the quintessence of all life and vitality) remains undiminished, so that nothing evil or destructive, not even Taswiscana, the personification of negative *otkon*, can harm him in the smallest degree. (Myth of the *Iroquoian Onondaga* people.)

(ii) NAYANEZGANI AND THOBADZISTSHINI

91 Very different in character is the story of the *Navajo* heroes mentioned earlier (**54–58**), whose journey to the home of the Sun-Bearer involves classic episodes of the hero's trial, familiar in stories from all parts of the world.

92 Leaving home early in the morning the twins set out on a sacred trail. A little after sunrise they noticed smoke rising from the ground near Dsilnaotil and discovered it came from the underground home of Spider-Woman, who welcomed them, asking who they were and where they were going. Four times they evaded her questions, but when she suggested they sought their father they tacitly admitted they did, saying they wished they knew the way to his *hogan*.

93 Spider-Woman warned them the trail was both long and dangerous. Moreover, far from welcoming them, their father might punish them for their intrusion. The twins were undaunted.

94 Spider-Woman told them the four particular dangers they would meet were clashing rocks that crushed travellers; knife-sharp reeds that cut them to shreds; cane cacti that tore them to pieces; boiling sands that engulfed them (cf. **13–14** and vol. 1 : 2.2. **353–362**). She gave the twins two life-feathers (feathers plucked from a living eagle) joined into a talisman called 'feather of the *anaye*', and also another life-preserving feather. She then taught them a spell that would subdue their enemies:

95 *Put your feet down with pollen. Put your hands down with pollen. Put your head down with pollen. Your feet are pollen. Your hands are pollen. Your body is pollen. Your mind is pollen. Your voice is pollen. The trail is beautiful. Be still.*

96 With the aid of Spider-Woman's charms and spell the youths survived all the perils of their journey and came at last to Tshohanoai the Sun-Bearer's *hogan*, a great, square, turquoise house built on the shore of a vast stretch of water.

97 At its entrance they were threatened first by a pair of huge bears, next by a pair of serpents, next by winds and finally by lightnings; but safely passed by them all, grasping their life-feathers and chanting the soothing words Spider-Woman had taught them.

98 On entering their father's *hogan* they saw a woman sitting in its western corner, two handsome youths in its northern, two beautiful girls in its southern corner. The girls immediately stood up and, without a word, came and wrapped Nayanezgani and Thobadzistshini into a bundle with four 'sky-coverings'—of dawn, daylight, dusk and night—and put them on a shelf, where they lay quietly waiting.

99 After a while a rattle at the door shook four times and Tshohanoai strode into the *hogan* carrying the sun upon his back. Taking it off he put it on the west wall of the house where it clanged for a while and then hung still.

100 Tshohanoai asked his wife who the two visitors were he had seen coming to the *hogan*. At first she refused to answer, but later said they claimed to be his sons, which made her wonder how truthful he had been in telling her he never visited anyone in the course of his daily journeys!

101 Angry, the Sun-Bearer took Nayanezgani and Thobadzistshini down from the shelf and, unrolling the bundle, tipped them out onto the floor. Then he picked them up and hurled them at each of the four sides of his house in turn, against great spikes and rocks; but the Spider-Woman's talismans preserved them. Next Tshohanoai tried to steam them to death in his sweat house (*sauna*); then to poison them with doctored tobacco, but the twins survived every trial and not only smoked the poisoned pipe to its end but commented on its sweetness.

102 Impressed by their insouciant courage the Sun-Bearer at last acknowledged them as his sons and welcomed them to his *hogan*. (*Navajo myth, Arizona.*)

Animal Heroes and Tricksters
103–127

(i) YETL THE RAVEN

103 In the beginning all was dark. In a lodge at the source of the River Nass lived Nascakiyetl (Raven-at-the-Head-of-Nass) who kept the stars, planets and light in his house. With him lived his daughter, attended by two menservants, Adawulcanak (Old-Man-Who-Foresees-All-the-Troubles-of-the-World) and Tliewatuwadjigican (He-Who-Knows-Everything).

104 Nascakiyetl created Heron—a very tall and very wise man; and then Yetl, the Raven, another good, wise man. Some say that Yetl's mother, Nascakiyetl's sister, had borne many sons but her brother had jealously killed them all. Advised by Heron, she therefore swallowed a red-hot pebble and so gave birth to Yetl, who was named after the impregnable stone Itc Ak and called TAqlikic (Hammer-father) because he was so tough and resilient. Nascakiyetl therefore made him the world's head man.

105 Others say Yetl was really the son of the man Kitkaositiyiqa, who gave him the strength he needed to make the world. He then transformed himself into a hemlock splinter, was swallowed by Nascakiyetl's daughter in her drinking water and so reborn as her son. He then stole the stars, planets and daylight from Nascakiyetl—as had been his intention.

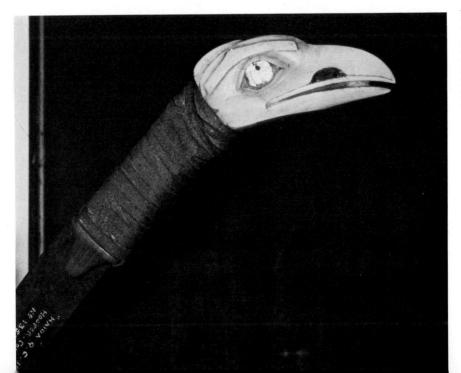

Nineteenth-century whalebone knife handle carved with a raven's head, inlaid with abalone shell, made by *Haida* Indians of the NW Coast. Hooper Collection, Watersfield. (*Photo: Werner Forman Archive.*)

Tlingit house screen, *c.* 1840, with the brown-bear clan-symbol. Denver Art Museum. (*Photo: Denver Art Museum.*)

106 He obtained fresh water for earth by stealing it from Petrel and scattering it over the world to form streams and rivers. As he was flying away with it, Petrel lit a fire underneath him and the smoke turned Yetl's white feathers to their present black.

107 When some people who were fishing refused to take him across a river he released the sun and they fled into the woods and sea in terror. As they ran they were transformed into the creatures whose skins they wore.

108 He went fishing with a Bear and Cormorant but cut off some of Bear's flesh, killing him and then tore out Cormorant's tongue to prevent him revealing the murder. Yetl also killed Bear's wife by tricking her into eating halibut bladders stuffed with red-hot stones, and trapped Deer in a pit and ate him.

109 He forced the old woman who governs the tide to make it rise and fall as it does nowadays. Then he again met Petrel and argued with him about which of them was the older. At last Petrel put on his fog hat so Raven was lost and had to admit defeat but he persuaded Petrel to let his hat go around the world.

110 Yetl persuaded a chickenhawk to steal fire for him and he stored it in red cedar and in some white stones (flints). He towed ashore the big house in which all fish lived and used some of them to feast his dead mother. The rest of them spread through all the world's waters.

111 By a trick, Yetl lured all but one of the killer-whales to their death and then boiled them down for their oil. A man was helping him do this, but Yetl stole the man's share of the oil, and when the man shut him in a grease-box and kicked it over the cliffs, the cunning Raven easily escaped death, since earlier he had persuaded the man to fasten the box with straw, instead of the customary rope.

112 Inviting all the 'little people' to a feast, Yetl waited until they were seated on mats and then shook the mats so that they all flew up into ordinary people's eyes, becoming their pupils.

113 He created the winds, putting the west wind in a house on a mountain peak and ordering it to hurt no one. Yetl created all the Indian peoples and the dog—who was at first a man until, seeing how quick he was, Yetl had

NW Coast copper mask of a killer-whale. British Museum. (*Photo: Photoresources.*)

second thoughts about him and changed him into an animal. He turned another man, who annoyed him, into the wild celery plant.

114 Yetl's biggest task was solving the problem of how to support the earth. Eventually, at low tide, he drained a pond of sea-water and, killing the beaver who lived in its depths, used one of its forelegs to prop up the earth, giving Hayicanke (Old-Woman-Under-the-Earth) responsibility for it. (Stories from the *Tlingit* Raven cycle.)

(ii) THE GREAT HARE OR RABBIT

115 The Great Hare or Rabbit is the chief figure in stories of the *Algonquian*-speaking tribes of the North American forests, to whom he is both demi-urge and culture-hero, as well as Trickster. He is given various names: Glooscap (*Micmac*); Manabush (*Menominee*); Manabozoho or Minabozho (*Chippewa*); Messou (*Montagnais*); Nanaboojoo or Nanibozho (*Potawatomi*).

116 Other important figures in the cycles are Hare's grandmother, the earth-goddess, called Nokomis by the *Menominee*, and his younger brother, who is also an animal—Lynx, Marten or Wolf. Stories about Hare and his brother (or brothers) often contain elements of the same myth as the *Iroquoian* tale of the rival twins Yoskeha and Taswiscana (**83–90**). In some stories the hero is not Hare but Rabbit. In others Rabbit is one of Hare's younger brothers. Longfellow incorporated many of the Hare stories into his poem about the legendary *Iroquoian* chief Hiawatha.

117 Nokomis's daughter bore twins but died in childbirth. One of the babies died too. Taking a wooden bowl (symbol of the heavens) Nokomis put it over the surviving twin to protect it. When she removed the bowl she saw the child was a little, white rabbit with long, trembling ears, Manabush.

118 Manabush was still young when he decided to steal fire to warm his grandmother and himself. Deaf to Nokomis's entreaties, he set off eastward in his canoe to the island where there lived the old man who owned fire. He arrived wet and cold outside the old man's wigwam. There he was noticed by the old man's two daughters who, taking pity on this poor little rabbit, picked him up, took him into the wigwam and put him near the fire to get dry. Manabush waited until they were busy and then, snatching a brand, hurried to his canoe. The old man and his daughters gave chase, but Manabush was too quick for them, paddling so fast that the glowing brand burst into flame as the air rushed past. Arriving safely home he gave it to his grandmother and Nokomis entrusted it to the Thunderers and their chief, Kineun, the Golden Eagle, who have guarded it ever since.

119 Manabush had a brother, Moqwaio, the Wolf. One day as he was walking across frozen water Moqwaio was dragged down under the ice by the malignant underworld spirits, the *anamaqkiu*. Four days Manabush mourned him. On the fifth he met his brother's shade and told him to go to the far west and build a big fire there, to guide the souls of the dead to their new home and to keep them warm.

120 Determined to avenge Moqwaio's murder, Manabush made war on the *anamaqkiu.* They were led by two great bear chiefs, whom Manabush tricked to their death. The *anamaqkiu* retaliated by raising a flood. Manabush climbed a huge pine tree growing on the summit of a mountain, but the waters still chased him. He made the tree grow to four times its normal height. Still the waters came on, reaching to his armpits; but then the Great Spirit intervened and arrested them.

121 The whole earth was covered with water. Manabush told the animals that he could create more land if he had so much as a speck of soil. First Otter, then Beaver, then Mink plunged down to look for some, but they all died in the attempt. At last Muskrat succeeded in bringing back a single grain of sand and with this Manabush recreated the earth.

122 In other versions of this flood story different creatures make the unsuccessful attempts to bring back some soil. In the *Montagnais* version the first attempt is made by Raven. All stories agree that it was Muskrat who succeeded.

123 In the *Potawatomi* Hare cycle Nanaboojoo is the eldest of four brothers born to a spirit father and earthly mother. The second brother is Chipiapoos, or Chibiabos, who is drowned by the evil, underworld spirits and becomes lord of the dead. The third is Wabasso. As soon as he saw light Wabasso fled far away to the north. There he became a white rabbit and is honoured as a great *manitou.* Nanaboojoo's fourth brother Chakekenapok (Flint) killed their mother (cf. **83**) and was slain by Nanaboojoo to avenge her. The fragments of his corpse were transformed into rocks, his intestines into vines and patches of flintstones mark the places where Nanaboojoo and he did battle.

124 Other stories in the various cycles tell of how Hare introduced the sacred rites and teachings of the medicine society, the *Midewewin*, and of his battles with various giants and other monsters. Perhaps his greatest feat, apart from recreating the earth, was his victory over the terrible water-

Birchbark pictorial record of a *Midewiwin* society seating-plan. *Ojibwa* Indians, Leech Lake, Minnesota. Field Museum of Natural History, Chicago. (*Photo: Werner Forman Archive.*)

monster who had been swallowing the people. In some versions of the myths this story is associated with the death of Hare's beloved brother, in others it forms a separate episode.

125 In the *Menominee* tales the fiend is a monstrous fish called Mashenomak or Misikinebik. Manabush allows himself to be swallowed by it and then, in company with all the victims who preceded him down its maw, holds a war dance in the monster's stomach, stabs its heart, and hacks his way out.

126 After his work was ended, Hare went away to the Village of Souls in the far west, where he now lives with his brother and grandmother, who had gone before him. Sometimes braves have journeyed there to visit him. One group of four, or, some say, seven, went and, after entertaining them, Hare offered each a wish. One man asked to be made a successful hunter, another a great warrior. The last of all wanted longevity, so Hare turned him into a stone—or, some say, a tree—so that he would remain for many generations to gaze upon.

127 A *Montagnais* story tells how Messou gave a warrior a little packetful of immortality, warning him he must never open it, but the man's inquisitive wife undid the packet and all the immortality flew away, which is why people now die. (Stories from *Algonquian* cycles of Hare myths.)

Death and the Spirit World
128–141

128 One story of death's origin is recorded in the preceding paragraph. In North American myths in general, death's inevitability is the consequence either of a deliberate choice made by a primal being, as in the *Eskimo* story (2), or arises accidentally as in **130**. Sometimes the primal being's choice is motivated by jealousy. We saw in **46** how Coyote determined that people should die, saying that otherwise the world would become overpopulated; but when his own son died, says a West Coast story, Coyote wanted an exception to be made for him! A similar choice based upon specious concern for mankind's happiness is recorded in the following story.

(i) SEDIT AND THE HUS BROTHERS
129 As a preliminary to creating man, Olelbis (The-One-Who-Sits-in-the-Sky) sent the two Hus (Buzzard) brothers to earth to build a stone ladder between it and Olelpanti (Heaven). The two Hus began work but were interrupted by Sedit (Coyote) who, professing wisdom, poured scorn upon Olelbis's plan. What would people have to do, he asked, but grow old, climb the ladder and come down young again? They would have no children or company since they would go up and come down alone. Their lives would be far happier if they could experience the joy of childbirth and the grief of death.

130 At length convinced, the two Hus dismantled the ladder, but the younger reminded Sedit that now he too would die and be buried in the ground, to rise no more.

131 Horrified, Sedit realised his mistake. 'What can I do?' he asked himself. Finally, in desperation he made himself a pair of wings from sunflowers (because they follow the course of the sun) and tried to fly up to Olelpanti; but the flowers withered and he crashed to earth and was killed.

132 Olelbis said Sedit had brought it upon himself and now all his people would similarly fall to the ground and die. (*Wintun* myth from the South West Coast).

(ii) A *PAWNEE* MYTH
133 Distracted with grief, a man whose wife and son had both died wandered over the prairie hoping to die himself. Scalped Men of his own tribe came upon him and begged Tirawa to have pity and allow the dead to return. Tirawa agreed on the condition that, during the four days that the dead and living were to camp side by side (as a kind of test), the bereaved father might not touch his dead son, though he could talk with him.

134 All the people of the tribe came together in their camp. Looking out over the prairie they saw a great cloud of dust moving quickly towards them and then the spirits of their dead passed before their camp.

135 When the bereaved man saw his son he could not contain his joy, but seizing and hugging the spirit to him, silently vowed he would never again let him go.

136 Everyone screamed. All the spirits vanished. So death continues.

(iii) A *KLICKITAT* MYTH
137 The following is typical of a number of stories about love between the dead partner of a marriage and the living survivor.

138 A young chief died and, as is customary, was buried on an island in the river; but, separated from his wife, his spirit could not rest. Nor could she forget him. One night he appeared to her in a vision and told her to come to him, so her father paddled her across to the island of the dead and left her there.

139 The woman was led to the spirits' dancing house and there found her husband, even more handsome than before; but when day dawned she woke up to find herself in a charnel-house clasped in the arms of a skeleton.

140 Screaming with horror she ran to her canoe and desperately paddled home. Her frightened people would not, however, allow her to stay but sent her back to the island.

141 Each night she enjoyed her husband's company and eventually bore a strikingly beautiful child. Its grandmother was sent for, but told she must on no account look at the baby until it was ten days old. However, the grandmother was so anxious to see the child that she disobeyed this injunction and peeped at the baby while it was asleep, and so the baby died and the spirits decided that dead souls should never again return to the living. (Myth of the South Western *Shahaptian Klickitat* people from lower Columbia.)

Ritual Myths
142–173

(i) *DELAWARE* MYTH OF THE ORIGIN OF THE CALUMET RITUAL (PEACEPIPE)

142 The peoples of the north decided to exterminate the *Delaware*, but while they were holding their war council a brilliant white bird appeared, hovering over the head of the chief's only daughter (cf. **176**). It commanded her to tell the warriors that the Great Spirit was both sad and angry that they were planning to drink the blood of his first-born the *Lenni-Lennapi*. If he was to be comforted they must wash their hands in the blood of a young fawn and then go in a body to the *Lenni-Lennapi* taking presents and the *Hobowakan* (peace-pipe). Having distributed their gifts, they should smoke the *Hobowakan* together, pledging eternal brotherhood.

143 In the *calumet* ceremony the pipe is lifted to the sky, the earth and the guardians of the four quarters, asking them to look kindly upon the supplicants and to confirm their pledges.

(ii) A *BLACKFOOT* MYTH OF THE BUFFALO DANCE

144 In hunting buffalo the Indians of the Plains lured them over a cliff and then slaughtered them on the rocks as they fell. A corral ensured that those who survived the fall uninjured did not escape.

145 Once, long ago, the hunters were unable to get the buffalo to the cliff's edge. Every time they tried, the animals turned away at the last moment. Soon the people were starving. A young woman noticing a herd grazing near the cliff's edge said, desperately, 'I will marry one of you if only you will jump!'

146 Immediately the herd leaped over the cliff and a huge bull, jumping the corral wall, came and claimed her as his bride.

147 When the rest of her people had finished butchering the wounded animals they missed the girl. Her father went to look for her, but the buffalo sensed his presence and summoning the other bulls attacked the man, trampling him to death.

148 The girl was distraught with grief. Her bull husband told her she was now experiencing the anguish his people felt when her relatives slaughtered his kinsfolk. Nonetheless he took pity on her, promising that both she and her father might return home if she could restore him to life.

149 Helped by a magpie, who after much searching, found a fragment of the trampled corpse, the girl charmed her father's body together and restored its life.

150 The buffalo people were astonished and their leader not only kept his word and allowed the girl and her father to go home but, before they went, taught them their dance and chant, so that in future the buffalo who were killed for food should also be restored to life, as the father had been.

151 The buffalo husband told them that the cult's sacred objects must be bulls' heads and buffalo-hide robes, which all the participating dancers should wear.

152 The purpose of restoring the buffalos' life was on the one hand to avoid the crime of slaying one's brothers and on the other to ensure the survival of the herds on whose meat the Indians were dependent.

(iii) THE *ZUÑI* MYTH OF THE CORN MAIDEN CEREMONY

153 This ceremony, one of the *Zuñis'* most sacred rites, is held every fourth August.

154 When the first people, the *ashiwi* (q.v.) came from the world below (cf. **29–46**), ten invisible Corn Maidens accompanied them for four years until, at Shipololo, the Place of Mist and Cloud, they were discovered by two witches who had been the last people to emerge from below. These presented the maidens with seeds of maize and squash.

155 The *ashiwi* continued their journey, but the Corn Maidens remained at Shipololo in a cedar bower roofed with clouds. Here they danced, each holding a beautiful *thlawe* (plumed underworld plant).

156 One day they were discovered by the twin gods Kowwituma and Watsusii, sons of the solar deity. The sun priest told the twins to bring the Corn Maidens to the people, which they did. So the Maidens came and danced before the people in a courtyard decorated with corn-meal paintings of clouds.

157 Gradually, as night came, everyone fell asleep; but still the Corn Maidens danced; then the flower and butterfly god Payatami came and saw them. He was enchanted by their loveliness, especially by the beauty of their leader, the Yellow Corn Maiden, but he frightened the dancers, who could read his thoughts, and when he too fell asleep, as day dawned, they fled home and were hidden under the wings of ducks in the Shipololo spring.

158 A great famine came and the people begged Kowwituma and Watsusii to find the Corn Maidens again. The *ashiwi* sat fasting in their *kiva* (temple) thinking only of the Corn Maidens and of rain.

159 The twin gods enlisted the help of Bitsitsi, their father's musician who, borne on the stars, descended to earth and telepathically conveyed the *ashiwi*'s prayers to the Corn Maidens, assuring them that if they did return to the people they would be treated honourably.

160 Led by Bitsitsi, the Maidens came again to the *ashiwi* and, each holding her *thlawe*, danced before the people from dawn till dusk to the music of Payatami's flutes and the singing of a choir.

161 Yellow Corn Maiden and Blue Corn Maiden, the older sisters, led the dance. First the Maidens on the north side of the courtyard passed west to join their sisters on the south and returned to their places; then those on the south side passed west to join their sisters on the north and returned to their places likewise. When the dance was ended the Corn Maidens went away and the *ashiwi* never saw them again.

Payatami—*Zuñi* gods of music, flowers and butterflies, *c.* 1900. Brooklyn Museum. (*Photo: Brooklyn Museum*.)

(iv) THE MYTH OF THE *NAVAJO HOZONI* CHANT

162 Although, in its images of the underground Snake People and their leader's marriage with the girl Glisma, this myth suggests a fertility rite, in fact, like all the other *Navajo* chants, whatever its original significance, its only known function is a medicinal one, being used by *shamans* in healing rituals.

163 Bear, Snake, Frog and Turtle went to an undersea village to capture two of its young women. Frog and Turtle were chosen for the kidnappers' rôles but were surprised in their attempt and had to kill the girls, whom they then scalped. The older one's hair was decorated with white shell jewellery, the younger one's with turquoise (cf. **53**).

164 Surviving the villagers' attempts first to roast them alive and then to drown them, Frog and Turtle rejoined Bear and Snake and all four set off for home.

165 En route they were met by eight men from their own village, who wanted the girls' scalps for themselves. Two of them suggested holding a shooting match and offered their daughters as the prize, thinking by this ruse to discover their relative strengths and who might be relied on as the most likely to wrest the jewelled scalps from their guardians. Bear and Snake protested that they were both far too old for such a match. Nonetheless, and much to all the others' chagrin, they not only won the shooting contest but also every one of the succeeding competitions that were suggested. No one, however, was willing to give Bear and Snake their prizes, so the whole company once more set off for home to hold a scalp dance.

166 Bear and Snake did not try to keep up with their younger companions, nor to join the dance. They made themselves a shelter outside the village and sat down to smoke. The delicious perfume of their tobacco, wafting into the village, enticed the two girls that were their rightful prizes to leave the dance and go to seek the perfume's source.

167 Bear and Snake now appeared in the guise of most handsome youths, Bear dressed in black, Snake in rainbow colours and both richly bejewelled. They agreed to let the girls taste their delicious tobacco. Bear gave his white shell pipe to the older girl, Snake his turquoise one to the younger. The fumes immediately anaesthetised them and when they woke next morning they found to their horror that the handsome youths of the previous night were now old men.

168 Glisma, the younger girl, tried to escape. She found the door guarded by snakes. Her fear seemed to excite them, but when she feigned calm indifference they allowed her to pass.

169 Knowing her relatives would kill her if they found her, Glisma waded downstream to hide her trail both from them and from Snake. Eventually, she came to the mountains near the Place of Emergence. As she circled them a lake appeared and Snake People approached her, asking where she had come from.

170 Glisma truthfully told them all that had happened and the Snake People rewarded her honesty by lifting up the lake like a lid and taking her down to their underworld home, assuring her that here she would be safe from Old Man Snake.

171 However in his youthful guise Snake reappeared at a feast and Glisma once more fell in love with him. He taught her all the words and painting rituals of the *Hozoni* chant and after two years, when she was beginning to feel homesick, told her she should now return home and teach the chant's rituals to her brother, so that he could become a healer.

172 Glisma was welcomed home, but her brother at first proved quite unable to memorise the *Hozoni* rituals in their proper sequence. She therefore marked each song as she repeated it with four maize kernels and left them overnight in the patterns in which she had set them. Next day they were collected and boiled and brought to her brother in a specially-made basket. The medicine was effective. Now he easily learned all the rituals.

173 Chanting, Glisma enacted rites with herbs, leaves and sand, making her brother into a great *shaman* and giving him the power to induct others into the sacred lore.

The Legend of Hiawatha (Haiohwatha) 174–178

174 Hiawatha or, more properly, Haiohwatha, was an *Iroquoian* leader who lived in the late sixteenth century. The stories in Longfellow's poem *Hiawatha* do not relate to this hero but derive from *Algonquian* myths (see 115–127).

175 The *Iroquoian* hero planned a peaceful union between all the various *Iroquoian* and *Algonquian* tribes, who had long been engaged in internecine warfare. His aim was not fully realised but he did succeed in uniting the *Iroquois* into a federation.

176 Hiawatha's plans were bitterly opposed by the great warrior and *shaman* Atotarho, whose head was covered with tangled serpents and whose anger so fierce that anyone who crossed his gaze fell dead. It is said that during one tribal council, Atotarho called down a huge white bird, which fell upon Hiawatha's only daughter and killed her.

177 After this terrible blow Hiawatha left home in a magic white canoe and travelled to the settlements of the *Oneida*, who chief, Dekanawida, became his great friend and ally. Together they converted both the *Mohawk* and *Cayuga* to Hiawatha's plan and then at last succeeded in persuading Atotarho to join them. So the great *Iroquoian* confederacy was formed and Dekanawida became its law-giver.

178 His work now done, Hiawatha stepped into his magic canoe and sailed away across the lake to the land of the souls, in the far west.

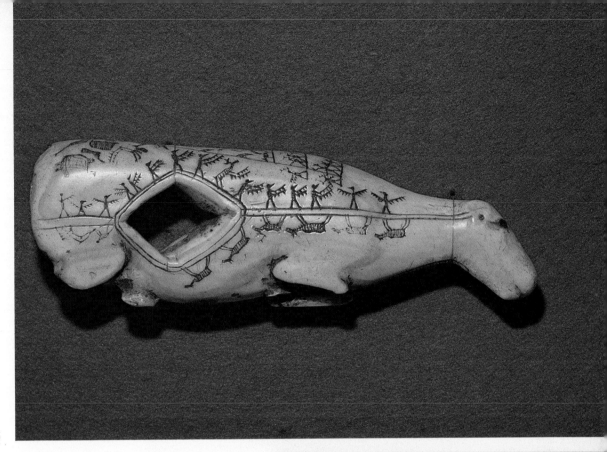

Alaskan Eskimo arrowshaft straightener engraved with *shamans* and hunters' prey. British Museum. (*Photo: Photoresources.*)

The head of a *Bella Bella* clan totem pole from the North West Coast of America. Horniman Museum. (*Photo: Photoresources.*)

Nineteenth-century *Crow* 'medicine-shield' of painted buffalo hide with crane and eagle-feathers attached to it. The picture was 'given' to the shield's owner in a shamanistic vision and it, rather than the shield itself, was believed to afford him protection. Field Museum, Chicago. (*Photo: Werner Forman Archive.*)

Hopi Indian carved and painted cottonwood *katsina* figures of the lightning and corn spirits. British Museum. (*Photo: Photoresources.*)

THE CARIBBEAN ISLANDS

Taïno Myths
179–184

THE FIRST PEOPLE AND THE HERO GUAGUGIANA

179 The first people came from two caves named Cacibagiagua and Amaiauva. Originally these had been guarded by a night-watchman called Marocael, but on one occasion he lingered outside after dawn and was caught by the sun's rays, which petrified him.

180 One of the other cave dwellers was named Guagugiana (or Vagoniona). He sent his servant Giadruvava out to look for a medicinal herb, but the sun also caught Giadruvava and turned him into a bird with a most beautiful song. On every anniversary of his capture he fills the night with his plaintive music, imploring his master to come to his rescue.

181 Grieved at Giadruvava's loss, Guagugiana decided to leave the cave himself. He summoned all the women among the First People to abandon their husbands and families and go with him, promising them untold riches.

182 The women complied, abandoning all but their infants-in-arms. Guagugiana led them to the island of Matenino and there left them, taking their children away with him.

183 According to some versions of the story, which survives only in fragmentary form, Guagugiana abandoned the children beside a stream or on the seashore, where their pleas to the earth for milk led to their being changed into the dwarf-like *tona*, or according to another version, into frogs.

184 On another journey Guagugiana met the sea-goddess Guabonito, who lived among the shells in the depths of the ocean. She taught him medicinal lore and the art of making sacred necklaces from *cibas* (white shells) and *guianos* (yellow shells).

Carib Myths and Legends
185–186

THE FIRST PEOPLE

185 At first the earth was very soft, but the rays of the sun gradually hardened it. The first man, named Louquo, came down from the sky and, after living on the earth for some time and producing many children, he returned to his sky home. When his descendants die they too ascend to the heavens, and there become stars.

THE LEGEND OF KALINAGO

186 Becoming tired of life among the *Galibi* (mainland *Caribs*), Kalinago set sail to find new lands and eventually came to Santo Domingo, where he settled and had many sons. They grew jealous of him and poisoned him. His soul entered into a terrifying fish, Atraioman, and his murderers, fleeing his wrath, were dispersed far and wide among the islands, where they slaughtered all the men, beheading the corpses and setting the severed heads up in caves, so that their own sons might recognise and honour their martial valour.

CENTRAL AMERICA

Myths of the Maya Peoples
187–231

CREATION MYTHS

(i) *Maya* Myth from Ancient Yucatán
187 Long ago in the eleven *ahau*, Ahmucencab (?night) covered the faces of Oxlahuntiku (Thirteen-gods) who was captured by Bolontiku (Nine-gods). Fire, salt, stones and trees were brought down to earth and Oxlahuntiku was knocked about and carried away. His serpent was taken from him and so was his *tizné* (black paint or soot). The first Bolon Dzacab (Guardian of the World) covered the earth with a thick layer of seeds and then went away to the thirteenth (highest) heaven.

188 After the serpent had been taken away, a great flood came and heaven collapsed onto the earth, destroyed by Cantultiku, the four Bacab (q.v.).

189 When the chaos ended, Cantultiku set Kanxibyúi on earth to reorganise it. Differently coloured trees were planted at each of the world's cardinal points and the heavens were propped up, and so the new world was completed.

190 Ahu-uc-cheknale (He-Who-Makes-Fruitful-Seven-Times) said the world had come from earth's seven bosoms. He descended from the heavens' centre to fructify Itzamkabain, the alligator-footed whale, and the four lights and four regions of the stars revolved as he came and lights, sun and moon awoke and so the world began.
(From the *Book of Chilam Balam of Chumayel*, Yucatán.)

(ii) A Creation Myth of The Quiché Maya, Guatemala
191 In the beginning the sky and sea lay tranquil in the silent dark. The creator Tepeu and the maker Gucumatz (Plumed Serpent), wrapped in green and azure, consulted with Hurakan, the Heart of the Sky, whose signs are the (sheet) lightning, the lightning flash and the thunderbolt, and they decided that the sea's waters should withdraw and earth appear, so that they might create men to glorify and honour them.

192 The waters withdrew and earth formed like a cloud and the mountains rose up like great lobsters, covered with cypress and pine trees. Gucumatz was elated.

193 Then he and Tepeu created animals and gave them their homes; but the creator and maker realised that these creatures fell short of perfection, for they had no language with which to glorify the gods; so they made men from damp soil. However these proved unsatisfactory too. Blind and lame, they were helpless and, although they could speak, lacked intelligence, and so were washed away.

194 Tepeu and Gucumatz consulted with Twice Grandmother and Twice Grandfather, Xpiyacoc and Xmucané, with Hurakan and with the sun. They divined with maize kernels and the red berries of the *tzité* plant and decided to carve some men from wood. However these lacked both intelligence and grace and did not honour their creators, of whom they remembered nothing, so the gods sent a heavy rain against them and four great birds to attack them. The birds were named Xecotcovach, Camalotz, Cotzbalam and Tecumbalam and each attacked a different part of the wooden peoples' bodies. All their animals and fowls, even their household utensils, turned against them, for they had been cruel masters. When they tried to shelter in trees, the trees drew away from them; when they tried to hide in caves, the caves closed themselves against them. So all the wooden people and their descendants were destroyed, except for the monkeys.

195 It seems that in the next age earth was peopled by the giant Vukub Cakix and his sons. They were conquered by the twin heroes Hunahpu and Xbalanqué (**225–231**).

196 Then, again, the gods came together to consider how the earth might be suitably peopled, and they learned that in the Place of the Division of Waters there grew white and yellow maize. These, they decided, were the materials they needed. The maize was ground and strengthened with nine broths brewed by Xmucané and so were formed the four brothers Balam Quitzé (Smiling Jaguar), Balam Agab (Night Jaguar), Mahucutah (Renowned Name) and Iqi Balam (Moon Jaguar).

197 The gods however found that this time they had done their work too well, for the brothers were so intelligent they seemed likely to rival their creators. Hurakan therefore breathed a cloud over the men's eyes, obscuring their sight of distant things and reducing their understanding to mortal dimensions. The brothers were then sent to sleep and four women brought to them to be their wives.

198 The people lived happily and peaceably together. They all spoke the same language and prayed to the same gods, those who had created them, asking for children and for light, because as yet there was no sun.

199 Time passed, but still no sun appeared and the people grew anxious, so the four brothers left their home in Tollan and went to Tulai Zuiva, the Place of Seven Caves and Seven Ravines. There they were each given a deity to preside over their clans. Balam Quitzé received Tohil; Balam Agab, Avilix; Mahucutah, Hacavitz; and Iqi Balam, Nicahtagah.

200 Tohil gave them fire and when rain extinguished his gift he rekindled it by striking his shoes together. Men of other tribes came shivering to beg for some of the fire, but they were not welcomed. Tohil demanded that in return for some of his gift they should embrace him 'under the armpit and under the girdle' (i.e. offer him human sacrifices).

201 Although the people were now warmer, they still lived in darkness, for still the sun did not appear, even though they prayed and fasted and watched unceasingly for his herald the Morning Star. At last, they decided they must resume their travels, otherwise they would never witness his birth.

202 Journeying through many lands they came at last to Hacavitz's mountain. There they burned incense and there they saw Morning Star rise and the birth of the sun. Animals and birds greeted him with joy and all the people prostrated themselves before him. As the sun grew strong he dried the damp earth and his rays, touching the old animal gods: lion, tiger and viper and the gods Tohil, Avilix and Hacavitz, turned them all to stone (cf. **179**).

203 Though the four brothers had succeeded in their quest and now lived in the light of the sun, moon and stars, they mourned their fellows, left behind in Tollan, who did not share their good fortune, and at length, foreseeing their end was near, the brothers took leave of their wives and children, saying that, now their work was completed, they would return home. So they vanished, leaving only the sacred bundle that must never be opened, the bundle called 'Majesty Enveloped'. (From the Guatemalan *Popul Vuh*.)

(iii) A Creation Story Of The Modern *Maya* Peoples, Yucatán
204 In the first time lived the dwarf *Saiyamkoob* (Adjusters), who built the cities that now lay in ruins. Food was brought down to them via a living rope that stretched from earth to heaven; but then the rope was cut, blood flowed from it and earth and sky were separated. All was yet dark, but when the sun appeared its rays turned the *Saiyamkoob* to stone. Their figures can still be found among their ruined cities.

205 A flood ended the first era; another destroyed that of the second people, the *Tsolb* (Offenders). Next came the age of the *Maya's* dominance; but their power too was destroyed by floods and so came the fourth age of the present, inhabited by a mixture of peoples.

206 Influences of the ancient Mexican concepts are clearly evident in this modern story of the world's successive eras, each destroyed by floods, while the image of the earth as child of the sky is graphically suggested by the 'umbilical cord' which originally joined them.

HUNAHPU AND XBALANQUÉ
(i) The Twins' Conception and Birth
207 Xpiyacoc and Xmucané had two sons, Hunhun Ahpu and Vukub Ahpu, the first of whom fathered the flute players Hunbatz and Hunchouen, who were skilled in every art.

208 Hunhun Ahpu and his brother were devoted players of the ball game, *tlachtli*, and willingly accepted a challenge by the lords of Xibalba (the underworld). Travelling down to that land they came eventually to a four crossways and were tricked by its guardian into choosing the black road. All

they found at its end were enthroned statues. Next they were tricked into sitting on red-hot stone thrones and finally, given torches, were taken to the Xibalban House of Gloom, with strict orders that they must not let the lights go out. Of course the torches quickly burned down and next day Hunhun Ahpu and Vukub Ahpu had to admit their failure. They were condemned to death.

209 Hunhun Ahpu's severed head was hung in the branches of a tree of gourds, which became taboo to the Xibalban people. However one girl named Xquiq dared to approach it, wondering aloud if picking one of its fruit would really prove fatal. Hunhun Ahpu's head asked her if she really wanted to pick fruit which were but death's heads. When she persisted he told her to stretch her hand out to him. Gathering all his strength he spat into it, impregnating her. He advised her to flee to the upper world to escape her own people's anger and when the Xibalbans tried to kill her Xquiq took his advice.

210 After successfully passing a test of maize picking she was accepted by Xpiyacoc as her daughter-in-law. Soon afterwards Xquiq gave birth to the twins Hunahpu and Xbalanqué.

Detail of a late ninth-century relief from the southern ball-court at El Tajín, Mexico, showing the sacrifice of a ball-player. (*Photo: Werner Forman Archive.*)

165

(ii) Their Early Adventures

211 From the very first Hunahpu and Xbalanqué were the most skilful magicians and when their jealous older brothers Hunbatz and Hunchouen plotted to kill them they transformed the pair into ridiculous monkeys.

212 Next the twins set magic tools to work to clear a patch of forest and make a field, but every night animals restored it to its former state. Keeping watch at night, Hunahpu and Xbalanqué saw animals and birds summon the felled trees to rise again and tried to trap the creatures. At first all they managed to catch were the tails of the deer and rabbit (which is why these are so short). Later they managed to trap a rat which, in exchange for its life, showed them where their grandmother had hidden their father's *tlachtli* equipment. Soon they too were enthusiasts of the game.

(iii) The Twins' Conquest of Xibalba

213 Feeling the earth tremble as Hunahpu and Xbalanqué played *tlachtli*, the lords of Xibalba, wondering who these new champions could be, sent their owl messengers up to challenge them. The twins accepted, but before setting off for Xibalba each planted a reed in their grandmother's house, saying that if any harm came to either his reed would wither and die.

214 Passing down into the underworld, Hunahpu and Xbalanqué crossed a deep ravine, a boiling river, a river of blood and then, beyond a fourth river came to the four crossways, where red, black, white and yellow roads met.

215 Like their father and uncle before them they followed the black road, but cautiously sent an animal named Xan ahead with orders to prick the leg of everyone he met. The two enthroned statues made no response, but each of the Xibalban lords exclaimed as they felt the prick and the others enquired the reason. In this way the twins learned every one of the lords' names and to their annoyed astonishment were able to address each in turn by his title: Hun Came, Vukub Came, Xiqiripat, Ahlalpuh, Cuchumaqiq, Chamiabak, Ahalcana, Chamiaholom, Patan, Quiqxil, Quiqrixgag and Quiqre.

216 Politely the twins refused to sit on the proffered stone thrones which had burned their father and uncle. When sent to the House of Gloom they preserved their torches by substituting red painted flames for the fire.

217 In the opening match of the ball game next day Hunahpu and Xbalanqué defeated the Xibalban lords, who, ever more incensed, now despatched them to the demonic House of Lances for the night with orders to bring them four vases of flowers next day. By promising to give them the flesh of all animals the brothers tamed the fiends and meanwhile persuaded ants to gather the flowers from the gardens of the underworld's rulers, Hun Came and Vukub Came.

218 Further trials followed. The twins survived the ordeals of the House of Cold by lighting pine knots, distracted the jaguars of the House of Tigers by throwing them bones and passed unscathed through the House of Fire. In the House of Bats however Hunahpu injudiciously raised his head from the ground and was immediately decapitated by the terrible bat-lord Camazotz.

219 Xbalanqué summoned all the animals to help him and the turtle which touched Hunahpu's bleeding trunk was immediately stuck to it. With the other animals' help Xbalanqué transformed it into a likeness of Hunahpu's head.

220 In this guise the brothers returned for the final ball game of their match, which they won with the help of a rabbit who, by distracting the Xibalbans' attention, gave Xbalanqué time to retrieve and restore his brother's head, which their opponents had hung up in the ball court for scorn.

221 Knowing that they would now be condemned to death the twins conferred with two magicians Xulu and Bacam and arranged to be resurrected; then they willingly mounted their funeral pyre. Their powdered bones were scattered on the underworld's sea and five days later the twins reappeared as poor fishermen. In this disguise they astonished the Xibalbans by their wonder-working powers, burning houses and immediately restoring them, even burning and restoring each other.

222 Soon they were summoned before the lords Hun Came and Vukub Came and obediently went through their marvellous repertoire. At length, on the

Zapotec clay mask of the bat-god known to the *Maya* as Camátoz. Note the feline features, relating the god to the deadly jaguar-god. Royal Scottish Museum, Edinburgh. (*Photo: Photoresources.*)

lords' insistence, having immolated and restored the rulers' dog, they agreed to burn the lords themselves, but of course did not restore their lives.

223 The other Xibalban princes fled in terror but all except one met the same fate, while their subjects were condemned to become potters living on the flesh of wild animals and sharing only bees with the civilised people of the upper world.

224 Taking the heads of their father and uncle the twins honoured them and placed them in the sky as the sun and moon.

(iv) The Defeat Of The Giants

225 In the days of the flood that destroyed the wooden men (194–195) lived Vukub Cakix (Seven Macaws), first of the giants, who boasted he was the sun of the world, while his offspring Zipacna (Mountain-maker) and Cabrakan (Earthquake) were equally arrogant, Zipacna claiming to move the earth, Cabrakan to overturn it and shake the sky. They were indeed very strong and could move mountains.

226 Vukub Cakix lived off the fruit of a tree he owned and, determined to destroy him, Hunahpu and Xbalanqué hid among its branches. When Vukub Cakix came to gather fruit they shot and wounded him in the cheek with a poisoned arrow, causing him intense pain. The heroes managed to escape, though he tore off Hunahpu's arm.

227 Posing as doctors, the twins now went to the giant's home offering to cure his pain, which they diagnosed as toothache, saying that if his bad teeth were drawn it would cease. Vukub Cakix protested that it was by virtue of his beautiful emerald teeth and silver eyes that he was king. He could not lose them. However, the heroes promised to substitute new teeth for the old and so had their way. They took out all the giant's emerald teeth, replacing them with ones of maize. They flayed the splendour from his silver eyes and, losing all his glory, Vukub Cakix faded and died.

228 Hunahpu recovered his arm which the giant's wife Chimalamat had been roasting on a spit and the heroes departed.

229 With the help of four hundred youths (cf. **255**) they next caught Vukub Cakix's son Zipacna in a pit-trap and hurled great trees down onto him. Believing him dead, they then built a house and celebrated their success, but at dead of night Zipacna rose up and tossed them, house and all, high into the sky, from which the youths fell and were buried until Hunahpu and Xbalanqué later rescued them and transformed them into stars.

230 The twins tried again to catch Zipacna, this time modelling a huge false crab which they placed in a deep ravine. Zipacna, who was inordinately fond of crab meat, was easily tricked into jumping down after it. The twins heaved mountains on top of him, trapping him there. So fierce were his struggles to escape that they then had to turn him to stone.

231 The third giant, Cabrakan, was tricked into eating poisoned roast fowl. So all three monsters met their end. (Stories from the *Popul Vuh*.)

The Aztec Empire
232–297

SUN MYTHS

(i) The Five Suns

232 Accounts vary as to whether two, three or four eras preceded that of the *Aztecs*, but it seems that four was the generally-accepted number. The most detailed version of this story is found in the *Historia de los Mexicanos por sus Pinturas*.

233 In the ninth (highest) heaven lived Tonacatecuhtli and his consort Tonacacíuhatl (Lord and Lady Nourishment). They had four sons, who seem originally to have been nature deities and gods of the four quarters, but later identified with gods of the empire's different peoples. The four were the red Camaxtli, chief god of the *Tlaxcala*; black Tezcatlipoca (q.v.), Smoking-Mirror, god of night and war-god of the great city of Tetzcoco; Quetzalcóatl, Green-Feathered-Serpent, wind-god and chief deity of the *Toltecs*; and the *Aztec* Huitzilopochtli.

Aztec greenstone 'mask' of Tezcatlipoca, 1507 A.D. Over one ear is a smoke-wreathed mirror, the god's symbol. Dumbarton Oaks Research Library and Collections, Washington. (*Photo: Dumbarton Oaks Research Library and Collections.*)

234 After resting for six hundred years, these deities created fire, a half-sun, a calendar and the man and woman Oxomoco and Cipactonal. They also made Mictlantecuhtli and Mictlantecuhtl, rulers of Mictlan the underworld, formed the twelve lower heavens, the sea, the water god Tlaloctecuhtli and his wife Chalchiuhtlicue and the sea monster Cipactli, from whom they formed the earth, Cemanahuac.

235 Seeing that half a sun gave but feeble light, the gods now completed it and Tezcatlipoca became Sun-Bearer and ruler of the First Sun era, whose giant inhabitants lived brutishly on acorns.

236 After 676 years Quetzalcóatl struck down Tezcatlipoca, who was transformed into a jaguar and ate all the giants. As Ursa Major he is seen in the night sky, still falling towards the waters into which Quetzalcóatl threw him.

Figure of Mictlantecuhtli, the Lord of Death. Museo de Antropologia de la Universidad Veracruzana, Jalapa. (*Photo: Werner Forman Archive.*)

Aztec stone head of the goddess Chalchiuhtlicue. British Museum. (*Photo: British Museum.*)

237 Quetzalcóatl recreated man and his era, that of the Second Sun, lasted another 676 years until Quetzalcóatl was struck down by Tláloc (q.v.) and a great wind and storm blew away almost all the people, transforming the remainder into monkeys.

238 After 364 years, the era of the Third Sun was ended by a rain of fire which only a few people managed to survive, in the form of birds.

239 Chalchiuhtlicue ruled the era of the Fourth Sun, during which maize was first introduced. This Sun ended after 312 years with a great flood, the surviving people being transformed into fish.

240 The gods then created four men, who helped Tezcatlipoca and Quetzalcóatl to lift up the heavens to their present position. The two deities then became rulers of the skies.

241 During all this time the first man, Piltzintechulti, son of Oxomoco and Cipactonal had survived, as had his wife, who had been born from a hair of the goddess Xochiquetzal. A son was now born to this pair and the gods created other people too, but as yet, apart from that afforded by their fires, these people had no light.

242 Quetzalcóatl therefore threw his own son, born of the goddess Chalchiuhtlicue, into a fire and he came forth as the Fifth Sun. Tlàloc threw his son into the fire's cinders and he emerged as the moon (a lesser light because the fire was now cooler).

243 The gods said the sun of this age should be fed with hearts and blood and so instituted war to provide sacrifices for him.

244 A variant story from the *Annals of Quauhititlan* says the first era, that of Atonatiuh, ended with the flood and transformation of people into fish. The age of the second, Jaguar Sun, Ocelotanatiuh, was the time of giants; then came the era of the Rain Sun, Quiyauhtonatiuh, ending in a volcanic deluge of fire and red-hot stones, which only a single pair of human beings survived. The age of the Fourth Sun, Ecantonatiuh, was destroyed by wind, while our own will end with earthquakes, famine, war and confusion.

245 Other extant versions, such as Camago's account of the *Tlascaltec* myth, make the present era the third of four. It seems that some of the confusion of the texts results from the absorption of *Toltec* stories about their supreme god, Quetzalcóatl, into others of later date.

(ii) The Birth Of The Sun and Its Rituals

246 One account of the origin of the sun sacrifices is given above. The following story, including details such as the hero's journey to the House of the Sun, seems to be based on very ancient material, for this theme of the journey and the concept of 'holy bundles' is a characteristic of primitive American Indian myths.

247 As the sun had not been shining for a long time the gods came together at Teotihuacán. They built a great fire and declared that the first of their servants to immolate himself should be honoured by becoming the sun.

248 The sacrifice took place and the gods waited, betting on the quarter at which Sun would appear. They guessed wrong and when he did emerge he remained stationary. Tlotli (Hawk) went to ask him to proceed on his way; but he refused to until they were all sacrificed. Citli (Hare) was so angry that he shot Sun but Sun threw the arrow back, wounding Citli in the forehead.

249 Recognising that Sun was indeed their superior, the gods now agreed to be sacrificed. Each took a green jewel, wrapped it in his clothes, like the heart in the body, and gave it to his followers; then Xólotl sacrificed each in turn, tearing out their hearts. Finally, he sacrificed himself.

250 One of the sacrificed gods was Tezcatlipoca, but soon after the rituals he appeared to one of his grieving devotees, Quetzalcóatl, and commanded him to go to the Sun's house and fetch musicians to make a feast for him.

251 Singing, Quetzalcóatl set out. Sun warned his people not to listen to this intruder, but some of them disobeyed and, captivated by his music, followed Quetzalcóatl back to earth, bringing with them the musical rites of the god.

252 This last section of the story would appear to be later than the rest, since Quetzalcóatl is represented as Tezcatlipoca's subordinate.

GODS OF THE *AZTEC* EMPIRE

253 The *Aztecs* had a very complex pantheon, as the deities of subject peoples became subordinate to those of the *Aztecs* themselves and in some

cases seem to have been assimilated to them. Thus, rather as in ancient Egypt, the great gods have many aspects and appear under various names. A number of them who were clearly of great ritual importance, such as Tláloc, Xipe Totec and Chalchiuhtlicue, play little part in such narratives as are known. For details of these and other important *Aztec* deities the reader is therefore referred to Part 3. Below are outline narratives of the great gods Huitzilopochtli, Xólotl, Quetzalcóatl and Tezcatlipoca.

(i) Huitzilopochtli

254 The Hummingbird-of-the-Left (i.e. the south) seems originally to have been the tribal god of the conquering *Aztecs*. With their rise to power he was given the rôles of both creator and war-god. The myth of his birth shows him as the all-conquering sun, driving moon and stars from the sky.

255 Coatlicue (She-of-the-Serpent-Woven-Skirt), the earth-goddess, lived on Coatepec (Serpent Mt.) with her daughter the moon-goddess Coyolxauhqui (She-Whose-Face-is-Painted-with-Bells), and her star-god sons the Centzonuitznaua (Four Hundred Southerners).

256 One day as she was doing penance on Coatepec a ball of feathers dropped onto Coatlicue, who placed it in her bosom, and so became pregnant. At Coyolxauhqui's instigation, the Centzonuitznaua planned to kill their disgraced mother; but as they came to do so, Huitzilopochtli sprang from the womb, armed with a blue shield and spear. His left leg was adorned with hummingbird feathers, his head with plumes. With a single blow of his serpent-torch, *Xiuhcoatl*, he killed Coyolxauhqui and, pursuing the Centzonuitznaua killed almost all of them too, except for the small remnant who managed to escape south to Huitzlampa, the Place of Thorns.

(ii) Xólotl

257 The god of twins and all the other deformed people (twins themselves were regarded as aberrations), who were sacrificed to the sun at the time of eclipses, Xólotl (Dog) is the sun's companion. This concept lay behind the practice of sacrificing a dog in the *Aztec* graves, for, just as Xólotl accompanied the sun, so the dog accompanied the soul of its master through the underworld, Mictlan, and carried it over Mictlan's nine rivers, the Chicunauhapan, to its final resting-place in Chicunauhmictlan.

258 As a solar deity Xólotl also governed the *Aztec* ball-game *tlachtli*, which, it is said, he himself played on a magical court (i.e. in the skies).

259 In many ways this deity resembles the Trickster of North American Indian myth and fable and seems to be a very ancient god, probably originating as the totemic ancestor of the *Chichimec* peoples (the Race of Dogs) who, according to one story, descended from the two survivors of the flood, a man and a bitch. The *Chichimec* war leader was Xólotl.

260 We have already seen Xólotl acting as the priest in the ancient ritual myth of the sun sacrifice (**249**). A variant of this story says that in the beginning, all being dark, two gods immolated themselves and were transformed into the sun and moon, but these remained motionless in the sky. The other deities therefore decided to sacrifice themselves to vivify the sun and moon. Xólotl refused and fled, transforming himself first into the twin-stalked (i.e. deformed) maize *xólotl*; then into a maguey plant, *mexolotl*; then into the lava *axolotl*, before eventually being caught and sacrificed. The sun and moon then began to move across the skies. In another myth Xólotl is the creator of man.

261 The earthly demi-gods, who had sprung from a stone knife born to the heavenly goddess Citalicue, asked their mother to let them create people to be their servants. She told them to ask Mictlantecuhtli to give them a bone or some ashes of the dead.

262 Xólotl went down to Mictlan and secured a bone but, in feeling with it, stumbled, dropped and broke it. Gathering up its fragments he brought them to earth, put them in a bowl and sprinkled them with gods' blood. On the fourth day a man emerged, on the eighth a woman, the first people.

263 This story, in what seems to be a later version, is also told of Quetzalcóatl.

(iii) Quetzalcóatl and Tezcatlipoca

264 In many of the known myths, Quetzalcóatl, the *Aztec* wind-god, is the adversary of the great Tezcatlipoca, Smoking-Mirror (q.v.). It seems that this enmity may possibly reflect struggles for supremacy among the various *Nahuatlan* tribes, Tezcatlipoca being the war-god of the great city of Tezcoco, which until the very end of the *Aztec* empire was one of its most powerful allies, while Quetzalcóatl was the principal god of the earlier Toltec civilization.

265 The plumed-serpent symbol is found among many American Indian peoples, from the *Hopi* and *Zuñi* to the north, as far south as the Andes, and

probably denotes that Quetzalcóatl was originally conceived of as a fertility-god of the rain clouds, for *quetzal* feathers symbolised the spring vegetation, while the serpent is both fertility and lightning symbol among peoples from all parts of the Americas south of the Arctic.

266 It is said that Quetzalcóatl was originally white-skinned—hence one of the reasons why the *Aztecs* were so ready to greet the Spanish Cortés as the returning Quetzalcóatl. However, the god is usually shown with a dark body, possibly symbolising rain clouds, though according to one myth he and Tezcatlipoca played a ball game against each other and the victor, Tezcatlipoca, expelled his vanquished rival to the east, where the sun burned him.

267 This story in which, as always in ancient Meso-American myths, the ball-game images the journey of the sun, is also a version of the legendary tale of Quetzalcóatl's expulsion from Tollan, which was, it is said, masterminded by Tezcatlipoca. Here myth and legendary history intertwine.

268 It is said that in the beginning the *Toltecs* came from the north led by the great god Mixcóatl (q.v.), Cloud-Serpent, and conquered large parts of central Mexico, where they built a great city. Mixcóatl married Chimalman (Prostrate-Shield) and their son was Our-Lord-One-Reed, Ce Actl Topiltzin.

Aztec relief from Tenoctlitlán shows the feathered serpent, with whom Quetzalcóatl is identified, between two year-symbols. (*Photo: Werner Forman Archive.*)

175

269 After his father's murder Ce Actl Topiltzin fled temporarily into exile, but then returned and killed his father's regicide and himself became the high priest of the city's god, Quetzalcóatl, whose name he adopted.

270 Under his inspired leadership a new city was built at Tollan. Some of its houses were of the most beautiful green stones, others of silver, yet others of shells, both white and coloured, of turquoise and of exquisite feathers. Everything prospered. Harvests were so abundant that small maize cobs were not used for food, but as fuel. Various shades of cocoa and cotton grew naturally, the cotton in red, yellow, blue, green, brown and orange, as well as white. Quetzalcóatl introduced writing and the calendar too.

271 Only snakes, birds and butterflies were sacrificed on the altars of this city, for Quetzalcóatl resolutely refused to sacrifice people, though evil fiends continually pestered him to do so. Eventually, at these fiends' instigation, a plot was hatched against him by the magicians Huitzilopochtli (**254–256**), Titlacuhan (a title of Tezcatlipoca), and their brother Tlacahuepan.

272 Disguised as a doctor Titlacuhan went to Quetzalcóatl, who had grown very depressed as a result of the fiends' torments, and offered to cure him. He tricked Quetzalcóatl into drinking wine and so breaking his priestly vow. One story says that while Quetzalcóatl was drunk he was also seduced and so lost his chastity too.

273 According to some versions he was banished from Tollan. According to others he decided to leave. Burning all the beautiful houses he had had built and burying all his treasure, he set out with his servants for his former home, Tlillan Tlapallan (Yucatán), promising to return to Tollan in the year 1519 (the date of the *conquistadores'* arrival).

274 On his journey eastward all his companions died of the cold; but at last, after many adventures, he himself reached the coast and set off on his serpent raft to Tlillan Tlapallan.

275 Although some stories identify the fall of Tollan with Quetzalcóatl's departure, according to others it survived for a further two hundred years, its last secular ruler being Huemac, whose disgrace and fall were also engineered by Tezcatlipoca, this time in the guise of a naked Indian who came hawking green peppers in the market place before Huemac's palace.

276 There he, designedly, caught the eye of Huemac's beautiful daughter who, never before having seen a naked man, became ill with desire for the Indian, whose name was Toueyo.

277 Huemac summoned Toueyo and said having made the princess ill he must also cure her. So Huemac married his daughter to this foreigner of the lowest class, making this Toueyo a prince of Tollan.

278 Catastrophe followed. The city was stricken first by drought and then by famine, for not only did all the rivers and wells dry up, but the granaries were invaded by vermin who devoured the corn. Tollan fell to its enemies.

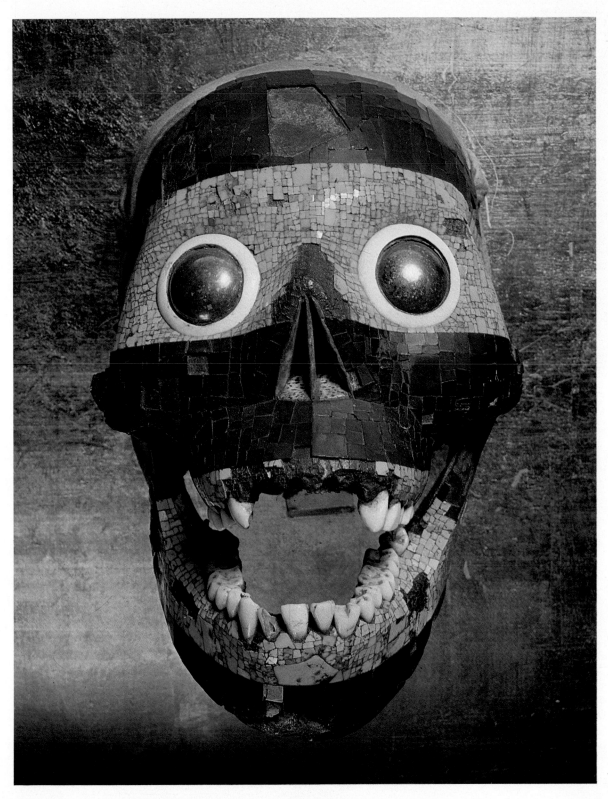

Aztec mask made from bands of lignum and turquoise laid on the front of a human skull. It possibly represents the god Tezcatlipoca. British Museum. (*Photo: Michael Holford*.)

Hammered gold plaque from Chimor engraved with fertility deities and staple foods – maize, yucca and sweet potato. Coll-Mujica Gallo, Lima. (*Photo: Michael Holford.*)

Leaves from the *Mayan Codex Tro-Cortesianus* (*Madrid Codex*) showing various deities performing agricultural rites. British Museum. (*Photo: Michael Holford.*)

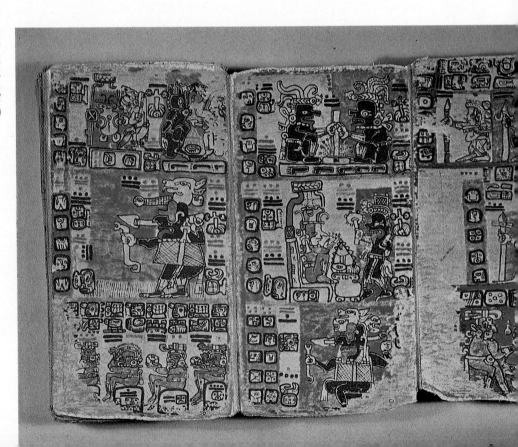

279 A variant story says that Tezcatlipoca-Toueyo led the Tollanese to victory against a neighbouring people and then by his magic intoxicated them at the victory celebrations, inducing them to dance over the edges of ravines and bridges and so fall to their deaths.

280 Accompanied by Tlacahuepan he came into the market place with Huitzilopochtli dancing on his head, drawing such a crowd that many were crushed to death. The remainder turned upon Tezcatlipoca and Huitzilopochtli and killed them. At Tlacahuepan's suggestion ropes were tied to the corpses to drag them into the ravine, but everyone who touched the ropes fell dead. So, its population decimated by these and similar magical devices, Tollan was easily overcome by its enemies.

AZTEC LEGENDS

(i) The Journey from Aztlan

281 The story of Quetzalcóatl's downfall seems to be, at least in part, legendary. The *Aztecs* themselves preserved many legends of their arrival in Mexico. One version says that, leaving their first home, Aztlan, which was an island, they came to Panotlan (Place-of-Arrival-by-Sea) and travelled to Tamoanchan where all but four of their *amoxaoque* (wise men) left them. The four who remained, Cipactonal, Oxomoco, Tlaltecuin and Xochicahuaca, invented the calendar so that the people might have a means of organising their lives.

282 From Tamoanchan they travelled to Teotihuacán, where they built pyramids to the sun and moon, sacrificed, and elected their first kings, who were thought of as gods. These kings were buried in Teotihuacán.

283 Leaving there, the people travelled to the Place of the Seven Caves, where they honoured their gods. Those with whom they had left Aztlan now departed, the *Toltecs* to Tollan, the *Otomi* to Coatepec, and other *Nahuatlan* peoples to other places, leaving only the *Aztecs*.

284 Huitzilopochtli, their god, led them to the *Colhuacan* city of Chaputepec, but they were driven out and their lord, Huitzilihuitl, captured and killed.

285 One story says they then went to Tizapan, another *Colhuacan* city, and fought as allies of the *Colhuacan* against Xochimilo, whom they defeated, but were soon after driven out of Tizapan. There are various explanations of their banishment.

286 It is said that their *Colhuacan* overlord required the *Aztecs* to bring him evidence of the number of the enemy they killed. They did so by cutting off all the ears of their victims and presenting them to the ruler, who was so horrified by this barbarity that he expelled them.

287 Another variant says that they captured, sacrificed and flayed the *Colhuacan* ruler's daughter (presumably in a ritual sacrifice to Xipe Totec, q.v.), and invited the ruler to a banquet which a priest attended, dressed in the girl's skin (a common practice in rites of Xipe Totec).

288 After many wanderings the *Aztecs* came to the Tezcoco and receiving a divine omen, as an eagle with a snake in its talons flew up from a nearby rock, they founded the city of Tenochtitlan.

(ii) The Return to Aztlan

289 The fifth ruler, Montezuma, decided to send messages to his ancestral homeland where, he had heard, Huitzilopochtli's mother yet lived. A sage named Tlacaelel described Aztlan as being near a sea-girt mountain named Culhuacan.

290 Led by spirits, the ambassadors eventually reached Culhuacan, where they found floating gardens and fisherfolk.

291 The fact that they could speak the native language caused surprise, but when they said they had come with gifts for the god Huitzilopochtli's mother Coatlicue, they were led to her steward and gave him their messages from Montezuma and Tlacaelel.

292 The steward asked who Montezuma and Tlacaelel were. Those who had left Aztlan had been leaders named Acacitli, Ahatl, Auexotl, Huicton, Ocelopan, Tecacatetl, Tenoch and Xomimitl, together with the four guardians of Huitzilopochtli (i.e. Cipactonal, Oxomoco, Tlaltecuin and Xochicauca, see **281**). The steward could not understand why these were not living since everyone who had remained in Aztlan yet lived. He asked who had killed them. The ambassadors explained their deaths and persuaded the steward to lead them to Coatlicue.

293 As they attempted to climb her mountain, their feet sank into the sand. The steward, who glided easily over it was again puzzled, asking why they were so heavy. They said they lived on meat and cocoa and the steward then realised that this luxurious diet had caused their former leaders to die. In Aztlan, where life was simple, people survived.

294 He took the messengers swiftly to Coatlicue, who, being in mourning for her son Huitzilopochtli's departure, was ugly and terrible to look upon. She sent him a message via the ambassadors, reminding him that before he left her he had prophesied that after leading the seven tribes into their new land and establishing them there, he would be conquered himself, as he had conquered others. He had promised that when this happened he would return to her.

295 Coatlicue gave them gifts for Huitzilopochtli and told them to remind him of his promise.

296 Dismissed, the ambassadors descended the mountain and as they went the goddess' steward explained that the people of Aztlan retained their youth because when they grew old they climbed the goddess' mountain and in doing so were renewed (cf. **129**). So the ambassadors returned to Montezuma.

297 Although presented as a journey to Aztlan, this embassy seems possibly to have gone in fact to Tezcoco, the great artistic and intellectual centre of early fifteenth-century Mexico, built around the 'floating gardens'— artificial islands—of Lake Tezcoco.

SOUTH AMERICA

The Inca Empire
298–328

CREATION MYTHS

(i) A *Chibcha* story from Columbia
298 In the beginning all was dark, because the light was contained within the creator Chiminigagué; then he expressed it and created four large birds to whom he gave the light, with orders to carry it all over the world, which he had made. Chiminigagué then created the sun Zuhé (Xuhé) and the moon Chiá.

299 Soon afterwards a woman named Bachúe or Furachogúe emerged from Lake Iguaque, near Tunja, carrying a young boy. When he was mature they married and their children populated the world, for Bachúe always bore either quadruplets or sextuplets.

300 The divine parents taught their children laws and all the arts of civilisation and then, adjuring them to live in peace, returned to the lake's waters in the form of serpents.

(ii) A *Chibcha* Flood Myth
301 The god Chibchacum, becoming very angry with the people, flooded the land. In response to prayers, the great spirit Bochica revealed himself in a rainbow. He struck the rocks and they opened, swallowing the waters and creating the great waterfall Tequendama.

302 Bochica sent Zuhé, the sun, to dry the land and Chibchacum went underground. Since then the world, formerly supported by pillars in Lake Guayacan, has rested on Chibchacum's shoulders. When he feels tired and shifts the load carelessly—which is quite often—there are earthquakes.

(iii) Two *Collao* Stories from Tiahuanaco
303 Long ago the people lived in darkness, praying for light. Suddenly the sun rose from the island in Lake Titicaca and soon afterwards a large, white, bearded man came from the south, changing hills into valleys, valleys into hills and summoning water from the rocks. He gave the people laws and told them to live peaceably together. He was named Ticci Viracocha by most of the Indians but in Collao they called him Tuapaca.

304 The earth was made by Con Ticci Viracocha, who emerged from Lake Titicaca; but afterwards he disappeared leaving everything in darkness. Con Ticci returned, rising from Lake Titicaca with a number of attendants and going to Tiahuanaco, there made the sun, moon and stars and then stone models of people of all ages and in every walk of life. He gave them all names and set them in a province, made of stone also.

305 Con Ticci then summoned his followers, who were called *viracocha*, and

179

told them to regard the stone models carefully and remember their names, for they would emerge from fountains, caves, rocks and rivers in various places and populate those regions. Now Con Ticci commanded all but two of the *viracocha* to go east and summon the peoples forth, give them names and assign them their provinces.

306 These *Collao* stories were collected in the sixteenth century, by which time the people of Tiahuanaco had no knowledge of that great city's founders, whom they regarded as mysterious giants. It is possible that these sixteenth-century peasants had been transported to Tiahuanaco by their *Inca* conquerors and we cannot tell how far their origin stories are representative of the earlier beliefs of this area.

307 The Spaniards who collected the tales were greatly impressed by that of the white, bearded teacher, whom they identified with St. Thomas the Apostle.

(iv) Con and Pachacamac

308 In the beginning the boneless Con came from the north, declaring himself to be a child of the sun. Simply by willing it he could move mountains.

309 Creating people he gave them all the necessities of life, but the people came to displease him and so he transformed their fertile land into desert where no rain ever fell, leaving them only the rivers by means of which they could, with great labour, irrigate their land.

310 Then came Pachacamac (Creator) son of the sun and moon and expelled Con, transforming all his people into monkeys; then he created a new race, the people of today, and gave them all they needed.

311 In gratitude for his goodness, the people worshipped Pachacamac as their god, establishing a temple to him near Lima. (From the account by Lopez de Gomara.)

312 Pachacamac's temple, whose cult continued in *Inca* times, was the site of an oracle and a centre of pilgrimage. It was an honour to be buried in its vicinity and archaeologists have uncovered many burial sites in the area.

313 Con seems to have been another version of the same deity, described elsewhere as Coniraya or Coniraya Viracocha, but it is possible that he was a separate god or culture hero whose story has been assimilated to that of Pachacamac. The accounts of these gods and culture-heroes exist in such fragmentary forms as to be impossible for us now to elucidate.

INCA STORIES OF THEIR ORIGINS

314 Several versions of the *Inca* origin story exist, but they can be divided into two main types, one in which the legend of the imperial house seems to have been assimilated to the myth of a god arising from Lake Titicaca; the other in which the *Inca* tale is combined with a, probably earlier, myth of man's origin from caves. Both types include details accounting for the *Inca* rulers' incestuous intermarriage and distinctive dress. Both explain the *Incas'* power by emphasising their superiority over all neighbouring peoples, who are depicted as little more than savages.

(i) Manco Capac and Mama Ocllo

315 In the beginning people lived like wild beasts. Taking pity on them, the sun, our father, sent to earth his two children, Manco Capac and his sister Mama Ocllo. He gave them a long golden rod ordering them to prod the earth with it in every place they stopped to eat or sleep. When they found a spot where the rod sank completely into the ground, they should stop there and found a city, bring the people under the laws of the sun their father, and teach them the arts of civilisation.

316 Manco Capac and Mama Ocllo came to earth on an island in Lake Titicaca and travelled north, stopping in various places, in none of which could the rod be buried. Their penultimate resting place was a village south of Cuzco, called Paccaritambo, Inn of Dawn, because it was from there that the children of the sun set out at dawn on the final stage of their journey.

317 Coming to the hill of Huanacauri, south of Cuzco, they stopped to rest and there found that the golden rod sank completely into the earth with a single blow.

318 They therefore went from this place to summon the people and teach them the laws of the sun our father, and the savages, impressed by the golden ornaments and clothes of the sun's children, were willing to believe and follow them.

319 Manco Capac taught them to build houses, irrigate and tend the soil, and to shoe themselves. His sister Mama Ocllo instructed the women in spinning, weaving and sewing.

320 So many came to the City of the Sun that it was divided, the upper part being Hanan Cuzco, the lower, Hurin Cuzco. (The version of Garsilaso Inca de la Vega.)

(ii) The Children of The Sun

321 Long ago, from a cave with three mouths at Paccaritambo, Inn of Origin, also called Tambotocco, Place of the Hole, emerged four brothers and four sisters or, say some, three brothers and three sisters. They came from the central one of the cave's three mouths and, according to some stories, followers who were to be the ancestors of other *Inca* clans, emerged from the other two mouths.

322 The names of the brothers and sisters are variously given. Pedro de Cieza de Leon says the *Inca* nobility told him the names were Ayar Ucho, Ayar Cachi Asauca, Ayar Manco and their sisters Mama Huaco, Mama Coya and Mama Rahua. Fray Martin de Monia, who had evidently heard various versions of the story, felt the most 'plausible' was that giving four brothers and sisters, the men named Huana Cauri, Cusco Huanca, Manco Capac and Topa Ayar Cachi, the women Topa Huaco, Mama Coya, Cori Ocllo and Ipa Huaco.

323 They were dressed in beautiful woollen tabards and cloaks, *tapacu*—the royal vesture of the *Incas*—and each of the men carried a gold sling. By their natural superiority they won immediate ascendency over the primitive tribes among whom they found themselves.

324 Travelling north they looked for a place to settle. One of the brothers, Ayar Cachi, climbed Mt. Huanacauri and, by slinging stones from its summit, split the surrounding hills and aroused the jealousy of his brothers, who luring him into a cave, entombed him there.

325 Proceeding on their way, the remaining brothers and sisters camped at Tambu Quiru, where they were visited by Ayar Cachi's spirit who, telling them to found a city at Cuzco, then turned himself into a stone on the top of Mt. Huanacauri, where he was thenceforward honoured as a god.

326 Another version says that not only Ayar Cachi but also Ayar Ucho became the cult stone, after first having taught Ayar Manco the *rite de passage* for adolescent youths.

327 Ayar Manco and his sisters went on to Cuzco, where they founded their city and Ayar Manco took the name Manco Capac.

328 In Fray Martin's account the oldest brother, Huana Cauri, chose to remain in Apitay, their first stopping place, and there he died, the mountain being named Huanacauri in his memory. The others proceeded to the city of Acamama and occupied it without resistance. Cusco Huanca became its first *Inca* king, changing its name to Cuzco. He was succeeded by his brother, the great Manco Capac.

Mochikan stories of Chimor
329–334

The Legend of Naymlap

329 Very long ago a fleet of *balsas* came to Lambeyeque (south of Cape Santa Elena), led by the great chief Naymlap, who was accompanied by his wife Ceterni and all his servants, Pitazofi his trumpeter, Ninacolla his throne-bearer, Ninagentue his cup-bearer, Fongasigde, who scattered powdered shells before the chief's feet, Ochocalo his cook, Xam the make-up man, and Llapchilulli, master of the wardrobe.

330 After landing the party immediately built a temple called Chot, in which they placed a green stone-carving of the king, which was therefore called *Llampallec*—'figure of Naymlap'.

331 At the end of his long reign, Naymlap disappeared, some said by flying up into the sky, and his grieving courtiers went to seek him, leaving their children to inhabit the land.

332 The tenth king after Naymlap was named Fempellec. He decided to move the statue *Llampallec* and was seduced by a fiend in woman's form. An unprecedented deluge ensued, followed by a famine. The priests therefore tied Fempellec hand and foot and threw him into the sea, bringing to an end

Twelfth-thirteenth-century gourd from Chimor inlaid with mother-of-pearl symbols of deities. Museum für Völkerkunde, Munich. (*Photo: Michael Holford.*)

Beaten gold funerary mask inlaid with emeralds, from Chimor. Mujica Gallo Collection, Lima. (*Photo: Michael Holford*.)

the rule of Naymlap's descendants. The valley then being without a governor was invaded by the *Chimu* leader Capac, who made Pony Massa its ruler.

333 This story, collected at the end of the sixteenth century, is believed to be of fairly late origin. It suggests not only the existence of a highly stratified theocracy, but also that the god-king was regarded as the son of the sea—hence perhaps his walking on powdered sea-shells. Possibly his death was followed by the ritual sacrifice of his courtiers, who 'went to seek him'.

334 Other stories from this part of the north-east coast of Peru also tell of the arrival of kings, or sometimes giants, from overseas. One, who came to the central Chimor valley of Moche, was named Tancanaymo. There are various theories as to where these visitors did originate, but the consensus of opinion is that they probably came from Ecuador.

184

Primitive South American cultures
335–355

CREATION STORIES

335 Stories collected from the primitive Indian peoples tell of the world's creation by creatures such as the beetle and of men's emergence from underground, like ants, as well as of anthropomorphic creator-spirits. The following selection of stories illustrates concepts from various parts of the continent.

(i) The Insect Men

336 Long ago men were very, very small and lived underground. They climbed to the earth's surface on a rope of *caraguata*—plant fibre. As there was hardly any food on the earth's surface, a dog soon gnawed through the rope, preventing the rest of the people from following their relatives.

337 The *Chamacoco* and other peoples then tried to climb into the sky up a huge tree but they all fell back to earth, which is why there are so few *Chamacoco* (Myth of the *Chamacoco* Indians of Bolivia.)

(ii) The Crocodile People

338 In the beginning trees bore fruit unceasingly, and all animals lived in peace. There were neither floods, nor droughts; even the waterfalls fell gently.

339 Adaheli, the sun, troubled that there were as yet no human-beings, descended to earth and soon afterwards people were born from the cayman (a form of alligator). The women were all beautiful but some of the men were so ugly that their fellows found them intolerable to look upon, so they separated, the ugly ones going east, the others west, each with their wives. (*Carib* myth from the Orinoco region.)

(iii) Karu and Rairu

340 In the beginning, in darkness, two men stumbled about, Karu and his son Rairu. Rairu tripped on a bowl-shaped stone, which his father told him to carry, so he put it on his head. It grew and grew, forming the sky.

341 Rairu knelt to his father, honouring him as the sky-maker, but Karu, perceiving his son to be more knowledgeable than he, grew angry and Rairu had to hide underground.

342 Karu discovered him and was about to despatch him when Rairu called out saying he had found people in the earth who would come and work for them. So the first people came up and were divided into tribes according to their colour and attractiveness. The lazy ones were turned into birds, bats, pigs and butterflies. (*Kadevo* myth, Brazil.)

(iv) The Star Creator

343 Long ago the world was inhabited by white, bearded men and the sun and moon were husband and wife. The men began to fight each other, so the sun and moon went up to the sky and sent down the red star (Mars), who became a giant and killed all the people. He then kneaded two lumps of clay and from them came a man and a woman, the ancestors of the *Ona*. (Myth of the *Ona* people, Tierra del Fuego.)

(v) Matvutsinim

344 In this story, the origin of man is combined with an aetiological ritual myth about the loss of immortality and the origin of the *Kuarup* rite.

345 At first Matvutsinim lived all alone; then he transformed a shell into a woman and made her his wife. She bore him a child and when she told Matvutsinim it was a son, he took the boy up and went away. Crying, the woman returned to her village in the lagoon and once more became a shell, while the grandchildren of Matvutsinim's son were the Indian people.

346 Matvutsinim wanted to restore his dead people to life so he cut three *kuarup* wood logs and decorated them with feathers, necklaces and threads. He called for a festival and singers with gourd rattles to plead to the *kuarups* to come to life.

347 At about midday the people wished to mourn the *kuarups*, who symbolised their dead, but Matvutsinim assured them that these *kuarups* were going to come to life, so there was nothing to mourn for.

348 Gradually as the second and third day passed, the *kuarups* did begin to come alive, and Matvutsinim would not let anyone look at them. When they were nearly complete, he told the villagers that everyone should now come out of their houses and laugh and rejoice near the *kuarups*—but anyone who had had intercourse with his wife the night before must stay away.

349 However one young man disobeyed; he was so anxious he had to see the *kuarups*. Immediately he emerged from his hut, the *kuarups* turned back into logs and so the dead never come back to life and the making of the *kuarups* is only a festival. (*Xingu* myth, Brazil.)

Drawing of *kuarup* logs by the *Xingu* artist Wacupiá. *Xingu, The Indians and Their Myths*, Villas Boas, pub. Souvenir Press.

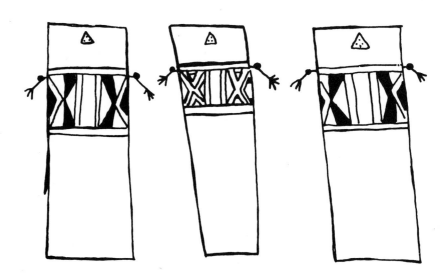

JAGUAR STORIES

350 The jaguar or puma is a creature found in carvings from many parts of South and Central America and archaeologists deduce that it played an important part in religious cults. However, references to the jaguar are extremely rare in the South American myths so far recorded, except among forest tribes and in eastern Bolivia, where the jaguar is indigenous. The following tale comes from the Bolivian *Yuracare* people.

351 One day when the youth Ulé was out hunting a jaguar killed him. His wife gathered the scraps of his body wishing to restore them, which she succeeded in doing, but Ulé caught sight of himself in a forest pool and saw that his face was disfigured—where a piece of flesh was missing. Despite his wife's pleas he went away, warning her not to look back. Unfortunately she did and, losing her way, stumbled into the jaguar's lair, where the jaguar mother took pity on her.

352 The four sons wanted to kill her and to test her obedience told her to eat the poisoned ants that infested them. The young woman deceived three of the sons by replacing the ants with seeds, but the fourth had eyes in the back of his head and saw what she was doing. He killed her.

353 From her body came the infant Tiri, whom the jaguar mother secretly cared for. When he grew up and went hunting, an animal he had wounded accused him of attacking harmless creatures, while living with his mother's murderers.

Mochican pottery trumpet in the form of a jaguar. N. Cummings Collection, Chicago. (*Photo: Giraudon.*)

187

354 Tiri ambushed the jaguar brothers and shot the first three, but the fourth jumped into a tree, summoning the stars, moon and sun to help him. The moon bent down and snatched him to her bosom, where he can still be seen. (*Yuracare* story, Bolivia.)

355 Among other primitive tribes, the jaguar, like the cayman, is sometimes a totem animal, while the Bolivian *Chiriguani* believe that the green tiger named Yaguarogui causes eclipses by trying to eat the sun and moon.

PART 3
Index and Glossary

The following abbreviations are used:
CA: Central America; NA: North America.

Bold numbers refer to the numbered paragraphs of Part 2 unless otherwise indicated.

A, God A (*Maya*, CA) depicted in the codices with naked vertebrae and skull, this god is usually identified with the death-god, named Ah Kinchel (q.v.), Ah Puch, or Hanhau, by the classical *Maya* and by the modern Yuacatec *Maya* called Yum Cimil. See also Mitnal.

Aba (*Choctaw*, SE Woodlands, NA) the great spirit.

Abirá (*Antioquia*, Colombia) the creator, according to sixteenth-century reports associated with the mother-goddess Dabeciba and opposed by the evil-one, Chanicubá.

Acacitli 292.

Acamama 328.

achachila(s) (*Aymará*, Bolivia) revered objects (cf. *huaca(s)*). They include the mountain peaks of the Bolivian cordillera, Illimani (q.v.), Ilanyau, Huayanu Potosí, Sicasica and Churuquilla (q.v.).

Achiyalatopa (*Zuñi*, Pueblo, NA) the Knife-feathered monster, a celestial giant with feathers of flint.

Acolnaucatl (*Aztec*, Mexico) another name for Mictlantecuhtli (q.v.)

Adaheli 339.

Adawulcanak 103.

Adekagagwaa (*Iroquoian* tribes, Woodlands, NA) the spirit of summer. In the winter he rests in the south, leaving his 'sleep spirit' to watch the earth. On the evening before he leaves for the south, he always promises the Earth Mother that he will return and when he does Hino (q.v.) will lower his voice, Ga-oh (q.v.) lock up his fierce winds and Gohone (q.v.) depart.

Adja see Adjassou-Linguetor.

Adja Bosu see Adjassou-Linguetor.

Adjassou-Linguetor (*Voodoo*, Haiti) a *loa* (q.v.), also referred to as Adja and Adja Bosu. Recognised by his protruberant eyes and ill temper, he lives under a tree by a spring, whose waters he governs.

Adjassou-Miro (*Voodoo*) a *loa*, probably a variant of Adjassou-Linguetor (q.v.).

Agaone (*Voodoo*) a *loa* (q.v.)

Agaou (*Voodoo*) a *loa* (q.v.) also called Agaou Tonné and Agaou Wédo; one of the Rada *loa* (q.v.). See also Damballa.

Agaou Tonné see Agaou.

Agaou Wédo see Agaou.

Agarou (*Voodoo*) a *loa*, possibly a variant form of Agaou (q.v.) but this is uncertain.

Agasu see Adjassou-Linguetor.

Age see Lomi Ago.

Agomme Tonnère see Ogoum Tonnère.

Agoué Oyo (*Voodoo*) a *loa* also referred to as Agué, Agué Woyo or Agwe Woyo, possibly of *Yoruba* origin.

Agriskoue see Airsekui.

Aguasu see Adjassou-Linguetor.

Agwe (*Voodoo*) the sea-goddess. See also Agoué Oyo.

Ah Kinchil (*Maya*, CA) the sun-god, possibly regarded as an aspect of Itzamna (q.v.). At night he travelled below the earth, possibly in jaguar form.

Ah Puch (*Maya*) the death-god. He may also have been called Cumhau and Cizin and was associated with Nacon and Ekahau (q.v.). See also God A and Mitnal.

Ahalcana 215.

Ahalpuh 215.

Ahatl 292.

Ahau Chamahez (*Maya*) one of the two 'medicine' gods, the other being Cit Bolon Tum. His name has been tentatively interpreted as 'Lord of the Magic Tooth'.

Ahkinshok (modern *Maya*, Yucatán) guardian-spirit of the day.

Ahkushtal (modern *Maya*) the goddess of childbirth.

Ahmakiq (modern *Maya*) a beneficent god who locks up the winds when they threaten to spoil crops.

Ahmucencab 187.

Ahsonnutli a variant of Estsanatlehi (q.v.).

Ahu-uc-cheknale 190.

Airsekui, Areskoui, Agriskone (*Huron*, Woodlands, NA) the great spirit. In times of extreme danger he is called upon as Airsekui Sutanditenr— Airsekui Saviour. He resembles, but is not the exact equivalent of, the *Algonquian* Kitshi Manito (q.v.). The first fruits of hunting and battle are offered to him.

Aktunowihio (*Cheyenne*, Gt Plains, NA) Wise-One-Below, a subterranean spirit, the earth's soul; cf. Heamma-wihio.

Akycha (*Eskimo*, Alaska) the sun-spirit.

Alawe see Laloué Diji, Maîtresse.

alec pong p. 130.

Alkuntam (*Bella Coola*, NW Coast, NA) assistant to Senx (q.v.) in creating mankind and the animals. She is said to be the daughter of a cannibal goddess who sucks men's brains out through their ears—possibly a personification of the mosquito, who, in many myths of this region is said to have sprung from the ashes of a cannibal goddess (see Sisiutl).

Aluberi (*Arawak*, Guyana) the great spirit a remote being, in contrast to the creator Kururumany (q.v.).

Amaiaua, 179.

Amalivaca (*Arawak*) a Trickster-hero.

Amarok (*Eskimo*, Greenland) a great wolf-monster living in the interior.

Amazons (Brazil) early Spanish visitors to Brazil were led to identify the Amazons of classical Greek mythology (see vol. 1: 2.2 **210** and **317**) with the women of Brazilian Indian tribes who fought beside their menfolk.

Amelia (*Voodoo*, Haiti) a *loa*, also called Maîtresse Amelia.

A'men (*Maya*, CA) *shaman*-diviners, with god-given powers to control cosmic forces. See also vol. 2: 3.1.

Amitolane (*Zuñi*, Pueblo, S West, NA) the rainbow-spirit.

Amminan (*Voodoo*, Haiti) a *loa* (q.v.).

amoxaoque 281.

Anago (*Voodoo*) a *loa* (q.v.) whose name derived from that of the W African *Nago* tribe i.e. the *Yoruba*.

anamqkiu **119–120.**

anaye **51, 56–57, 94.**

angakok (pl. *angakut*) (*Eskimo*) *shaman(s)*, men or women helped by many, or a single very powerful, *tornak* (q.v.). See **13–15** and also vol. 2:3. 1.

angakut see *angakok*.

Angpetu Wi (*Dakota*, Gt Plains, NA) the sun-spirit.

Anguta (*Eskimo*) the father of Sedna (q.v.). A shadowy being, Anguta lives in his daughter's undersea realm, to which he drags down the dead with his maimed hand. According to some stories it was he who, having rescued his daughter from her abductor, then threw her overboard to save himself. See **10**.

Aningan (*Eskimo*) the moon-spirit.

anishinabeg (*Chippewa*, Woodlands, NA) the helpless primordial people upon whom the good Minabozho (q.v.) took pity.

anitsutsa (*Cherokee*, Woodlands, NA) the star-spirits of the Pleiades.

Annals of Cakchiquel p. 125

Annals of Quauhititlan **244**.

Anpao (*Dakota*, Gt Plains, NA) the spirit of dawn.

Antoine, Saint (*Voodoo*, Haiti) St Antony, the Catholic saint who features as a *loa* (q.v.) in some *Voodoo* cults.

apachita(s) see *huaca(s)*.

Apitay 328.

Apoyan Tachu (*Zuñi*, Pueblo, S. West, NA) the Sky-Father. See Awitelin Tsita.

Arada (*Voodoo*, Haiti) a *loa* (q.v.) whose name derives from that of the W African tribe, *Allada*.

Areskoui see Airsekui.

Arkoanyó see Valedjád.

Arnakuagsak 9.

Arnarkusuagsak 9.

Arnarquagssaq variant of Arnarkusuagsak (q.v.).

Aroteh (*Tupari*, Brazil) one of the primitive *vamoa-pod* (q.v.). He and his companion Tovapod lived in a tent. The first men, who were underground beings, came and stole the two *vamoa-pod's* food and, in seeking the thieves, Aroteh and Tovapod tracked them to a hole, in which they dug. Streams of people poured out, until the two *vamao-pod* stopped the hole up again. These first men were tusked and Tovapod removed the tusks and webbing, giving the people their present beautiful teeth, hands and feet.

Arunaua a variant name of Tuapaca (q.v.).

Ashiwanni (*Zuñi*, Pueblo, S West, NA) the rain priesthood, the most important religious group, comprising fourteen rain-priests, two priests of the bow and a fertility-priestess. Together with the sun-priest and the two leaders of the *Kotikili* (q.v.), the *Ashiwanni* represent the earthly counterparts of the Council of the Gods that meets in Kothluwalawa (q.v.). See also *ashiwi*.

ashiwi (Zuñi) the rain priests of the *Ashiwanni* (q.v.). The name is also that of the first people to emerge from the

underworld. Originally these were ugly, smelly creatures with webbed feet and hands, mossy bodies, long ears, and short, hairless tails. These ugly defects were remedied by the gods who guided them to the earth's surface. See also **154–155, 158–161.**

Assez Media (*Voodoo*, Haiti) a *loa* (q.v.).

Atacrou (*Voodoo*, Haiti) a *loa* (q.v.).

Ataentsic (*Iroquoian* peoples, Woodlands, NA) the earth-goddess, grand-daughter of the Ancient Bodied One (The-Chief-Sky-Ruler) and wife of the celestial Chief-Who-Holds-the-Earth. She came to earth with her daughter Gusts-of-Wind when her husband unjustly suspected she had been unfaithful to him. See also **84–85, 88.**

Atahocan (*Montagnais*, Woodlands, NA) the Great Spirit as the creator of all things.

Ati Dangné (*Voodoo*, Haiti) a *loa* (q.v.).

Atira 63.

Atlatonan (*Aztec*, Mexico) a goddess and one of the wives of Tezcatlipoca (q.v.).

Atonatiuh 244.

Atotaho 176, 177.

Atraioman 186.

Atse Estsan 30, 36–37, 48–50.

Atse Hastin 30, 36–37, 38, 41, 48–50.

Atseatsan variant of Atse Estsan (q.v.).

Atseatsine variant of Atse Estsan (q.v.).

Auexotl 292.

Aunyainá (*Tupari*, Brazil) an evil sorcerer of old. Tusked like a boar, he fed on children until one day, when he was out hunting his neighbours, the *vamoa-pod* (q.v.) escaped to the skies by climbing a long creeper. He tried to pursue them, but a parrot gnawed through the creeper and he fell to the ground and was killed. Caymans (alligators) and iguanas grew from his arms and legs, all kinds of small lizards from his fingers and toes.

Aurora Borealis see Baxbakualanuchsiwae and **16**.

Avilix 199, 202.

Awitelin Tsita (*Zuñi*, Pueblo, S West, NA) 'Fourfold-containing-Earth-Mother'. According to some myths she was created by Shiwanokia (q.v.) from spittle; according to others Awonawilona (q.v.) in the form of the sun created both Awitelin Tsita and Apoyan Tachu (the sky) from sea foam.

Awonawilona (*Zuñi*) the androgynous supreme power, first expressed in Sun-Father, but pervading all things, cf. Wakonda. As the Sun-Father and Moon-Mother travel across the sky their faces are hidden by shields. Awonawilona gradually withdraws and then replaces the veil which hides the Moon-Mother's shield. This is why she

is not always visible.

axolotl **260.**

Ayar Cachi, Ayar Cachi Asauca **322, 324–326.** See also Topa Ayar Cachi.

Ayar Manco 322, 326–327. See also Manco Capac.

Ayar Ucho 322, 326.

Azaca Si see Mambo Zacca.

Azaka Baing Baing see Mambo Zacca.

Azaka Mede see Mambo Zacca.

Aztec(s) pp. **125–128**; **233, 253, 254, 257, 264, 266, 281–297.**

Aztlan 281, 289–297.

B, God B (*Maya*, CA) the deity most often found in the codices, shown with a long nose, protruding teeth and tongue and in association with serpents, weather symbols and symbols of the cardinal points. He is usually believed to represent the Chac (q.v.).

Bacabs (*Maya*, CA) four deities who guarded the divisions of the 260-day calendar. See also **188**.

Bacam 221.

Bachué 299–300.

Badé (*Voodoo*, Haiti) also referred to as Badé-si or Gbadé, this *loa* (q.v.) is of W African origin.

Badger 38, 45.

badjican(s) (*Voodoo*) assistant(s) to the *houngan* (q.v.).

baka(s) (*Voodoo*) zombie(s) (q.v.) transformed into animal shapes by their wicked masters.

balam (*Maya*, CA) guardians of the world's cardinal points, red in the east, white in the north, black in the west, yellow in the south, green in the centre.

Balam Agab 196–203.

Balam Quitzé 196–203.

Balongahoya see Pookonghoya.

balsa(s) (Bolivia and Peru) boat(s) made of *balsa*. See **329.**

Baquicie (*Voodoo*, Haiti) a *loa* (q.v.).

'Batala (*Voodoo*) otherwise Obatala or Grand Batala; a *loa* (q.v.) derived from the Nigerian *Yoruba* god Orishanla— see vol. 2: 3.3 p. 185.

Bats, House of 218.

Baxbakualanuchsiwae (*Kwakiutl*, NW Coast, NA) the cannibal spirit, here a male deity (among other peoples the spirit is usually female). He is thought of as living in the Arctic. The 'cannibal pole' of his house, its place of honour, is said to be the Milky Way or, sometimes, to be the rainbow. Red smoke rises from his house. Some commentators think he originated as a war-god symbolised by the Aurora Borealis. He is one of the two chief tutelary spirits of the *Kwakiutl*, the other being Wixalagilis (q.v.).

Bazo (*Voodoo*, Haiti) also called Bosu, Bosu-Cessé or Kadia-Bosu, a *loa* (q.v.) thought to be of W African origin.

Bazon-Mainnain probably a variant of Bazo (q.v.).

Bear 108, 163, 164–167. See also Great Bear.

Beaver 121.

Binaye Ahani 51.

Bitsitsi 159–160.

Black Body 35, 40, 48–49.

Blue Body 35, 40, 48–49.

Blue World 31–32.

Bochica (*Chibcha*, Colombia) the supreme being, with whom the culture-hero Chimizapagna or Nemterequeteba was sometimes identified. An invisible spirit, Bochica expressed himself in the sun, Zuhé. See also **301–302**.

Bois l'en Dingué (*Voodoo*, Haiti) a *loa* (q.v.).

Bokwus (*Kwakiutl*, NW Coast, NA) wild spirit of the woods, who draws spirits of the drowned to his home.

Bolodjoré (*Voodoo*) a *loa* (q.v.).

Bolon Dzacab (*Maya*, CA) otherwise Bolon Zacab, one of the deities associated with genealogies. Some think his name may mean 'Many Matrilineages'. See Kanu-u-Uayeyab and **187**.

Bolontiku 187.

bope (*Bororo*, Brazil) evil spirits who attack the dead. During the eight-day funeral ceremony the tribe therefore impersonate the *bope*. The ritual ends with the secret removal of the corpse to the river. The flesh is scraped off, leaving the bones clean. The soul then escapes to become embodied in a frog, bird or deer.

Borrommée (*Voodoo*, Haiti) a Roman Catholic saint regarded as a *loa* (q.v.) by some *Voodoo* cultists.

Bosu see Bazou.

Bosu-Cessé see Bazou.

Bow Priests (*Zuñi*, Pueblo, S West, NA) members of the warrior class and guardians of the twin war-gods. At death they are believed to ascend to the skies, where the flight of their arrows is seen as lightning.

Brave (*Voodoo*, Haiti) a *loa* (q.v.).

Brer Rabbit p. 121.

Bright Star 64, **66**, 68–69, 70, 71, 76, 78. See also Venus.

Buffalo Dance **144–152**.

Bumba *loa* (*Voodoo*) the group of *loa* deriving from deities of the Congolese *Bumba* tribe.

Busk festival (*Creek*, Woodlands, NA) an anglicisation of the *Creek puskita* ('fast'). The festival is the great New Year celebration, held in late summer

Kwakiutl mask of Bokwus. Denver Art Museum. (*Photo: Denver Art Museum.*)

when the first maize has ripened. New fire is kindled, all used dishes and household goods are destroyed and replaced by new ones and there is a general amnesty for all criminals except murderers.

C, God C (*Maya*, CA) one of the divinities shown in the *Mayan* codices. He is thought to be a sky-god, possibly Xaman Ek or the spirit of Ursa Major.

Cabrakan 225, 231.

Cachimana (Orinoco region, Venezuela) the Great Spirit, who is opposed by the more active Trickster Iolokiamo.

Cacibagiagua 179.

Caesars, City of (Chile) mythical city of gold, said to exist by the shores of a mountain lake. It has an inexhaustible tobacco plantation and no one who lives there has to work. It will become generally visible only at the end of the world. The concept of this city seems to combine elements of the El Dorado legend and the Christian concept of the new Jerusalem, 'the Golden'. Its name may derive from memories of an expedition to find the golden city of El Dorado, led by the sixteenth-century explorer César.

calumet ceremony 142–143.

Camago 245.

Camaxtli (*Aztec*, Mexico) the god of Tlacale, an aspect of Xipe Totec (q.v.). See also **233.**

Camazotz 194, 218.

Canicubá see Abira.

Cannibal Mother see Tsonoqua and also Baxbakualanuchsiwae and Istepahpah.

Cantultiku 188–189.

Capac 332.

Cari (*Collao*, Bolivia) one of two legendary chieftains, the other being Zapana. It is said they engaged in internecine warfare as a result of which the *Inca* were easily able to conquer their realm.

Carrefour, Maît(re) Carrefour (*Voodoo*, Haiti) a *loa* (q.v.).

Cassé Brisé (*Voodoo*) a *loa* (q.v.).

Catherine, Sainte (*Voodoo*) the Roman Catholic saint, regarded as a *loa* (q.v.) by the *Voodoo* cultists.

Cavillaca see Coniraya.

Ce Actl Topiltzin 268–269.

Celia, Sainte (*Voodoo*) the Roman Catholic saint, regarded as a *loa* (q.v.) by the *Voodoo* cultists.

Cemanahuac 234.

cemis see *zemis*.

Centéotl (*Aztec*, Mexico) the corn-god, son of Tlazoltéotl (q.v.) and husband to Xochiquetzal (q.v.).

Aztec basalt statue of the goddess Chalchiuhtlicue. British Museum. (*Photo: Michael Holford.*)

Centzonhuitznáua (*Aztec*) the 400 stellar gods of the southern sky, sometimes referred to as the Four Hundred Southerners; cf. Centonmixixcoa and see also **255, 256.**

Centzonmixixcoa (*Aztec*) the 400 stellar gods of the northern sky; cf. Centzonhuitznáua.

Centzontotochtin (*Aztec*) the *pulque* (q.v.) gods, the 'Four Hundred Rabbits'. They include Patecatl, lord of *ocpatli*, the *peyote* from which the intoxicating drink is made.

Cha-u-Uayeyab (*Maya*, CA) the guardian god of the cities' eastern gates during Muluc years, which were governed by the eastern Bacab (q.v.). A god named Kinich Ahau presided over the centre of the town in these years. See also Ek-u-Uayeyab, Kan-u-Uayeyab, Zac-u-Uayeyab.

Chacmool figures (*Toltec*, Mexico) seated figures of gods at the great *Toltec* centre of Tula.

Chacs (*Maya*, CA) four fertility- and rain-gods, honoured in spring together with the Bacabs, and at the March festival of the great rain-god Itzamma (q.v.). The early writer Landa said the name *Chacs* was also given to the four old men chosen each year to assist the priests. The gods lived at the world's four quarters and were manifest in thunder and lightning.

Chahuru (*Pawnee*, Gt Plains, NA) the water-spirit.

Chakekenapok 123.

Chalchiuhtlicue (*Aztec*, Mexico) Lady-of-the-Turquoise-Skirt, goddess of running water, the sister of Tláloc. She was an ambivalent deity, governing shipwrecks and death by drowning, but also presiding over the cleansing baptism of infants in a rite that impressed the Spaniards as Christian in its implications. The goddess' emblems were maize and snakes. See also **234 239, 242, 253.**

Chalchiutotolin an aspect of
Tezcatlipoca (q.v.).

Chamacoco 337.

Chamiabak 215.

Chamiaholm 215.

Chan-Chan p. 130.

Chantico (*Aztec*) the hearth-goddess, also
associated with volcanic fire.

Chaputepec 284.

Chavin p. 128.

Chavin de Huántor p. 128

chenoo (*Abnaki* and *Micmac*, Woodlands,
NA) stone giants, a concept common to
all the *Iroquoian* tribes. Unversed in
archery, these monsters used rocks as
missiles and in fights among themselves
uprooted trees to use as clubs.
Occasionally a man managed to tame a
chenoo. Being mighty hunters they
were very useful to their *shaman*
masters.

Chenuke see Kwanyip.

Chiá 298.

Chibchacum or Chicchechum (*Chibcha*,
Colombia) the earth-god, patron of
farmers and merchants. See also
301–302.

Chibiabos 123.

Chicama p. 129.

Chichimec(s) pp. 125, 127, **259.**

Chicomecóatl (*Aztec*, Mexico) an early
fertility-goddess, the *Aztec* corn-
goddess. Her name means Seven
Snakes. See also Xilonen.

Chicuna (Panama) the supreme being of
Panamanian Indians during the last
century.

Chicunauhapan 257. See also Mictlan.

Chicunauhmictlan 257. See also
Mictlan.

Chilam Balam of Chumayel, the Book
of pp. 125, 223 and **187–190.**

Chilchi (*Zuñi*, Pueblo, S West, NA) an
important *kachina* (q.v.).

Chimalamat 228.

Chimalman 268.

Chiminigagué 298.

Chimor (Chimu) pp. 130–131, **329–334.**

Chipactonal 281, 292.

Chipiabos 123.

Chipiripa (*Curra* or *Cueva*, Costa
Rica) the rain-god.

chixu (*Pawnee*, Gt Plains, NA) the spirit
of the dead, i.e. ghost.

Chot 330.

Chucuito p. 131.

Chulavete (*Cora*, Mexico) the Morning
Star, one of these people's most
important deities.

Churuquilla, Mt. (*Aymará*, Bolivia) one
of the two *achachilas* of Sucré, the
other being Mt. Sicasica. It is said that
they embody a pair of male and female
spirits and occasionally that of Sicasica
manifests itself as a seductive but

Aztec stone figure of the goddess Chicomecóatl wearing maize cobs in her
headdress. British Museum. (*Photo: Michael Holford.*)

de Landa, Diego p. 125.

Delgeth 51.

Dent Friand (*Voodoo*) a *loa* (q.v.).

deohako (*Iroquois*, Woodlands, NA) the spirits of cultivated plants, especially corn, beans and squash.

Desaguadero, River see Thunupa.

Desportes, Monsieur (*Voodoo*, Haiti) a *loa* (q.v.).

Dévis Pas Pressé (*Voodoo*) a *loa* (q.v.).

Diable Tonnère (*Voodoo*) Thunder Devil, a powerful *loa* (q.v.).

diablesse(s) (*Voodoo*) fiendish spirit(s) of women who died as virgins. They are compelled to purge this 'sin' by living in the woods for many years before God will admit them to Heaven.

Diejuste, Monsieur (*Voodoo*) a benevolent *loa* (q.v.).

Difficile Clérmeil, Monsieur variant of Président Clérmeil (q.v.).

Diji see Laoué-Diji, Maîtresse.

Dismiraye (*Voodoo*) a *loa* (q.v.).

Djeneta (*Chippewa*, Woodlands, NA) a mythical giant.

Dohkwibuhch (*Snohomish*, NW Coast, NA) the creator-trickster.

Dokibatl (*Chinook*, coast, S West, NA) the Trickster. He was responsible for the flood.

Doquebuth (*Skagit*, coast, S West, NA) the second creator of the world, son of two of the five people who rode out the great flood in a canoe, into which they had loaded two specimens of everything on earth (an aspect of the tale probably influenced by Christian teaching). In a *shamanistic* trance Doquebuth was instructed by Old Creator how to remake the earth and people on it.

Dosu-Dosua (*Voodoo*, Haiti) a *loa* (q.v.).

Dreamers, the (NA) a cult led by Smohalla (born c. 1820), based on a mixture of Roman Catholic and Indian beliefs. In c. 1860 he was challenged by a rival *shaman*, Moses, who left him for dead beside a river. Carried downstream by floodwaters, Smohalla was rescued by a white farmer and wandered through the South East and into Mexico before returning home to Oregon. He claimed to have died in the river and conversed with the Great Spirit who had expressed disgust at Smohalla's having foresaken his own religion for that of the white man. His miraculous return convinced many that he was the Great Spirit's chosen messenger. He claimed that since the Indians were the first men to have been created by the Great Spirit, the earth belonged to them and it was their responsibility to stop its defilement by the whites. The cult, which took its

Fragment of *Aztec* pottery figurine showing the wind-god Ehécatl. (*Photo: Werner Forman Archive.*)

name from the *shamanistic* trances of its followers, proved a major obstacle to government policy.

Ducá (*Xingu*, Brazil) a form of jaguar or puma, father of the hero Sináa.

Dumballah variant of Damballa (q.v.).

Dzarilaw (*Haida*, NW Coast, NA) the Bear Chief's son who married a human wife, Rhpisunt, who bore him two sons, before her brothers tracked down Dzarilaw and killed him. As the men approached, Dzarilaw taught his wife the sacred bear-song. Cf. **144–152**.

Dzerlarhons (*Haida*) the Volcano-Woman; also a Frog-Woman.

Dzhe Manito (*Chippewa*, Woodlands, NA) the Good Spirit, next in importance to the Great Spirit, Kitshi Manito (q.v.). His servant is Minabozho, (q.v.).

E, God E (*Maya*, CA) a maize-god in the codices, possibly to be identified with Yum Kaax (q.v.).

Earth Mother see Ataentsic, Awitelin Tsita, Ethinoha, Cihuacóatl, H'llraru, Nokomis, Pachamama, Shiwanokia, Tlazoltéotl, pp. 121 and 9.

Ecantonatiuh 244.

Ehécatl (*Aztec*, Mexico) wind-god, an aspect of Quetzalcóatl (q.v.).

Eithinoha (*Iroquois*, Woodlands, NA) the earth-goddess. Her daughter is the corn-maiden Onatah (q.v.).

Ekahau (*Maya*, CA) the Black Captain, the black-faced god of travellers and merchants also associated with the gods of death and war, possibly because trade was a dangerous business often involving war.

Ekkekko (*Quecha*, Peruvian-Bolivian borders) the god of good fortune, depicted as a cheerful, pot-bellied dwarf carrying all sorts of domestic goods. His cult is especially associated with annual fairs called *Alacitas*, held at Cochambamba, Oruro and La Paz.

Ek-u-Uayeyab (*Maya*, CA) the god who guarded cities' western gates during the malign Cauac years, governed by the western Bacab (q.v.). The cities'

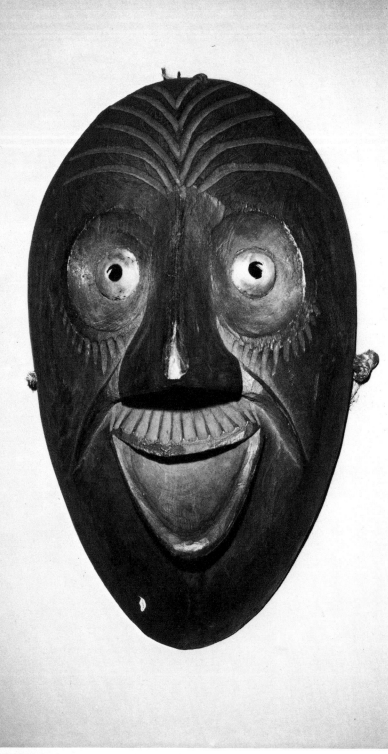

Iroquoian False-Face Society mask. Peabody Museum of Salem. (*Photo: M. W. Sexton.*)

centres were guarded by Zac-Mitun-Ahau. See also Chac-u-Uayeyab, Kan-u-Uayeyab, Zac-u-Uayeyab.

El Dorado the Gilded Man or Gold Man, a figure of persisting legend that has induced innumerable hopefuls to seek his treasure. The story of El Dorado, the great priest-king whose body was covered in gold-dust, almost certainly derives from garbled stories of the *Inca* which the first *conquistadores* received from primitive tribes. El Dorado has been associated with Lake Guatavita (q.v.) and with the mythical Lake Parima that, until von Humboldt disproved it, was said to lie beyond the Orinoco in a land named Manoa or Omoa. See also Caesars, City of the, and Paititi.

El Lanzón p. 128.

Ellal (*Puechlo*, Patagonia) the evil-one.

Emisiwaddo (*Arawak*, Guyana) one of the two wives of the creator Kururumany, the other being Wurekaddo (q.v.). Her name means She-Who-Bores-Through-the-Earth and she is identified with a species of ant, suggesting a creation myth in which the earth results from anthills.

Erzilie, Erzulie (*Voodoo*, Haiti) a very important *loa* (q.v.) of W African origin. Many variants of her name are recorded. The goddess of sexual love, she is a very beautiful, amorous woman, but also identified by devotees with the Christian Mater Dolorosa.

Estanatlehi 53, 54, 56, 57, 59, 60.

Etienne, St. (*Voodoo*) the Roman Catholic Saint Stephen, regarded as a *loa* (q.v.) by *Voodoo* cultists.

Evening Sky 20–21, 23.

F, God F (*Maya*, CA) a war-god depicted in the codices, probably to be identified with Nacon (q.v.).

False-Face Society (*Iroquois*, Woodlands, NA) an organised group of *shaman* healers, supervisors of religious rituals. They cure the sick with the aid of large wooden masks, of which there are twelve basic types. The members of the Society always function as a group, going through a grotesque, noisy dance at the house of the sick person, scattering ashes over him, shaking turtle-shell rattles and chanting incantations. The masks are called 'faces' not 'masks' because they are portraits in which the spirits are manifest. A 'face' is 'discovered' as the *shaman* carves his vision of the spirit into a living tree-trunk and then cuts the face free. Red-painted 'faces' were carved in the mornings, black-painted

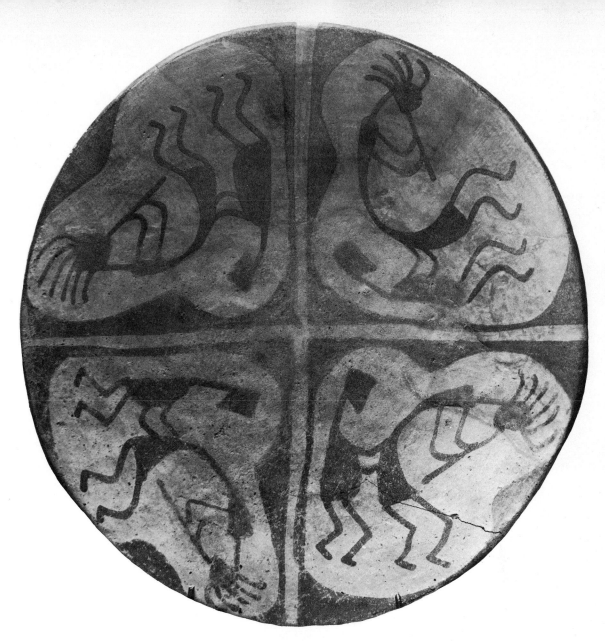

Tenth-century bowl from Snaketown, Arizona, decorated with dancing flute-players, possibly precursors of the *Hopi* Flute Dancers. Arizona State Museum. (*Photo: Werner Forman Archive.*)

ones in the afternoons. The False-Face medicine society is more properly called the *Hadigonsa Shano*.

Fat God, the (Mexico) an apparently important deity of the period A.D. 300–900. His significance is unknown but images of him have been found throughout the region.

Feathered Serpent see Plumed Serpent.

Fempellec 332.

Firavitoba see Nompanem.

Fire, House of **218**.

Fire Drill see Olelbis.

Flute Dance (*Hopi*, Pueblo, S West, NA) a biennial summer rite alternating with the Snake Dance (q.v.). The sun-spirit, who takes an important part in the ritual, is represented by a disc circled with ribbons and eagle feathers.

Fongasigde 329.

Four Earthquake (*Aztec*, Mexico) the era of the Fifth Sun. See **244**.

Four Ocelot (*Aztec*) the era of the First Sun. See **235–236**.

Four Rain (*Aztec*) the era of the Third Sun. See **238**.

Four Water (*Aztec*) the era of the Fourth Sun. See **239**.

Four Wind (*Aztec*) the era of the Second Sun. See **237**.

Frog 163–164.

Furachogué 299.

G, God G (*Maya*, CA) a solar deity of the codices, thought to represent

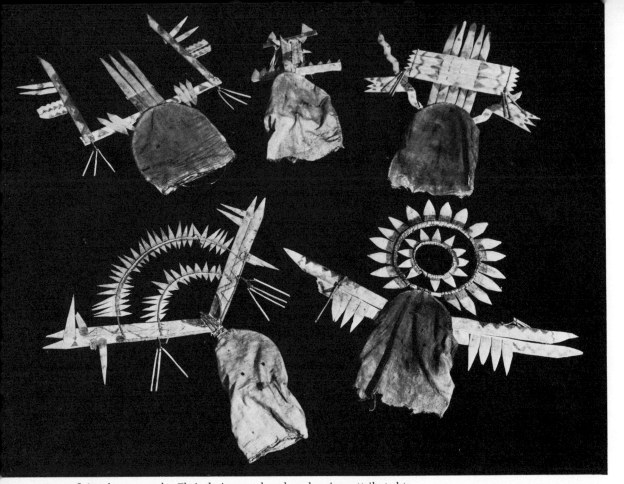

A set of *Apache gans* masks. Their designs are based on drawings attributed to the *gans* spirits. Maxwell Museum of Anthropology, Albuquerque. (*Photo: Maxwell Museum of Anthropology.*)

Kinichahau (q.v.).

Galibi **186.**

Ganga (*Voodoo*, Haiti) a *loa* (q.v.) probably of HIndu origin, see vol. 3: 5.3.

gangan (*Voodoo*) an inferior *shaman*, one unable to reach *hougan* (q.v.) status.

gans (*Apache*, Gt Plains, NA) mountain-spirits sent by the Great Spirit to teach the *Apache* all the arts of civilisation. Distressed by the people's corruption of their teaching, the *gans* went away to live in caves. They are impersonated in the *Gans Dance* by four dancers and an attendant clown.

Gans Dance see *gans*.

Ga-oh (*Iroquois*, Woodlands, NA) the wind-giant. His house is guarded by a bear, whose prowling brings the north wind; a panther, whose whining brings a strong westerly; a moose, whose breathing brings the wet east wind; a fawn, whose returning to its mother brings a gentle south wind.

Garsilasco Inca de la Vega p. 132

Georges, St. (*Voodoo*, Haiti) the Christian saint regarded as a *loa* by *Voodoo* cultists.

Geyaguga (*Cherokee*, Woodlands, NA) the moon-spirit.

Ghost Dance(s) (NA) the origin of these revivalist rituals bears a striking resemblance to that of the Melanesian Cargo Cults (see 7.1.). The first wave of dances began in 1870 among the *Paiute* of the California-Nevada border, led by the prophet Wodziwob, who foresaw that spirits of ancestors would return on a large train (the railroad had just been opened), announcing their arrival with an explosion. All the whites would be swallowed up in a cataclysm, leaving their goods for the Indians. The Great Spirit would then return to live among them. The dances Wodziwob had been taught in a vision would, it was said, hasten this millennium. The second series of dances began in 1890 inspired by Wovoka, son of Wodziwob's assistant. The tribes of the Gt Plains became involved and the cult was taken up by the disaffected *Sioux* who, under their great leader Sitting Bull, distorted Wovoka's teaching

(which was peaceable) and spread the belief that the dances would also cause a landslide and engulf the whites, while the dancers' specially decorated 'ghost shirts' would be invulnerable to bullets. The movement culminated in the massacre of the *Sioux* at Wounded Knee, 29 December 1890.

Giadruvava 180–181.

Gitche Manito a variant of Kitshe Manitou (q.v.).

Glendenwitha see Sosondowah.

Glisma (*Navajo*, S West, NA) culture-heroine. See **162–173.**

Gloom, House of 208, 216.

Glooscap 115.

Gluscap variant of Glooscap (q.v.).

Gohone (*Iroquoian* tribes, Woodlands, NA) the spirit of winter, an old man who raps the trees with his club. In the coldest frosts his blows can be heard as the trees split. See also Adekagagwaa.

Gougoune or Gugune variant of Ogoun (q.v.).

Grand Batala see 'Batala'.

Grand Bois (*Voodoo*, Haiti) together with Oraji Brisé one of the very powerful *loa*

Kwakiutl mask representing the monstrous Hokhokw. Private Collection, Kansas City.

Hunchouen 207, 211.

Hunhun Ahpu 207–209.

Hurakan 119, 194, 196–197.

H'Uraru (*Pawnee*, Gt Plains, NA) the earth, called 'atira', 'Mother'.

Hurin Cuzco 320.

Huruing Wuhti (*Hopi*, Pueblo, S West, NA) the primordial women of the east and west, between whom the sun journeyed. Together they created the earth and all its creatures, including man.

Hus Brothers 129–130.

Huti Watsi Ya (*Huron*, Woodlands, NA) the star-spirits of the Pleiades.

Huxley, Francis pp. 128, 223.

I, Goddess I (*Maya*, CA) a goddess depicted in the codices with serpentine headdress, taloned arms and a skirt decorated with crossed bones. She is probably to be identified with Ix Chel (q.v.).

Iatiku (*Acoma*, Pueblo, S West, NA) one of the two sisters who created man, the other being Nautsiti. Cf. Estanatlehi and Yolkai Estsan.

Iavurê-cunhã (*Xingu*, Brazil) a tiny forest-spirit.

Ibo (*Voodoo*, Haiti) a *loa* (q.v.) whose name derives from that of the Nigerian *Ibo* (*Igbo*) tribe. He is very handsome and friendly, but of secondary importance. Sometimes he is referred to as Ibo-léle.

Ibo loa (*Voodoo*) Voodoo cult gods and spirits deriving from the pantheon of the Nigerian *Ibo* (*Igbo*).

Iboroquiamio (*Guyana*) the personification of evil among the Guyanese, according to the seventeenth-century missionary Ruiz Blanco.

Idlirvirissong (*Eskimo*, Greenland) evil-spirit, cousin to the sun-spirit.

Igaluk (*Eskimo*, Alaska) the moon-spirit.

Igaranhã (*Xingu*, Brazil) a very powerful spirit who takes a canoe's shape. He can help people, but can also do them great harm.

Iguagué, Lake 299.

Ilamatecuhtli see Cihuacóatl.

Illimani, Mt. (*Aymará*, Bolivia) an *achachla* (q.v.) regarded as the protective spirit of La Paz. It is said that Illimani was especially favoured by Viracocha (q.v.), which made the neighbouring (volcanic) Mt. Mururata grumble jealously. Annoyed, Viracocha slung a stone at it and decapitated it. Its peak flew through the air and, descending, formed Mt. Sajama.

Imaymana Viracocha (*Inca*, Peru) one of the creator, sun-god's two sons,

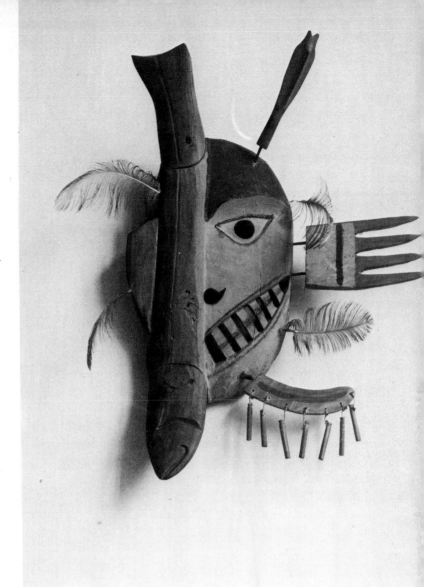

Eskimo *inua* mask representing the spirit of the salmon. Musée de Guimet, Paris. (*Photo: Hamlyn Picture Library.*)

according to one myth. The other was Tocapo Viracocha. Their father sent Imaymana to traverse the mountains and valleys naming trees, flowers and plants and teaching people their properties. Tocapo was given a similar task in the plains. Imaymana had absolute power. At the end of his work he ascended to the skies.

Inagi-utasunhi (*Cherokee*, Woodlands, NA) the malign twin, cf. Taswiscana.

Inca pp. 131–133 and **306, 314–328.**

Ingersuit (*Eskimo*) 'Fire-people', who dwell on the verge of sea and land, among the ice-cliffs. They are divided into the friendly Pug-nosed People and

the hostile Noseless, who drown sailors.

Inglesou see L'inglesou.

Inktonmi (*Dakota*, Gt Plains, NA) Spider, the Trickster.

Inomème, Maîtresse (*Voodoo*, Haiti) a *loa* (q.v.).

Inti (*Inca*, Peru) the sun-god. See p. 133.

inua (pl. *inue*) 'owner', indweller'. Even air has its *inua*, so have strength and appetite. The soul is the *inua* of the body. The *inue* are normally invisible but sometimes manifest themselves as light or fire, the sight of such a manifestation being an omen of death. An *inua* who helps or guards a man is called a *tornak* (q.v.). *Inue* of the sea are a sort of mermen, those of the stars and planets were once people, but now illuminate the skies of which they are the 'owners'—see p. 116 and **4** and cf. *manitou, orenda, wakonda* and 7.1: *mana*.

Iolokiamo see Cachimana.

Iouskeha, variant of Yoskeha (q.v.).

Ipa Huaco 322.

Iqui Balam 196–203.

Isakakate (*Crow*, Gt Plains, NA) the Great Spirit.

Isakawuate (*Crow*) Old Man Coyote, the Trickster.

Ishtinike (*Ponca*, Gt Plains, NA) the Trickster-hero. The meaning of his name is unknown.

Isitoq (*Eskimo*) a *tornak* (q.v.) whose name means 'Giant-eye'. His thick, coarse hair stands on end. Each of his eyes is divided by a large mouth containing one long tooth at the top between two shorter ones. He helps to find people who have broken taboos.

Istepahpah (*Creek*, Woodlands, NA) man-eating monster.

Itc Ak 104.

Itsike (*Osage*, Gt Plains, NA) the Trickster-hero. The meaning of his name is unknown.

Itzamkabain 190.

Itzamná (*Maya*, CA) thought to be the head of the *Mayan* pantheon, he is depicted as an old man with a prominent Roman nose and seems to have been particularly honoured as the inventor of writing and patron of learning (which was confined to the priesthood). His wife was Ix Chel (q.v.).

Itzlacoliuhqui (*Aztec*, Mexico) Carved-Obsidian-Knife—an aspect of Tezcatlipoca (q.v.).

Itzli (*Aztec*) Stone-Knife, a symbol of Tezcatlipoca (q.v.).

Itzpapálotl (*Aztec*) a stellar goddess of agriculture.

Ix Chel (*Maya*, CA) the Rainbow Lady. It is thought that she was the early *Mayan* moon-goddess, patroness of weaving, childbirth and medicine, but in the Dresden Codex she is depicted with snaky locks and clawed hands and feet, suggesting that after the *Toltec* conquest she was identified with the *Aztec* Coatlicue (q.v.). Ix Chel was the wife of Itzamná and seems to have been regarded as the mother of the *Mayan* pantheon. See also Ix Ch'up.

Ix Ch'up (*Maya*, CA) the moon-goddess of the *Toltec* period, possibly regarded as the consort of Ankinchil (q.v.). See also Ix Chel.

Ixcuina (*Aztec*, Mexico) Four-Faces, an

Drawing of Jakuí by Wacupiá. *Xingu, The Indians and Their Myths*, Villas Boas, pub. Souvenir Press.

aspect of Tlazoltéotl (q.v.).

Ixtab (Maya, CA) the goddess of the hanged. She received their souls in paradise.

Ixtlilton (*Aztec*, Mexico) the god of healing, feasting and games, Little-Black-Face.

Jacques Majeur (*Voodoo*, Haiti) the Christian St. James the Great, regarded as a *loa* (q.v.) by Voodoo cultists.

Jacunâum (*Xingu*, Brazil) the fish that swallows the moon. The Villa Boas brothers have suggested it may be the *crenicichla*.

jaguar gods pp. 123, 128, 129 and **218, 236, 350–355**; Ducá, Paititi, Tepeyoltotl, Tezcatlipoca.

Jakuí (*Xingu*, Brazil) an extremely important spirit living in a village at the bottom of rivers and pools. Ritual flutes are held not only to manifest Jakuí but actually to *be* him.

Jakuí-katu (*Xingu*) a small wooden mask thought of as a 'child' or a manifestation of Jakuí.

Jakuiaép (*Xingu*) a mask denoting the Jakuiaép spirit who lives on the river bed.

Jean, St. (*Voodoo*, Haiti) the Christian St.

John the Apostle, regarded as a *loa* by *Voodoo* cultists, to whom he is a stern but nervous spirit, always on the move. He rules the thunder and earthquakes.

Jean Baptiste (*Voodoo*) St. John the Baptist, the Christian saint, regarded as a *loa* by Voodoo cultists.

Jean Brigand (*Voodoo*) a *loa* (q.v.).

Jean Crabe, Maître (*Voodoo*) a *loa* (q.v.).

Jean Délé (*Voodoo*) a *loa* (q.v.).

Jean Féro (*Voodoo*) a *loa* (q.v.).

Jeune Gens Direct (*Voodoo*) a *loa* (q.v.).

jogah (*Iroquois*, Woodlands, NA) dwarf nature-spirits, who are divided into three tribes, the *Gahonga* (Stone-throwers) of rocks and rivers; the *Gandayah*, who tend the earth's fertility; the *Ohdows*, or underground people, who control the monstrous underworld spirits and prevent them from fulfilling their desire of coming up to the surface to see the sunlight.

K, God K (*Maya*, CA) deity shown in the codices with an extraordinarily long, distorted nose. Possibly he is to be identified with Kukulcan (q.v.).

Kablunait (*Eskimo*, Greenland) legendary white people, possibly a memory of early Scandinavian settlers.

Kadia-Bossu see Bazou.

Kahit (*Wintun*, coast, S West, NA) the primordial wind-god. He looks like a huge bat and carries a whistle in his mouth. See also Olelbis.

Kalasasaya p. 129.

Kanati (*Cherokee*, Woodlands, NA) the first man, ancestor of the *Cherokee*. His wife was Selu.

Kan-u-Uayeyab (*Maya*, CA) the god whose statue guarded cities' gates during the Kan years, governed by the southern Bacab (q.v.). A statue of a god called Bolon Dzacab was placed in the city centre in these years. See also Chac-u-Uayeyab, Ek-u-Uayeyab; Zac-u-Uayeyab.

Karous, Maîtresse (*Voodoo*, Haiti) a *loa* (q.v.).

kasip see Temaukel.

Kastsatsi (*Acoma*, Pueblo, S West, NA) the rainbow-spirit.

kachina(s) or *katcina(s)* (i) (*Zuñi*, Pueblo, S West, NA) a generic term originally, it seems, limited to a group of spirits personifying the beneficent powers of nature. Each clan has its own. The *katchinas* visit the Pueblo villages annually, when they are impersonated by masked and costumed men. The *katchina* masks were objects of great veneration and often burned on the death of the individual owner.
(ii) (*Hopi*, Pueblo, S West, NA) generic term for benevolent natural powers such as the sun's 'medicine'. See also Katsinas.

Katchina Mana (*Hopi*, Pueblo, S West, NA) one of the two spirits of the sprouting maize. The other is Kerwan.

Kathatakanave (*Walapai*, Mexico) Taught-by-Coyote, the first man who, together with Coyote (q.v.) emerged from the Grand Canyon. Kathatakanave prayed to the sky-spirits to make him companions, but Coyote, in interrupting the spell, spoiled it.

Katsinas (*Acoma*, Pueblo, S West, NA) the younger children of Iatiku, fertility- and rain-spirits.

Kchemnito (*Potawatomi*, Woodlands, NA) variant of Kitshi Manito (q.v.).

Keckamanetowa (*Fox*, Gt Plains, NA) the gentle creator-spirit.

Kelok (*Miwok*, S West, NA) a winged giant who killed Wekwek (q.v.) with red-hot stones, but was himself slain by the trickster Coyote (q.v.). From his corpse came the fire that engulfed the first world.

Hopi painted wooden *katchina* figure, *c.* 1850. Its eyes are said to symbolise rain clouds, its eyelashes rain. Private Collection. (*Photo: Werner Forman Archive.*)

Kemush 16–24. See also Kumush.

Keneun (*Iroquois*, Woodlands, NA) Golden Eagle, chief of the Thunderbirds (q.v.), an invisible spirit whose flashing eyes cause lightning while thunder comes from the beating of his great wings. See also **118**.

Kenos (*Ona*, Tierra del Fuego) the first man and *Ona* culture-hero.

Kerwan see Katchina Mana.

Ketchimanetowa (*Fox*, Gt Plains, NA) the Great Spirit.

Ketchkatch 17.

Ketqskwaye (*Huron*, Woodlands, NA) Grandmother Toad, the creatrix.

Ketsi Niousak (*Abnaki*, Woodlands, NA) the personification of absolute goodness, in contrast to the evil Matsi Niousak.

Khuno (*Aymará*, Bolivia) the god of snowstorms. Some Indians settling in the high *yunga* valleys on the eastern slopes of the cordillera, polluted the sacred peaks of Illimani and Illampu (qq.v.) with smoke from the fires they were using to clear the forest for cultivation. Khuno assailed them with torrential storms and landslides (? erosion caused by deforestation). Coming out of the caves in which they had taken refuge, the Indians could find nothing to eat. In desperation they tried the brilliant leaves of a shrub, which gave them such euphoric energy they were able to return home to Tituanco. The shrub was the coca (q.v.), knowledge of which was thus spread.

Kiaklo (*Zuñi*, Pueblo, S West, NA) a mythical hero who visited Pautiwa (q.v.) and warned the *ashiwi* (q.v.) that the gods were coming to give them the breath of life, so that after death they could go to the dance-house-of-the-gods, Kothluwalawa, before returning to the underworld from which they had emerged.

kia-pod (*Tuparu*, Brazil) the heavenly spirits, with whom only the *shaman* can communicate. From them he receives the magical yellow *pagab* seeds that he uses to bewitch and kill his enemies.

Killer-of-Enemies (*Apache*, Gt Plains, NA) the culture-hero and also the principle of life.

Kina rites (*Yahgan*, Tierra del Fuego) a ghost rite from which women are excluded, because, it is said, originally they dominated their men folk by wearing spirit masks which deceived and frightened the men. The trick being discovered, all but one of the women were killed and ever since the men have worn the masks and ruled the women.

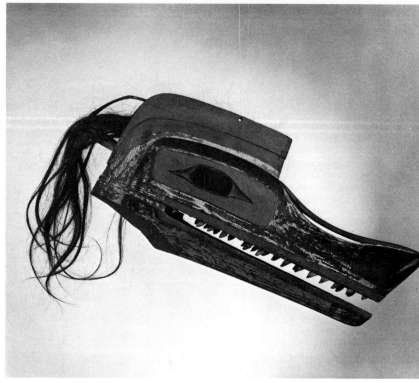

Late eighteenth-century *Nootka* wolf headdress used in *Klukwala* rites. Denver Art Museum, Denver, Colorado. (*Photo: Denver Art Museum.*)

Kinich Ahau (*Maya*, CA) a solar deity usually identified with God G (q.v.) of the codices. See also Cha-u-Uayeyab.

Kinich Kakmo (*Maya*) the sun-god, symbolised by the brilliant macaw.

kinno (*Tupari*, Brazil) the people who were left underground when Aroteh (q.v.) and Tovapod dug out the first men. They will come up to repopulate the earth when all its present inhabitants have died.

Kiousa see Oki.

Kisani 35, 37.

Kishá Manido (*Menominee*, Woodlands, NA) variant of Kitshi Manitou (q.v.), also known as Masha Manido.

Kisin (*modern Maya*, Yucatán, CA) the evil earthquake-spirit who lives beneath the earth. Disliking the rain sent by the good Yumchakob, Kisin also raises winds to drive it away. His realm is a purgatory in which all souls, except those of soldiers killed in battle and women dying in childbirth, spend some time. Suicides are doomed to remain there eternally.

Kitshi Manitou (*Chippewa*, Woodlands, NA) the Great Spirit, translated as 'Master-of-Life' or 'Great Mystery'.

kiva **158.** See also *Kiva* groups.

Kiva groups (*Zuñi*: Pueblo, S West, NA) the six religious societies of the *Zuñi*: the Sun-priests; the *Uwanami* (Rain-makers); the *Katchinas* (q.v.); the *Katchina* priests; the priests of the War-gods (see **156, 158–159**) and those of the Animal-gods. They meet in the *kiva*—that is communal houses/temples in which the secret rites of the various fraternities and cults are held. Women are admitted to the *kiva* only in special circumstances when the rite calls for their presence.

Klamath, Lake **18.**

Klehonoai 50, 61.

Kloketen rite (*Ona*, Tierra del Fuego) an initiation rite comparable with the *Yahgan Kina* (q.v.). Its origin is similarly explained.

Klukwala (*Nootka*, NW coast, NA) the Wolf Society, whose rites resemble a simplified form of the Kwakiutl *Hamatsa* (q.v.).

K'makamtch (*Klamath*, Gt Plains, NA) Old Man, the creator-trickster. Cf. Kemush.

Kobath (*Skagit*, coast, S West, NA) Mt. Baker, one of the two mountains that was not submerged in the great flood, the other being Takobah (Mt. Rainier).

Koil 17.

Kokopelli (*Hopi*, Pueblo, S West, NA) a
fertility *katchina*.

Koloowisi (*Zuñi*, Pueblo, S West,
NA) the plumed serpent. Among the
Zuñi, as among so many other peoples,
the serpent has a dual significance,
both chthonic and celestial—associated
with death, but also with lightning and
fertility. Koloowisi is depicted with
maize and water streaming from his
mouth. The neighbouring *Hopi* call him
Palulukoñ (q.v.).

Komokwa (*Kwakiutl* and *Haida*, NW
Coast, NA) the sea-god, living in a
great underwater home supported by
living sea-lions. He controls the killer-
whales, who provide the food for his
feasts, and at very high tides comes
ashore attended by his sea creatures.
Any mortal who can journey to
Komokwa's house receives the right to
use his masks, dances and songs. This
right can be bequeathed to members of
one's lineage.

Konakadset (*Tlingit*, NW Coast, NA) a
mythical hero of renowned strength.
He is usually depicted as an aquatic
wolf with some killer-whale features.
The *Haida* call him Wasco.

Koshari (*Sia*, Pueblo, S West, NA) the
first man.

koshpik (*Yahghan*, Tierra del Fuego)
spirits of the dead. They fly
away to the east.

Kothluwalawa (*Zuñi*, Pueblo, S West,
NA) the dance-house of the gods,
where the deities hold their council.
The souls of all dead men and of those
few women who are inducted into the
Kotikili kiva (q.v.) during their lives,
have right of access to Kothluwalawa.
See also *Ashiwanni*.

Koti (*Creek*, Woodlands, NA) the Water-
frog, a helpful spirit.

Kotikili kiva (*Zuñi*, Pueblo, S West,
NA) the society of those who
impersonate the *katchinas*. It includes
all the men and a few women.

Kowwituma 156, 158–159.

Koyemshi (*Zuñi*, Pueblo, S West,
NA) the Mudheads, two of the *Zuñi*
Katchina priests. They wear mud-
daubed masks with bulging eyes, a
gaping hole for the mouth and the face
covered with warts. They are believed
to be the offspring of an incestuous
union. Licensed clowns, they are
agents for the expression of otherwise
repressed hostility to the ceremonies.
See also *Kiva* groups.

Kuarup ritual (*Xingu*, Brazil) funeral rite.
See 346–349.

Kukucan (*Maya*, CA) the wind-god,
thought to be God K (q.v.) of the

Kwakuitl mask of Komokwa. John H. Hauberg Collection, Seattle.

codices.

Kukumatz (*Mohave*, Mexico) one of the
twin sons of the Earth-Mother. His
sibling is Tochipa. They raised the
skies, set the cardinal points and
organised the land. See also Hokomata.

Kulimina (*Arawak*, Guyana) the
creatrix of women. See also
Kururumany.

Kumush 24–27. See also Kemush.

Kururumany (*Arawak*) the creator of
man and origin of all goodness.
Descending to earth, he found that
people had become corrupt, so
ordained that they should die like
snakes and other vermin, instead of
enjoying immortality. His wives were
Emisiwaddo and Wurekaddo. See also
Kulimina.

Kutoyis (*Blackfoot*, Gt Plains, NA) hero
and wonderchild. He was found by an
old couple who had put a clot of
buffalo blood in a pot to cook. Hearing
crying from the pot, they looked inside

and found Kutoyis. On the fourth day
after this, he told the people to tie him
to their lodge poles one after the other,
so that he could grow and become a
man. They obeyed and after being tied
to each pole in turn, he was fully
grown.

Kwanyip (*Ona*, Tierra del Fuego) a
culture-hero, the vanquisher of the
evil-one, Chenuke. He battled
constantly against an invisible, black,
man-eating giant (? personification of
death).

La Silène–La Baliene (*Voodoo*, Haiti) a
loa (q.v.).

Lacroix, Baron (*Voodoo*) a *loa* (q.v.).

Lalakoñti (*Hopi*, Pueblo, S West, NA) a
September ritual conducted by women
invoking the goddesses of growth and
of corn to give a good harvest. The
participants dance with baskets around
the two Lakone girls, who wear

205

Drawing of *mamaé* spirits by Wacupiá. *Xingu, The Indians and Their Myths*, Villas Boas, pub. Souvenir Press.

brave. He climbed to the Eagle's home beyond the sky and, helped by Spider-Woman (q.v.) overcame Eagle's enemies, the Bumble Bees and Tumbleweeds. He also tricked the Indians into gambling away all their treasure and took it back to the skies by means of ropes made of lightning. Cf. **52**.

Mudheads see Koyemshi.

Mururata, Mt. see Illimani, Mt.

Mushmush 17.

Muskrat 121, 122.

Mustamho (*Mohave*, Mexico) the grandson of the Earth-Mother and Sky-Father, and creator of the first people. When the land was later flooded he carried all its people in his arms until the waters subsided.

Mutsoyef (*Cheyenne*, Gt Plains, (NA) Sweet-Medicine, a culture-hero credited with the introduction of most of the *Cheyenne*'s rituals and customs. As a youth he was handsome, but strange in manner. After marriage he and his wife travelled to the Sacred Mountains by the Black Hills where, with other specially-selected wise men of all the peoples on earth, he became a pupil of the Great Spirit, Maiyun, who gave him four arrows and taught him how to use and care for them. Two have mysterious power over buffalo, two over humans. These were the Spirit's great gifts to the *Cheyenne* for, when the buffalo arrows were pointed at the animals, they became baffled and helpless and so easy prey to the hunters. The two other arrows, pointed at enemies, blinded and confused them. The story thus records the *shaman's* initiation and evokes a vivid image of the *shaman's* magical rôle in the buffalo hunt, a rôle like that recorded in primitive paintings from many parts of the world.

Naápatecuhtli (*Aztec*, Mexico) a Tlaloque—see Tláloc.

Nacon (*Maya*, CA) the war-god, honoured at a Pax (May) festival of which, it is thought, the *Holkan Okot* (Dance of Warriors) formed a part. Nacon is associated both with the death-god Ah Puch and with Ek Ahau (qq.v.).

Nagaitcho (*Kato*, NW coast, NA) the Great Traveller. With Thunder's help he repaired the original sky, supported the heavens on pillars (establishing the four quarters) and flooded the world. The present earth then came down from the north in the form of a great horned

creature. Walking underground, pausing here and there to look up and so making land rise above the floodwaters, the earth carried Nagaitcho between its great horns. When it reached the far south, it lay down. Nagaitcho arranged its head properly and daubed clay between its eyes and over each of its horns. He lay reeds on the clay, more clay over them and in that planted trees, shrubs and grass. On earth's head he made the mountain peaks.

Nago loa (*Voodoo*, Haiti) *loa* (q.v.) deriving from gods of the Nigerian *Yoruba* people.

Nago Shango (*Voodoo*) an important and powerful *loa* (q.v.), of lively appearance derived from the *Yoruba* thunder-god Shango (see vol. 2: 4.3. p. 186).

Nahuatlan pp. 125, 133 and **264, 283**.

nahurak (*Pawnee*, Gt Plains, NA) the animal-spirits. They lived in five houses, *Pahuk, Nakiskat, Tsurapako, Kitsawitsak, Pahua*, the first being the most important.

Nambo-Nansi (*Voodoo*, Haiti) a *loa* (q.v.) derived from the W African *Ashanti* and *Fon* peoples' trickster-hero Anansi.

Nanaboojoo 115, 123.

Nane Chaha see Nanih Waya.

Nanibozho 115.

Nanih Waya (*Choctaw*, Woodlands, NA) the mound in Winston County, Mississippi, said to be the end of the tunnel through which the *Choctaw* emerged from the underworld, accompanied by Grasshopper. However, Grasshopper Mother, who stayed behind, was killed by men, and the *Choctaw* persuaded the Great Spirit, Aba, to close the tunnel's mouth, imprisoning her murderers below, where they were transformed into ants.

Nanook, Nanue (*Eskimo*) Ursa Major and the Pleiades.

Na'pi (*Blackfoot*, Gt Plains, NA) Old Man, the creator.

Nascakiyetl 103–104, **105**.

Nass, River 103.

Nautsiti see Iatiku.

Nayanezgani 54–56, 58, 91–102.

Naymlap p. 130 and 329–332.

Neegyauks (*Tlingit*, NW Coast, NA) Volcano-Woman and a frog-spirit, the *Tlingit* version of the *Haida* Dzelarhons.

Negakfok (*Eskimo*, Alaska) the cold-weather-spirit, represented in a ritual dance by a man wearing a sad-faced wooden mask. The expression is sad because the spirit must leave the people as spring comes. Negakfok masks were carved from driftwood and

Wooden Eskimo mask of Negakfok. Museum of the American Indian, New York. (*Photo: Museum of the American Indian, Heye Foundation*.)

burned each year at the end of the rite even though driftwood, the only timber available, was very scarce and so extremely precious.

Nemterequeteba (*Chibcha*, Colombia) a culture-hero who came from Venezuela 140 years before the Spanish conquest. He was depicted as an old, bearded, long-haired man, similar to Thunupa (q.v.) of whom he may be a version. He is also called Sugumonxe or Sugunsúa (Disappearer) and Chimizapagua (Chiminigagua's messenger). Sometimes he is identified with the sun, Zuhe, or with the supreme being, Bochica (qq.v.). He was pursued by the goddess Huitaca (q.v.) and according to some stories changed her into an owl or into the moon.

Nerrivik 9, 11–15.

Nesaru (*Arikara*, Gt Plains, NA) the great creator. Having made the earth and peopled it with supermen Nesaru found that they were foolish and scorned the gods, so he drowned them, taking care to preserve in a cave the animals, whom he liked, and the maize plant. He then created Mother Corn and sent her to find the people who were imprisoned in the underworld and lead them into the light of day.

Nhenebush (*Ojibway*, Woodlands, NA) the Trickster—of human appearance. He marked the birch as his own, forming the delicate patterns on its bark that command the Thunderers' (q.v.) respect. (The birch bark is not only waterproof but highly resistant to fire, hence, unlike the forest pines, it is not easily set alight if struck in a thunderstorm.)

Nicahtagah 199.

Night Chant (*Navajo*, S West, NA) the most popular of the *Navajo* rituals. It can only be held in winter when snakes are hibernating. It lasts nine days and involves the preparation of ritual sweat-houses, sand paintings of the spirits, the sprinkling of sacred masks with life-giving pollen and water. The ceremonies end with a great masque of the spirits and prayers to the 'dark bird who is lord of pollen' (i.e. the thunder cloud).

Niltshi 34, 60.

Ninacolla 329.

Ninagentue 329.

Nipinoukhe (*Montagnais*, Woodlands, NA) the spirit of spring. He shares the world with the winter-spirit Pipounoukhe. When their time in one part of the earth draws to its close they reciprocally change places in a rite called *Ahitescatoneh*.

Noh Ek (*Maya*, CA) the spirit of the Great Star, (i.e. of Venus).

Nohochakyum (*Lacandones*, Yucatán) the chief deity of this people, probably deriving from the ancient *Maya* Chac (q.v.). Dwelling in the eastern sky, he is served by the spirits of the stars and planets. His subordinate brothers rule the other quarters of the heavens. Of them, the most powerful is Usukun (q.v.). At the end of the world Nohochakyum will gird himself with the serpent Hapikern, whose breath will draw all the people to him, and then kill them.

Nokomis 116, 117–118.

Nompanem (*Chibcha*, Colombia) legendary divine king to whom Bochica or the culture-hero Nemterequeteba (q.v.) taught all the arts of civilisation and religion. He was succeeded by his brother-in-law Firavitoba.

Noogumee (*Micmac*, Woodlands,

Painted wooden mask of the *Kwakiutl* spirit Noohlmahl. Originally it was decorated with human hair. British Museum. (*Photo: British Museum.*)

NA) variant of Nokomis (q.v.).

Noohlmahl (*Kwakiutl*, NW Coast, NA) the fool, a character in the winter *Hamatsa* ritual.

Noohlum ritual (*Kwakiutl*) a rite including masked dancers, but they were not, as in other *Kwakiutl* rituals, possessed by the spirits whose masks they wore.

North West Coast, North American Indians of the pp. 117–18.

Nowutset (*Sia*, Pueblo, S West, NA) sister of Utset and, like her, created by the primordial spider Sussistinnake (q.v.). Nowutset was the mother of people other than the Indians. Though stronger than their mother, Utset, she was less intelligent and lost a riddle game with her. Utset then killed her and drew out her heart.

Nueva corónica y buen gobierno p. 132.

Nukuchyumchakob see Yumchakob.
Nuliajoq 9.
Numokh Mukana (*Mandan*, Gt Plains, NA) the first man.
Nunhyunuwi (*Cherokee*, Woodlands, NA) a man-eating stone giant.

Obatala see 'Batala.
Ocelopan 292.
Ocelotanatiuh 244.
Ochocalo 329.
Ockabewis (*Chippewa*, Woodlands, NA) the culture-hero.
Ogoun (*Voodoo*, Haiti) a *loa* (q.v.) derived from the W African *Yoruba* war-god (see vol. 2: 4.3. p. 185). To the *Voodoo* cultists he is both warrior and blacksmith and is especially fond of rum and tobacco. He is also called Agomme Tonnère and sometimes depicted in the likeness of the Christian St. George—the thunder- and warrior-god being especially associated among almost every people with the slayer of the dragon-serpent monster.
Ogoun Tonnère a variant of Ogoun (q.v.).
Ogun Balanjo a variant of Ogoun (q.v.).
Ogun Ferraille a variant of Ogoun (q.v.).
Ohoyo-osh Chishba (*Choctaw*, Woodlands, NA) the Corn Mother.
Oí (*Xingu*, Brazil) strange, legendary people. Very tall, they always sang choruses as they walked and constantly spied on the *Xingu*. Although they always carried great clubs over their right shoulders they never attacked anyone, just watched them.
Oke Hede (*Mandan*, Gt Plains, NA) the evil one of the first twins.
Oki (*Oumas*, Woodlands, NA) the sun-spirit, whose image watched over the bodies of dead chiefs, who were said to be his descendants. He was also called Kiousa.
Oklatabashih (*Choctaw*, Woodlands, NA) Mourner-of-the-People, the sole survivor of the flood.
Old Man see Na'pi.
Old Man Acorn (*Wintun*, coast, S West, NA) he fertilised the earth after it had been recreated by Olelbis (q.v.). following the flood.
Old Man of the Ancients 16–27.
Olelbis (*Wintun*) He-who-sits-above, first known living in Olelpanti (though, it is said, he may have previously lived elsewhere) with two old women—his grandmothers, who helped him to build a paradisal sweat-house, roofed by the entwined branches of six oaks and walled with screens of flowers. After the first world was set on fire by

Aztec stone carving of Ometecuhtli in his aspect as Tonacatecuhtli. Museum für Völkerkunde, Basle. (*Photo: Werner Forman Archive.*)

Shooting Star, Fire Drill and Buckeye Bush—to avenge the theft of Flint—Olelbis, on the advice of his grandmothers, had the sky propped up and then summoned Kahit, the wind-spirit, and Mem Loimis, the water-goddess, to extinguish the fire, which they did by flooding the earth. Olelbis then recreated the world. See also Old Man Acorn and **129–132**.
Olelpanti 129, 131.
Olmec pp. 123, 128
Omacatl see Tezcatlipoca.
Omecíhuatl (*Aztec*, Mexico) the wife of Ometecuhtli (q.v.).
Ometecuhtli (*Aztec*) an important, though rather remote god, Lord of Duality, the equivalent of Tonacateculitli (q.v.). His wife is Omecíhuatl.
Ometéotl (*Aztec*) the bisexual omnipotent creator.
Ometochtli (*Aztec*) Two Rabbit, an

important *pulque* (q.v.) god. See also Centzontotochtin.
Omeyocan (*Aztec*) Place-of-the-Twofold—home of the creative deities Ometecuhtli and Omecíhuatl. From here, souls descend to be born into the lot consigned them at the world's beginnings.
Omoa see El Dorado.
Ona 343.
Onatah (*Iroquois*, Woodlands, NA) the corn-spirit, daughter of Eithinoha (q.v.). Once, when she went out to collect dew, Onatah was captured by the spirit of evil, who imprisoned her in darkness below the earth, but after a search, the sun-spirit found and rescued her.
Ondoutaete (*Huron*, Woodlands, NA) the war-god.
orenda (*Iroquois*, Woodlands, NA) a good, indwelling spirit, contrasted to the *otkon*. See **90**.

Orion 6.

Oshadagea (*Iroquois*, Woodlands, NA) Dew Eagle, one of Hino's (q.v.) warriors. He lives in the western sky and carries a dew-pond in the hollow of his back. When evil fire-spirits attack the earth, he flies out and scatters his dew upon the scorched land, restoring its verdure.

otkon see *orenda* and 90.

Otomi 283.

Owasse (*Menominee*, Woodlands, NA) the bear-chief of the *anamaqkiu*. See 119ff.

Oxheheon (*Cheyenne*, Gt Plains, NA) the Sun Dance. The name means roughly 'New-Life-Lodge'.

Oxlahuntiku 187.

Oxomoco 234, 241, 281, 292.

Ozoun Elou Mandja, Maît'(re) a variant of Ogoun (q.v.).

---

pabid (*Tupari*, Brazil) a soul of the dead. It emerges through the pupils and crosses the land of the dead over the backs of two crocodiles and two huge snakes. Great jaguars try to frighten it but are powerless to harm it. Eventually the soul reaches Mani-mani River and the dead realm, where it is received by its chief *shaman* Patobkia (q.v.). After initiation rites the *pabid* joins its fellows in their large circular huts. They sleep standing up and do no work since Patobkia produces food magically. Much of their time is spent in dancing, adorned with feathers.

Paccaritambo 316, 321.

Pachacamac see Coniraya and 310–313.

Pachacuti, the *Inca* pp. 131, 133.

Pachamama (Peruvian-Bolivian borders) the earth-goddess to whom *coca* is offered to ensure good crops and to win her blessing for a new home.

Pachayachachic (*Inca*, Peru) the creator, according to one writer, and the father of Imaymana Viracocha and Tocapa Viracocha (qq.v.). He appointed Manco Capac (q.v.) as king and said Manco was to regard him as his father.

pagab see *kia-pod*.

Pah 64, 70.

Paititi (*Guaraní*, Paraguay) the land of gold, ruled over by El Gran Moxo and said to lie in Lake Cuni-Cuni, guarded by a jaguar-lizard Teyú-Yaguá. The tale almost certainly arose as a result of marauding raids upon outposts of the *Inca* empire.

pajé (*Xingu*, Brazil) *shaman*-healer.

Palulukoñ (*Hopi*, Pueblo, S West, NA) the great plumed serpent. See Koloowisi.

Panotlan 281.

paqok (modern *Maya*, Yucatán) night-wandering fiends who attack women.

Pariacaca (*Quechua*, Peru) after a great flood, five falcons were born from golden eggs on Mt. Condorcoto. They changed into men, Pariacaca and his brothers. He was a great lord of wind and storm and expelled Huallallo Caruincho (q.v.), making him flee into the forests. Huallallo turned himself into a bird and hid on Mt. Tacilluka. Pariacaca's sons attacked the mountain with thunderbolts and Huallallo fled again, hiding behind a great double-headed snake. Pariacaca petrified it, so Huallallo finally had to flee to the forests and there he remained. Pariacaca's sons then returned to Mt. Lamallaka and, summoning all the people, established their father's cult in that place.

Parichata, Mt. (*Aymará*, Bolivia) one of two peaks—the other being Tati-Turqui, honoured as the tutelary *achachilas* (q.v.) of Potosi. It is said that when the silver mines of Parichata were open, the Indian labourers prayed to the mountain to help them against their Spanish masters. The spirit of the mountain transformed all its beetles into mules which, at dead of night, carried away all the silver so the mines had to close and the *Aymará* were no longer worked to their deaths.

Parima, Lake, see El Dorado.

Pasikola (*Creek*, Woodlands, NA) Rabbit, the Trickster (q.v.).

Patécatl (*Aztec*, Mexico) the god of medicine and husband to Mayahuel (q.v.). He was an important *pulque* god. See Centzontotchtin.

Patobkia (*Tupari*, Brazil) the chief *shaman* of the dead souls (*pabid*, q.v.). When the *pabid* arrives in the village of the dead it is blind. Patobkia sprinkles pepper juice in its eyes to make it see. He then gives it unfermented *chicha* (beer) and afterwards leads it to the giant *shaman* rulers of the village, Vaugh'eh and Mpokálero. Male *pabid* must have ritual intercourse with Vaugh'eh, female ones with Mpokálero, before being allowed to join their new companions.

Pauahtuns (*Maya*, CA) four deities of unknown significance.

Pautiwal (i) (*Zuñi*, Pueblo, S West, NA) the lord of the dead.
(ii) (*Hopi*, Pueblo, S West, NA) the sun-spirit.

Payatami 157, 160.

Paynal (*Aztec*, Mexico) messenger of Huitzilopochtli (q.v.).

Pelado Peak 49.

Petalesharo (*Pawnee*, Gt Plains, NA) a

famous late nineteenth-century hero, who is said to have stopped the sacrifice of a captured *Comanche* girl when, according to the old *Pawnee* ritual, she was about to be torn to pieces and buried in the fields to honour the fertility-spirit Morning Star.

Petrel 106, 109.

Petro loa (*Voodoo*, Haiti) a group of spirits whose rites are said to have been introduced from San Domingo by one Don Pedro (hence the name). Their emblem is the whip and Huxley suggests they originated in response to slavery. Easily annoyed, and then malign, they have red eyes and make those whom they possess writhe and grimace in an ugly fury. The *Petro loa* are in strong contrast to the dignified and benevolent *Rada* (q.v.). They visit stern and overwhelming punishment upon those who fail promptly to pay for their services.

Peyote cult (NA) a blend of traditional Indian and Christian belief involving ritual use of the hallucinogen *peyote*. The cult is organised in the Native American Church.

Philomène, Maîtresse (*Voodoo*) the Roman Catholic St. Philomena, regarded as a *loa* (q.v.) by *Voodoo* cultists.

Pie, Papa (*Voodoo*) St. Peter as a *loa* (q.v.). A grave soldier who lives at the bottom of ponds and rivers, he is very powerful. Floods are his work.

Pié Anfalo (*Voodoo*) a *loa* (q.v.).

Pié Damballa a variant of Damballa (q.v.).

Pillan (*Araucan*, Chile) the storm-god.

Piltzintecuhtli (*Aztec*, Mexico) Young Prince, a title of Tonatiuh (q.v.). See also Xochiquetzal and 241.

Pinga (*Eskimo*) a female spirit. Her abode is unknown and she appears only in necessity. A strict housekeeper, she watches carefully over men's actions, especially over their treatment of hunted animals.

Pipounoukhe see Nipinoukhe.

Pishumi (*Acoma*, Pueblo, S West, NA) the spirit of disease.

Pitazofi 329.

Place of the Dark 21.

Pleiades see *anitsutsa*, Huti Watsi Ya and 5.

Plumed Serpent pp. 124, 125 and see also Koloowisi, Mixcóatl, Paluton, Quetzalcóatl.

Poïa (*Blackfoot*, Gt Plains, NA) the Star Boy, Scarface, son of the Morning Star and the earthly Soatsaki (q.v.). As a youth he fell in love with a chieftain's daughter but his scarred face repelled her, so he journeyed to the home of the sun to ask him to remove the blemish. *En route* Poïa killed seven evil birds who threatened his father's life. Sun rewarded him by not only removing the scar but teaching him the rites of the Sun Dance and giving him a flute and song to enchant his beloved. Poïa was ordered to teach the *Blackfoot* the rituals of the Sun Dance, which he did before returning to the sky with his bride. He is the planet Jupiter.

Polik Mana (*Hopi*, S West, NA) the butterfly kachina.

Polisson, Monsieur (*Voodoo*, Haiti) a *loa* (q.v.).

Pollen Boy 49.

Pong Massa 332.

Pookonghoya (*Hopi*, Pueblo, S West, NA) one of the twin sons of the solar spirit and brother to Balongahoya. They are the *Hopi* equivalents of Maasewe (q.v.) and Uyuwyewe, of Nayanezgani and Thobadzistshini, see 54–56, 91–102.

Poopo, Lake (*Quillaca*, Bolivia) a lake sacred to the moon and as the original parent of these Indians.

Popul Vuh pp. 125, 223 and 191–203, 207–231.

Poshaiyangkyo (*Zuñi*, Pueblo, S West, NA) the first man and culture-hero.

Poshaiyanne (*Sia*, Pueblo, S West, NA) the son of a virgin, Poshaiyanne was a great *shaman* and skilful gambler, winning all the *Sia* people from their chief (cf. 52). He proved a benevolent ruler and brought his people an abundance of game and riches. Eventually, promising to return, he left them. Jealous enemies killed him but he was revivified by the touch of a downy eagle feather ('life feather', see 94). One day he will return. Some commentators see this as a northern version of the Quetzalcóatl (q.v.) myth but the theme is of course common to peoples in all parts of the world.

pueblos, Indians of the pp. 119–120.

Pukeheh (*Havasupi*, Mexico) the daughter of the good Tochopa. When her uncle, the jealous Hokomata (q.v.) flooded the earth, Tochopa sealed Pukeheh in a hollow log and so enabled her to survive. When the flood receded, she emerged and bore two children, a boy fathered by the sun-spirit and a daughter fathered by a waterfall. These two became the parents of the world's present inhabitants.

pukwudjie(s) (*Algonquian*, Woodlands, NA) dwarf nature-spirit(s).

pulque (*Mexico*) an hallucinogenic beverage made from the sap of the *maguey* plant, and used in rituals. See also *peyote*.

Purrunaminari (*Maipuri*, Guyana) the creator. His wife is Taparimarru, their son Sisiri.

puskita see *Busk* festival.

Qalanganguase (*Eskimo*) a crippled orphan left alone while his fellow villagers went hunting. The spirits of his parents and younger sister came to comfort him but his sister left her departure too late and her shadow was glimpsed by the villagers. They challenged Qalanganguase to a *shamanistic* singing duel and then, binding him to the house posts, left him dangling. His parents came and summoned him and villagers never saw him again.

Qamaits (*Bella Coola*, NW Coast, NA) the chief deity of this tribe, who are exceptional among the NW Coast Indians in conceiving this principal spirit to be feminine. Qamaits is a great warrior and at the beginning of time is said to have fought the mountains that had rendered earth uninhabitable. She reduced them to more manageable proportions. Qamaits lives at the eastern end of the upper heaven beyond a bleak prairie. Behind her house is the pool of Sisiutl (q.v.). This goddess is not offered prayers and is said rarely to visit the earth. When she does so sickness and death result. Of more immediate importance to the *Bella Coola* are the subordinate spirits led by Senx (q.v.).

Querranna (*Sia*, Pueblo, S West, NA) the second man. Cf. Koshari.

quetzal 265.

Quetzalcóatl pp. 124, 125, 127 and 233, 236–237, 240, 242, 245, 250–252, 253, 263, 264–275.

Quiqre 215.

Quiqrixgag 215.

Quiqxil 215.

Quiyauhtonatiuh 244.

Rabbit, see p. 121 Wabus and 115–127.

Rada loa (*Voodoo*, Haiti) the chief deities of the *Voodoo* pantheon, originating from Benin (Dahomey). In contrast to the *Petra loa* (q.v.) the *Rada* are dignified and benevolent, organised into a hierarchy that still reflects the hierarchical organisation of the ancient kingdom of Dahomey.

Raimondi Stele p. 128.

Rairu 340–342.

Raphaël (*Voodoo*) the Roman Catholic St. Raphael, regarded as a *loa* (q.v.) by *Voodoo* cultists.

Ravagé (*Voodoo*) a *loa* (q.v.).

Raven p. 121. See also Yetl and 122.

Red World 29, 31.

revenant(s) (*Voodoo*) spirit(s) of the dead who, feeling for some reason neglected, return to plague their living relatives.

Rhpisunt (*Haida*, NW Coast) the Bear-Mother—wife of Dzarilaw (q.v.).

Rock-Crystal Boy 49, 60.

Rock-Crystal Girl 49.

Sacred bundles (NA) bundles of ritual objects, sometimes referred to as 'medicine bundles'. Cf. 7.2. 160 and see 65.

Saiyamkoob 204.

Sajama, Mt. See Illimani, Mt.

Sakuru 64, 70.

Samedi, Baron (*Voodoo*, Haiti) the important *loa* (q.v.) of the cemetery.

San Francisco, Mt. 49.

San Juan, Mt. 49.

Santeria (*Cuba*) the worship of African deities predominantly *Yoruba* in origin.

Sargant, William pp. 128, 223.

Sedit 129–132.

Sedna 9–10, 13–15.

Selu see Kanati.

Senotlke (*Squawmish*, NW Coast, NA) the snake-monster that is an important totem of this region. See Sisiutl.

Senx (*Bella Coola*, NW Coast, NA) the creator and sun-spirit, known as the Sacred One and Our Father. He rules the House of Myths in the lower heaven where all the gods subordinate to Qamaits (q.v.) live. In his creative work he is helped by Alkuntam (q.v.).

Seqinek (*Eskimo*) the sun-spirit.

serviteur (*Voodoo*, Haiti) one who becomes possessed by a *loa* (q.v.) during cult ceremonies.

Shakanli (*Choctaw*, Woodlands, NA) the serpent-monster.

Shakuru (*Pawnee*, Gt Plains, NA) the sun-spirit.

shaman pp. 113, 116, 120, and 173, 176. See also A'men, *angakok*, False-Face Society, *gangan*, *hougan* and vol. 2: 3.1.

Shango (*Voodoo*, Haiti) an important *loa* (q.v.) derived from the *Yoruba* lightning-god. See vol. 2: 4.3. p. 186.

Shasta, Mt. 17.

Shel 19–23.

shilup (*Choctaw*, Woodlands, NA) a spirit. Cf. *manito*.

Shilup Chito Osh (*Choctaw*) the Great Spirit.

Shipololo 154, 155, 157.

Shiwanni (*Zuñi*, Pueblo, S West, NA) a primordial being who, with his wife Shiwanokia (q.v.), existed below the Great Spirit Awonwilona (q.v.) and the Sun-Father and Moon-Mother. After

Hide painting of the Sun Dance, the Plains Indians' greatest ritual. Brown Museum, Providence, Rhode Island. (*Photo: Werner Forman Archive.*)

Awonawilona had created the clouds and oceans, Shiwanni decided he too would like to create something beautiful and decided to make lights for the sky when Moon-Mother slept. From his saliva he made multicoloured bubbles, blowing them upwards to become the stars.

Shiwanokia (*Zuñi*) the primordial goddess, wife of Shiwanni (q.v.). After he had created the stars, she made the Earth-Mother, Awitelin Tsita, from saliva.

shtabai (modern *Maya*, Yucatán) demons who may take male or female forms. In the latter they entice men to their ruin. Cf. *paqok*.

Sibu (*Bribri* and *Borcua*, Panama) the Great Spirit.

Sicasica, Mt. see Churuquilla, Mt.

Sila Inua (*Eskimo*) Lord of Power, a personification of the mythical animistic power which *shamans* can command and use.

Simba-La Source (*Voodoo*, Haiti) a *loa*, probably a variant of Simbi—see Simbi Laoka.

Simbi Laoka (*Voodoo*) a *loa* (q.v.) derived from the Congolese deity Simbi.

Sinchi Roca (*Inca*, Peru) legendary second ruler of the *Incas*. It was said that his mother dressed him magnificently and placed him in a cave mouth, having started a rumour that the sun was about to send the people a leader. Gulled by his splendid appearance the people accepted him. Some tell this story of Manco Capac (q.v.). Possibly the legend refers to an early rite.

Sio Calako (*Hopi*, Pueblo, S West, NA) a mythical giant.

Sio Humis (*Hopi*) a rain-spirit.

Sipapu (*Zuñi*, Pueblo, S West, NA) the hole through which the *Zuñi* emerged from the underworld.

Sisiri see Purrunaminari.

Sisiutl (*Kwakiutl* NW Coast, NA) the name of one of the most important totemic beings of the NW Coast Indians. Sisiutl is depicted as a serpent monster with three heads: snake ones at either side of a human one. It can change itself into a poisonous fish at will, but is a powerful friend to those it favours and *shamans* make powerful 'medicine' from pieces of its 'body'. Its skin is so tough that it turns the keenest knife, but it can be pierced by a holly leaf. The *Kwakiutl's* neighbours the *Bella Coola* say the Sisiutl's home is in a lake behind the dwelling of the supreme goddess Qamaits (q.v.). It seems, like the Plumed Serpent (q.v.) of

the south, to have been a water-deity.

siudleratuin (*Eskimo*) the spirits of the dead.

skoyo (*Sia*, Pueblo, S West, NA) generic term for mythical man-eating monsters.

Skyamsen (*Tlingit*, NW Coast, NA) the Thunderbird (q.v.).

Snake 163, 164–171.

Snake Dance, the (*Hopi*, Pueblo, S West. NA) a biennial rain- and fertility-festival alternating with the *Flute Dance* (q.v.). It includes both secret and public rites involving live snakes. the celebrants belong to two societies, the Snake Priests and the Antelope Priests. The ritual celebrates the marriage of Snake Youth—probably a sky-god—with the underworld Snake Girl, whose offspring included both reptiles and the human ancestors of the *Hopi* Snake Clan. At the close of the rites, the snakes are taken into the fields and released to carry the people's prayers for rain and good harvests to the underworld fertility-spirits.

Snake Girl see *Snake Dance*.

Snake People 162, 169–170.

Snake Youth see *Snake Dance*.

Sneneik see Tsonoqua.

Soatsaki (*Blackfoot*, Gt Plains, NA) Feather-Woman, the mother of Poïa (q.v.).

Sobo, Sobo-si (*Voodoo*, Haiti) a *loa* (q.v.) probably derived from a W African deity. He looks like a handsome soldier.

Solongo loa (*Voodoo*) spirits deriving from gods of the Congolese *Solongo* people.

Solophine (*Voodoo*) a *loa* (q.v.).

Sosondowah (*Iroquois*, Woodlands, NA) the hunter Great-Night. He chased the spirit Sky-Elk, who had wandered down from the heavens to graze, and followed it right back to the highest heaven, beyond the sun. There he was caught by Dawn who made him her watchman. Looking down to earth one day he fell in love with the beautiful Gendenwitha and descended to woo her, first in the spring, as a bluebird, then in the summer, as a blackbird, finally, in the autumn, he came as the night-hawk and carried her away. Dawn, annoyed by his excursions, tied him to her door posts and transformed Gendenwitha into a star which she set in Sosondowah's forehead, forever beyond his reach.

Sousson-Pannan (*Voodoo*, Haiti) a very ugly *loa* (q.v.) covered with sores. He lives in the air. He is both wicked and pitiless and especially fond of drinking not only spirits but blood.

South West, North American Indians of

the pp. 119–120.

soyoko (*Hopi*, Pueblo, S West, NA) generic term for mythical monsters.

Spider Woman 92–96, 101. See also Hahi Wügti, Mountain Chant and Sussistinnako.

Sun Dance, the (Gt Plains, NA) the chief ritual of the Plains Indians, this annual festival usually lasted eight days, culminating in the building of a symbolic lodge representing mankind's home. In its centre was a pole denoting earth and heaven, decorated with symbols of the elemental powers. Warriors who had vowed themselves to the sun-spirit danced around the pole to which they were attached by ropes skewered under their pectoral and shoulder muscles. This ritual torture was not an essential element of the ceremony among all tribes. In some, it and all similar rites were forbidden, as to them any sign of blood during the ceremonies was a dire ill omen. The Dance ended with prayers to the Sun-Father, Earth-Mother and Morning Star (the fertility-spirit) to bless the celebrants.

Sun, Gateway of the p. 129.

Sun Halo 19, 20, 23.

Sun, Pyramid of the p. 129 and **282.**

Sussistinnako (*Sia*, Pueblo, S West, NA) Spider, the magical first being who created the mothers of mankind as two sisters, Utset, mother of the Indians, and Nowutset, mother of everyone else (qq.v.). Spider also created rain, thunder, lightning and the rainbow. See also Spider-Woman.

Sutalidihi (*Cherokee*, Woodlands, NA) the sun-spirit.

Swaikhway ceremony (*Cowichan*, NW Coast, NA) ritual enacting the myth of a boy who, diving into a lake, came down upon the roofs of its spirits' house. They gave him magical power and when he returned home he brought the *Swaikhway* mask with him.

Swaixwe (*Cowichan*) a sky-being who descended to live in terrestrial lakes.

Taapac see Thunupa.

Tacuilla see Urus.

Tahit (*Tlingit*, NW Coast, NA) the god of fate who lives in the northern heaven.

tahmahnawis (*Chinook*, coast, S West, NA) supernatural power.

Taikomol (*Yuki*, coast, S West, NA) He-Who-Goes-Alone, the creator.

Takoboh see Kobah.

Takuskanskan (*Dakota*, Gt Plains, NA) the Trickster (q.v.) and wind-spirit.

Tamacauí (*Xingu*, Brazil) a legendary chief of immense physique and strength. He routed his people's enemies single-handed until one day all the hostile tribes united against him. His people were massacred, but Tamacauí fought on. At length, running short of arrows, his foes tried to crush him bodily, but one by one he fought them off and killed them until, as evening drew on his strength began to wane and he started to sink into the marsh. Overpowered and killed, he yet had the victory, for those of his enemies who ate him were poisoned by his flesh and all died too.

Tambotocco 321.

Tambu Quiru 325.

Tamoanchan 281, 282.

Tamosi (*Carib*, Guyana) Ancient One, the supreme being, also called Tamosikabotano, Ancient-One-the-Sky.

Tamosikabotano see Tamosi.

Tancanaymo p. 130 and 334.

tapacu 323.

Taparimarru see Purrunaminari.

TAqlikic 104.

Tarhuyiawahku (*Iroquois*, Woodlands, NA) the giant upholder of the skies.

tasoom (*Cheyenne*, Gt Plains, NA) the individual's spirit. After separating from the body at death it journeys to the sky home of Heammawihio (q.v.), via the Ekutsihimmiyo (Hanging Road, i.e. the Milky Way), suspended between heaven and earth.

Taswicana 83–90, 116.

Tatu-Karaiá (*Xingu*, Brazil) a legendary people discovered by former *Xingu* explorers. They lived underground and were detected by the columns of smoke issuing from their homes. The *Xingu* killed them all as they came to the surface.

Taureau (*Voodoo*, Haiti) Bull, a *loa* (q.v.).

Taxet (*Haida*, NW Coast, NA) House Above, a sky-god who receives the souls of those who die by violence.

Taylor, Mt. 49.

Tchakabech (*Algonquian*, Woodlands, NA) a dwarf whose parents were eaten by an underworld bear-chief and the Great Hare. He climbed a tree up into the sky and, being enchanted by the beauty of the heavenly realm, decided to return to fetch his young sister, building houses en route for her to rest in. On their journey to the sky the sister's child broke off branches below them so that none might follow them. Tchakabech caught the sun. One version of the story says he did so with a noose of his sister's hair. There was no day on earth until a mouse nibbled through the noose and released the

Cowichan (*Salish*) wooden comb decorated with a figure of Swaixwe. British Museum. (*Photo: British Museum.*)

sun.

Tcochkut, (Tcüchkuti) *kachina* (*Hopi*, Pueblo, S West, NA) the glutton-priest.

Tcolawitze (*Hopi*) the fire-spirit.

Teçacatetl 292.

Tecciztécatl (*Aztec*, Mexico) He-Who-Comes-From-the-Sea-Snail, a title of Metzitli (q.v.).

Tecumbalam 194.

Tehabi (*Hopi*, Pueblo, S West, NA) the Mudhead clown. See Koyemshi.

Temaukel (*Ona*, Tierra del Fuego) like the neighbouring *Yahgan's* Watauineiwa (q.v.), this supreme being is a disembodied spirit, the sustenance of the universe and its moral order. He lives above the stars and dead souls—*kaspi*—go to him.

Temazcalteci see Chiuacóatl.

Tenoch 292.

Tenochtitlan p. 127 and 288.

Teotihuacán 247 and 282.

Teoyaomqui (*Aztec*, Mexico) the god of dead warriors.

Tepeu 191–197.

Tepeyollotl (*Zatopec*, Mexico) Heart-of-the-Mountain, the earthquake-god, depicted in jaguar form.

Tepoztécatl (*Aztec*, Mexico) the tutelary god of Tepoztlan, said to be the son of a virgin.

215

Panel from the *Codex Fejervary-Mayer* shows Tezcatlipoca fishing for the Earth monster with his foot as bait. The date symbols with dots denote eras which Tezcatlipoca dominated. Liverpool City Museum. (*Photo: Werner Forman Archive.*)

Tequendama 301.

Teteoinnan (*Aztec*) Mother-of-the-Gods, an aspect of Tlazoltéotl (q.v.) See also Chiuacóatl.

Tezacatzontécatl (*Aztec*) an important *pulque* god, Straw-Covered-Mirror, possibly to be identified with the *Toltec* Chacmool figures. See also Centzontotochtin.

Tezcatlipoca (*Aztec*) Smoking-Mirror, a solar deity and tutelary god of Tezcoco. His name comes from his emblematic mirror with a spiral of smoke ascending from it. It enabled Tezcatlipoca to see all that happened in the heavens, on earth and in the underworlds. Often it replaces one of his feet—which he was said to have lost by catching it in an underworld door. The many aspects of the god reflect his rôle as symbol of the all-encompassing sky—and also his absorption of many lesser deities. Thus he is Yoalli Ehecatl—Night Wind; Telpochtli—the Youth; Omactl—Two Reeds; Ruler-of-Feasts. As Iztli-Tezcatlipoca he personifies the knife of human sacrifice. In the spring of each year a youth who had been honoured as his embodiment was sacrificed to the sun. An early manuscript shows Tezcatlipoca presiding over the four cardinal points, each of his aspects being differently coloured—red (east), blue (south), black (north), white (west). See also 233, 235–236, 240, 250, 252, 253, 264, 266–267, 271, 275–280.

Tezcoco p. 127 and 233, 264, 288, 297.

Theelgeth 51.

thlawe 155, 160.

Thobadzistshini 54–56, 58, 91–102.

Thomas, St. see Thunapa and 307.

Thunderbird (NA) see p. 122. A particularly important totem among NW coastal tribes, where, it is said, lightning flashes from its eyes and it feeds on the monstrous killer-whales. See also Keneun, Oshadagea, Skyamsen and 118.

Thunderers p. 122.

Thunupa (*Collao, Inca* empire) a culture-hero also called Tonapa and Taapac. Stories about him are preserved in muddled form as the Thunupa tale was assimilated to that of the *Inca*'s origin and also to that of Viracocha (q.v.), while the Augustinian fathers who recorded it were prone to identify Thunupa with Christian figures, particularly St. Thomas. Thunupa was said to have arrived from the north, long ago, with five disciples, or alone, carrying a large, wooden cross. He preached peace, sobriety and

Stele of the Teotihuacán period, from the neighbouring city of Atzcapotzalco, shows the water-god Tláloc. (*Photo Werner Forman Archive.*)

because, it is said, he was regarded as being elevated above these things (cf. Tloque Nahuaque). His wife was Tonacacíhuatl (q.v.). See also 233.

Tonantzin see Cihuacóatl.

Tonapa see Thunapa.

Tonatiuh (*Aztec*) a solar-god, the eagle and heavenly warrior. He was much more important in cults than the theologically superior Ometecuhtli, Tloque Nahuaque and Tonacatecuhtli (qq.v.). Closely associated with the great gods Huitzilopochtli and Tezcatlipoca (qq.v.), he was also called Piltzintecutli.

Topa Ayar Cachi 322. See also Ayar Cachi.

Topa Huaco 322.

tornak (pl. *tornait*) (*Eskimo*) an *inua* (q.v.) who has become a man's helper or guardian spirit. The most powerful *inue* are those of bears and stones. If a bear *inua* becomes a man's *tornak* it may swallow him and regurgitate him as an *angakok* (shaman). The Greenland *Eskimo* had a vague belief in a powerful ruler of the *tornait* called Tornasuk (Great Tornak), who enabled the *shamans* to control their *tornait* helpers.

Tornasuk see *tornak*.

Tornit (*Eskimo*, Greenland) 'Inlanders'— large people, taller and stronger than the *Eskimo* though less skilled at handling boats and hunting. They are associated with a quarrel in which an *Eskimo* youth killed a *Tornit* by boring a hole into his head with a crystal drill. The remaining *Tornit* fled and became the *Eskimo's* enemies. They sometimes steal *Eskimo* women when there is a thick fog, but are not really dangerous as they always hide from the *Eskimo* men and are terrified of their dogs.

totem(ic) pp. 118 and **259**. See also pp. 37–38.

Toueyo 276–278.

Toussaint, Monsieur (*Voodoo*, Haiti) a *loa* (q.v.).

tova-pod see Aroteh.

Toxint dance (*Kwakiutl*, NW Coast, NA) masked dance ritual miming the decapitation of a woman.

Tracas (*Voodoo*, Haiti) a *loa* (q.v.)

Trickster, the see Amalivaca, Cachimanc, Coyote, Dohkwibuhch, Dokibatl, Isakawuate, Ishtinike, Itsike, K'mukamtch, Nehenebush, Takuskanskan, Wisagatcak, Wakdjunkaga, Wigit and pp. 121–122 and **259**.

Tsantsa (*Jivaros*, Ecuador) a ritual performed after a head-hunting raid. The warrior is washed in chicken's blood, and the *tsanta* (shrunken head)

Aztec statue of the solar-god Tonatiuh. The symbol on his back denotes an earthquake. Museum für Völkerkunde, Basle. (*Photo: Werner Forman Archive.*)

stuck on a lance. At the height of the ritual the men dance around it flourishing spears and re-enacting the kill. The purpose is to triumph over the dead man's evil spirit and transform it into a good, helpful one. A *Jivaros* is not regarded as mature until he has captured the soul of an enemy and so enabled those of his loved ones to rest from their sad wanderings.

Tsegihi (*Navajo*, S West, NA) a sacred place referred to in the great *Night Chant* (q.v.).

Tsenta (*Huron*, Woodlands, NA) the *Huron* equivalent of Yoskeha.

Tsetseka (*Kwakiutl*, NW Coast, NA) the winter, or supernatural season, at which everything is changed, names, chants and ways of singing them. The Bakoos (summer) names of the clans and tribal ranks are altered to others relating them to the spirits.

Tshanahale 51.

Tshohanoai 50, 54, 55, 56, 59, 96–102.

Tsichtinaka (*Acoma*, Pueblo, S West, NA) the leader who brought the people up from the underworld.

Tsiskagili (*Cherokee*, Woodlands, NA) the Red Crayfish. After the primordial animals had raised the earth from the floodwaters and descended to it, they set the sun to cross it just overhead every day so that their new home might be illuminated; but at first they fixed it too low in the sky and Crayfish was badly scorched, which is why his shell is scarlet and his meat inedible.

Tsolb 205.

Tsonoqua (*Kwakiutl*, NW Coast, NA) the Cannibal Mother, an important figure in clan rituals. Called by neighbouring tribes Baxbakualanuchsiwae and Sneneikulala, she lived in the woods feeding on corpses and on stolen children, but was killed by the Sky-Youth with whose reflected image she had fallen in love.

Tsotil (*Navajo*, S West, NA) one of the

Kwakiutl mask, *c.* 1870, of the ogress Tsonoqua. Mr and Mrs Morton I. Sosland Collection.

Basalt statue of the Aztec goddess Xilonen. Private Collection. (*Photo: Hamlyn Picture Library.*)

Detail from the *Codex Borbonicus* shows the goddess Xochiquetzal (*left*). Library of the Chamber of Deputies, Paris. (*Photo: Hamlyn Picture Library*.)

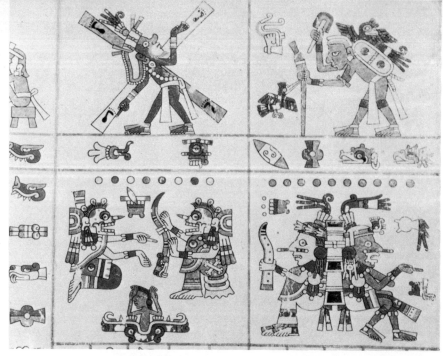

Page from the *Codex Fejervary-Mayer* showing Yacatecuhtli, god of merchants, carrying a crossroads symbol, and merchants with quetzal feathers. Liverpool City Museum. (*Photo: Werner Forman Archive.*)

derivation.

Yacatecuhtli (*Aztec*, Mexico) the god of merchant adventurers.

Yagis (*Kwakiutl*, NW Coast, NA) sea-monster that overturns canoes and eats their crews.

Yaguarogui 355.

Yananamca Intanamca (*Quechua*, Peru) deities or culture-heroes of the early seventeenth-century Indians. They were said to have been conquered by the cruel Huallallo (q.v.). Their story, recorded by the priest Francisco de Avila, is associated with the legend of the Indians' expulsion from the fertile valleys of the cordillera to its barren highland plateau.

Yanauluha (*Zuñi*, Pueblo, S West, NA) the first priest.

Yáotl (*Aztec*, Mexico) Enemy, a title of Tezcatlipoca.

Yaxche (*Maya*, CA) the tree of heaven under which good souls rejoice.

yei 52, 53, 60.

Yeitso 51.

yek (*Tlingit*, NW Coast, NA) all-pervasive spirits, cf. *inua*.

Yellow Body 35, 40.

Yellow-Corn Girl 49.

Yellow World 33–34, 38.

Yetl p. 121 and 104–114.

Yimantuwinyai (*Hupa*, coast, S West, NA) the creator Old-One-Across-the-Ocean, who seems to be a volcanic deity. At his birth there was a metallic ringing noise, smoke appeared on the mountainside and pieces of rotten wood, thrown up by someone, fell into his hands, creating fire.

Yiyanitsinni (Navajo, S West, NA) the upholders of the heavens.

Yoaltl Ehecatl see Tezcatlipoca.

Yolkai Estsan 53, 54, 60, 61.

Yolkaiaisn, variant of Yolkai Estsan (q.v.).

yoyolche (modern *Maya*, Yucatán) giant night-spirits. Heroes tremble as they pass.

Yum Cimil see God A.

Yum Kaax (*Maya*, CA) the maize-god.

yumbalamob (modern *Maya*, Yucatán) beings living in the first of the seven heavens. Their especial charge is the protection of Christians. Invisible by day, at night they keep watch beside the crosses set at each of a village's cardinal points, guarding against the evil forest-spirits. They slice the wind with obsidian knives. They resemble the ancient *Aztec* deity Tezcatlipoca (q.v.).

yumchabob (modern *Maya*) bearded old men living in the sixth heaven. They are partial to tobacco and are lords of the rain. They seem to be derived from the classical *Maya* Chacs and Kukucan (qq.v.). They receive their orders from El Grand Dios, the Great God of the Christians, who lives in the seventh (highest) heaven.

Yzamna see Zac-u-Uayeyab.

Za see Zadieu.

Zac-u-Uayeyab (*Maya*, CA) the god who guarded cities' northern gates during the malign Ix years, ruled by the northern Bacab (q.v.). At these times

the centre of the cities was guarded by Yzamna. See also Chac-u-Uayeyab, Ek-u-Uayeyab, Kan-u-Uayeyab.

Zadieu (*Voodoo*, Haiti) a *loa* (q.v.) sometimes referred to as Za and possibly deriving from a W African god. He may be a variant of Zahi or vice-versa.

Zahi (*Voodoo*) a *loa* (q.v.) possibly a variant of Zadieu (q.v.).

zanges (*Voodoo*) an alternative generic term for the *loa*, spirits and deities of the *Voodoo* cultists. It derives from the Christian French *les anges*—angels.

Zapana see Cari.

zemis, pl. *zemes* (*Taïno*, Caribbean) generic term for deity.

Zipacna 225, 229–230.

zobops (*Voodoo*) the formally organised order of male sorcerers.

zombie(s) (*Voodoo*) (i) a generic term for the spirits of the dead.
(ii) more specifically, those killed by sorcerers or who, having died naturally, are resurrected by evil *houngans* (q.v.). Dominated by their wicked masters, the *zombies* have lost their souls to them and can be made to perform any evil.

zombie(s) errant(s) (*Voodoo*) spirit(s) of people killed in accidents. They spend their days in the woods and walk the roads by night until they have completed the term of earthly life originally assigned to them by God.

Zotzilha Chimalman (*Maya*, CA) the bat-god of darkness, who fights Kinich Ahau, the sun (q.v.).

Zuhé see Bochica and **298**.

PART 4

Bibliography

*ALEXANDER, HARTLEY BURR *North America*. Vol. 10 of *Mythology of All Races*, ed. Louis Herbert Gray. New York: Cooper Square Publications. 1916/1964.
—— *Latin America*. Vol. 11 of *Mythology of All Races*, ed. Louis Herbert Gray. New York: Cooper Square Publications. 1920/64.

BRITON, DANIEL G. *The Maya Chronicles*. Philadelphia: Library of Aboriginal American Literature. 1882.
—— *The Annals of the Cakchiquels*. Philadelphia: Library of Aboriginal American Literature. 1885.

BROWN, JOSEPH EPES (ed.) *The Sacred Pipe. Black Elk's Account of the Seven Rites of the Oglala Sioux*. Penguin Books. 1971.

CARPENTER, E. *Eskimo*. Oxford University Press. 1959.

CATLIN, GEORGE *Letters and Notes on the Manners, Customs and Condition of the North American Indians* (1841). Dover Publications. 1977.

CIEZA DE LEON, PEDRO DE *The Travels of Pedro de Cieza de Léon . . . The Hakluyt Society*. 2 vols. 1883.

CLARK, ELLA E. *Indian Legends of the Pacific Northwest*. University of California Press. 1953.

COE, MICHAEL D. *The Maya*. Penguin Books. 1971.

*COE, RALPH T. *Sacred Circles. Two Thousand Years of North American Indian Art*. The Arts Council of Great Britain. 1977.

DORSEY, GEORGE A. and KROEBER, ALFRED L. *Traditions of the Arapaho*. Chicago: Field Columbia Publications 18. Anthropology Series vol. 5. 1903.

FAGG, WILLIAM *Eskimo Art in the British Museum*. British Museum Publications. 1970.

GOETZ, D. and MORLEY, S. *Popul Vuh. Translated from the Spanish . . .* William Hodge. 1970.

GRINNELL, GEORGE BIRD *Blackfoot Lodge Tales*. New York: Charles Scribner's Sons Ltd. 1892.

HOEBEL, E. ADAMSON *The Cheyennes— Indians of the Great Plains*. Holt Rhinehart & Winston. 1960.

HUXLEY, FRANCIS *The Invisibles*. Rupert Hart Davis. 1966.

JUDSON, K. B. *Myths and Legends of Alaska*. Chicago University Press. 1911.

KATZ, FRIEDRICH *The Ancient American Civilisations*. Weidenfeld and Nicolson. 1972.

W. KRICKEBERG, H. TRIMBORN, W. MÜLLER and O. ZERRIES *Pre-Columbian American Religions*. Weidenfeld and Nicolson. 1961.

LÉVI-STRAUSS, CLAUDE *The Raw and the Cooked*. Jonathan Cape. 1970.

MARCELIN, M. *Mythologie Vodu*. Haiti: 1953.

MARKHAM, CLEMENTS R. *Rites and Laws of the Yncas*. Hakluyt Society. 1873.

MARRIOT, ALICE and RACHLIN, CAROL K. *American Indian Mythology*. Mentor Books. 1972.

MASON, J. ALDEN *The Ancient Civilisations of Peru*. Penguin Books. 1957.

MATTHEWS, WASHINGTON *Navaho Legends*. Memoirs of the American Folklore Society. Vol. 5. 1897.

O'KANE, WALTER COLLINS *The Hopis*. University of Oklahoma Press. 1953.

OSBORNE, HAROLD *South American Mythology*. Paul Hamlyn. 1968.

*PETERSON, FREDERICK *Ancient Mexico*. George Allen & Unwin. 1959.

RADIN, PAUL *The Trickster*. New York: Shocken Books. 1972.

ROYS, RALPH L. *The Book of Chilam Balam of Chumayel*. Carnegie Institution of Washington. Publication 438. 1933.

SARGANT, WILLIAM *The Mind Possessed*. Heinemann. 1973.

SIMPSON, GEORGE EATON 'The Belief System of Haitian Vodun.' *American Anthropology*. Vol. 47. 1945.

*STEWART, JULIAN *Handbook of South American Indians*. Washington: Smithsonian Institution, Bureau of American Ethnology. 1944–50.

*STEWART, JULIAN and FACON, LOUIS C. *Native Peoples of South America*. McGraw Hill. 1959.

THOMPSON, SMITH *Tales of the North American Indians*. Harvard University Press. 1929.

VAILLANT, G. C. *The Aztecs of Mexico*. Penguin Books. 1965.

VILLAS BOAS, ORLANDO and VILLAS BOAS, CLAUDIO *Xingu, the Indians and Their Myths*. Souvenir Press. 1973.

*VON HAGEN, VICTOR WOLFGANG *The Ancient Sun Kingdoms of America*. Thames and Hudson. 1962.

*These books contain useful, detailed bibliographies.